SOCIAL ENTERPRISE IN EMERGING MARKET COUNTRIES

Social Enterprise in Emerging Market Countries

No Free Ride

Nicole Etchart and Loïc Comolli

palgrave
macmillan

First published in 2013 by
PALGRAVE MACMILLAN®
in the United States—a division of St. Martin's Press LLC,
175 Fifth Avenue, New York, NY 10010.

Where this book is distributed in the UK, Europe and the rest of the world,
this is by Palgrave Macmillan, a division of Macmillan Publishers Limited,
registered in England, company number 785998, of Houndmills,
Basingstoke, Hampshire RG21 6XS.

Palgrave Macmillan is the global academic imprint of the above companies
and has companies and representatives throughout the world.

Palgrave® and Macmillan® are registered trademarks in the United States,
the United Kingdom, Europe and other countries.

ISBN: 978–1–137–37327–4

This publication contains information prepared by sources outside NESsT,
and opinions based on that information. NESsT strives to provide accurate
information and well-founded opinions, but does not represent that the
information and opinions in this publication are error free.

This publication is for informational purposes, and NESsT is not engaged
in providing legal, accounting, or other professional advice. As professional
advice must be tailored to the specific circumstances of each situation,
the information and opinions provided herein should not be used as a
substitute for the advice of a competent professional.

NESsT does not undertake to update this publication.

*NESsT promotes the social, political, economic, and religious rights of all
people and does not discriminate on the basis of gender, race, national
origin, mental or physical disability, sexual orientation, or political or
religious opinion or affiliation.*

Library of Congress Cataloging-in-Publication Data

Comolli, Loïc.
    Social enterprise in emerging market countries : no free ride / by Loïc
Comolli and Nicole Etchart.
        pages cm
    Includes bibliographical references and index.
    ISBN 978–1–137–37327–4 (hardback)
        1. Social entrepreneurship—Developing countries. 2. Social
responsibility of business—Developing countries. I. Etchart,
Nicole. II. Title.

HD60.5.D44C66 2013
658.4'08091724—dc23   2013025821

A catalogue record of the book is available from the British Library.

Design by Newgen Knowledge Works (P) Ltd., Chennai, India.

First edition: December 2013

10 9 8 7 6 5 4 3 2 1

We would like to dedicate Social Enterprise in Emerging
Market Countries: No Free Ride *to the individuals
who are our daily inspiration: to the NESsT Enterprises for
their commitment to providing sustainable solutions to overcome
systemic poverty and inequity; to the NESsT staff for their
incredible energy, creativity, and hard work without which
NESsT would not be possible; and finally, to our spouses
Alex and Laila for their love and constant support.*

CONTENTS

ILLUSTRATIONS

BOXES

DIAGRAMS

FIGURES

GRAPHS

TABLES

FOREWORD

The world used to be so much simpler. Businesses were only expected to focus on making profit for owners. And governments and grant-funded nonprofits took care of social problems that free markets did not solve. They existed in a *bifurcated world* filled with mutual suspicion.

But a major, global shift in the last few decades has complicated that simple picture. Our social and environmental challenges have grown beyond the capability of government and charity to address them. And businesses focused solely on maximizing financial returns are pushing the limits of their legitimacy among concerned citizens, employees, and shareholders.

The social enterprise movement has sprung up as a rejection of the bifurcated worldview. Social enterprise leaders are inherently optimistic, focused on harnessing the resources and expertise of business approaches to the social purpose of mission-focused work. This optimistic vision has caught the imagination of a generation of pioneers who are charting new territory, developing innovative approaches to addressing a range of social challenges.

This work is not for the weak willed. It's hard enough to make money in business, but social enterprise leaders seek to create sustainable organizations serving customers that mainstream business leaves behind. And it's hard enough to raise grant funds to sustain a charitable organization, but social enterprise leaders seek to sustain and grow their organizations without relying on handouts. And social enterprise leaders set out to do this work in a world set up to support business and charity, but not their combination.

But they no longer set out alone. Decades of experience are beginning to map the contours of what it takes to run a successful social enterprise, and what governments and other supporters can do to ensure smoother sailing. In this context, *Social Enterprise in Emerging Market Countries: No Free Ride* is a timely contribution not only to social enterprise practitioners, but also to all of us with a stake in seeing social enterprises succeed.

The insights in this book are grounded in the practical experience of real social enterprise leaders in emerging markets, understood from an insider's view. These are not just the good news stories so often celebrated at conferences and in feel-good news items that are more inspiring than they are helpful to inform a reasoned discussion about what we can all do to create the conditions for their success to be replicated. Instead, this book affirms the promise of social enterprise without sugarcoating the commitment and patience we will need to realize it.

Individual social enterprises, and the inspiring leaders who run them, have fueled early interest in the potential of this movement. Many of its supporters are drawn to social enterprise exactly because it offers the promise of opening new channels of impact without having to rely on slow and frustrating process of changing the practices of established governments and funders. But the authors of this book make clear that ignoring the systems within which these enterprises operate will ultimately stifle the movement's success.

We cannot keep social enterprise open only to those heroes willing and able to succeed despite the lack of support. We need to create a new set of systems to support an integrated, social enterprise, approach, just as existing systems support those working on either side of the bifurcated world. This will require governments to create regulatory and policy frameworks that recognize the ambitions of social enterprise leaders to blur the lines of business and charity. It will require universities to acknowledge the ambition of their students to learn business principles in policy and social work schools and social impact strategies in business schools. And it will require investors and donors to fill the vast spectrum between profit-maximizing investment and purely charitable donations with new investment approaches and products and to overcome the risk aversion that currently constrains too many from investing in early-stage social enterprises.

Social Enterprise in Emerging Market Countries: No Free Ride makes clear that building this support system is going to require patience and insight. And we must ground this work in an understanding of the macro conditions in which any social enterprise operates. Operating in emerging markets presents unique challenges and opportunities for social enterprise leaders. A book focused on lessons from experiences learned under these conditions offers a unique contribution.

As social enterprise leaders in the second decade of the twenty-first century, we stand on the shoulders of an earlier generation who set out from comfortable shores of the bifurcated world with a conviction that they could build a new way to address social challenges. We get to do what we do because they were able to generate tailwinds of enthusiasm for their early successes. But we owe it to these pioneers, and to the communities still left unserved, to confront the difficulties we face now and the challenges ahead so that we can work together to build a stronger social enterprise system that will ease the path for those who follow.

ANTONY BUGG-LEVINE
CEO Nonprofit Finance Fund and co-author,
*Impact Investing: Transforming How We Make
Money While Making a Difference*

About NESsT

Founded in 1997, NESsT develops and invests in social enterprises that solve critical social problems in emerging market countries. The organization supports pioneering early-stage enterprises, which pilot new business models and approaches to tackle social issues. Because of their innovative models, NESsT Enterprises create new markets that can be replicated and catalyze changes in behavior or within the broader system.

NESsT uses a long-term portfolio approach to develop social enterprises. We provide business-planning support in order to identify and select the best ideas. We launch the most promising enterprises and we incubate them with capacity support and tailored financing. We then scale those enterprises with patient investments to multiply their impact.

NESsT has invested USD 8 million in capacity and financial support to launch over 130 high-impact social enterprises. NESsT Enterprises have directly improved the quality of life of 320,000 marginalized people.

As a thought leader, NESsT has been at the forefront of social enterprise development, conducting extensive research and disseminating many publications on best practices. We have organized numerous forums on this topic, and are the founder of Social Enterprise Day, an annual event that focuses on fostering an enabling environment for the sector. We leverage our thought leadership to promote policies that further increase the impact of social enterprise.

The organization has six country offices, representative offices in San Francisco and London, and works throughout Central Europe and Latin America. The majority of staff are emerging market professionals and we count on the support of over 300 volunteer business advisors to mentor our enterprise portfolio. NESsT's consulting services have taken our work to 48 countries for over 100 clients to advance social enterprise.

PREFACE

Two decades ago, when NESsT was created with a mission to develop social enterprise in emerging market countries, there were very few actors interested in this topic. The notion of developing sustainable, entrepreneurial solutions to social problems was either met with resistance from those who felt that this should be the work of the government, or bemusement by those who felt that anything social could not really be profitable or sustainable. Today, the landscape is quite different. Social enterprise has appeared on the agendas of a wide range of actors in the social change sector. In the past few years, there has been a plethora of impact investing funds that have emerged ready to invest in social enterprises. Pioneer donors have begun to provide philanthropic support to social enterprise development. Certain governments and corporations have begun to assess whether to incorporate social enterprise in their programs. And slowly but surely, there are more and more social enterprise support structures being created.

The recognition of and enthusiasm about social enterprise is highly encouraging for the development of the sector. The fact that well-respected philanthropic organizations are becoming interested in building the field, and basing their support on research findings, proven models, and best practices, is very promising. Although there has been an overemphasis on scaling, there is now recognition that scaling is hard, and not always possible, and that the potential impact of social enterprise even at a smaller scale can be quite dramatic in emerging markets where systemic poverty and inequality persist.

But this enthusiasm and hopefulness is coupled with some anxiety. The risks are that social enterprise could become a passing trend and that the support won't be at the levels and for as long a period that is truly needed to build this sector; that once again, the willingness to accept some failure and its accompanying lessons will be overridden by quick fixes, outputs as opposed to impact, and numbers as opposed to real life changes.

The response to this can only be to embrace and confront the challenging opportunity that is in front of us with the confidence that we are on the right track. *Social Enterprise in Emerging Market Countries: No Free Ride* provides a road map of what needs to happen for social enterprise to flourish and have long lasting impact. It demonstrates that if all stakeholders work hard to create the enabling environment we know is needed, supported social enterprises will become the industry norm for overcoming our most daunting social problems.

NICOLE ETCHART AND LOÏC COMOLLI

ACKNOWLEDGMENTS

Loïc Comolli is co-CEO of NESsT and is responsible for the overall strategic direction of NESsT and mobilizing financial resources to fund the organization's growth. Loïc is part of NESsT's Investment Committee and provides strategic advice on the growth of the NESsT Enterprise portfolio. In addition, he provides training and consulting to nonprofit organizations, donors, and international organizations on financial sustainability, social enterprise, business planning, and related topics.

Nicole Etchart is the cofounder and co-CEO of NESsT, where she leads NESsT's strategy, growth, and impact worldwide including entrance to ten countries, diversification of the portfolio to new target markets, and the use of diverse financial instruments. Nicole is responsible for the development of NESsT's new initiatives as well as its capacity and investment strategy and tools. She manages key donor relations and oversees a senior management team to carry out NESsT's goals while maximizing the organization's resources and impact. Nicole is also author, editor, or a contributor to numerous publications and articles on social enterprise and impact investing in emerging market countries.

Contributing Writers:
    Sebastian Gatica
    Geoff Schwarten
    Éva Varga

Research Team:
    Shareena Mundodi
    Francisco Silva

Content Contributors:
    Roxana Damaschin-Tecu
    Gonzalo San Martín
    Mónica Vasquez del Solar
    NESsT Portfolio Managers

Editorial Team:
    Kerry Dudman
    Bill Gardiner
    Nicolas Mendoza

Legal Research Contributions:
Brons & Salas Abogados (Argentina)
Mattos Filho, Veiga Filho, Marrey Jr. e Quiroga Advogados (Brazil)
Morales & Besa (Chile)
Rebaza, Alcázar & De Las Casas (Peru)

Graphic Design, Illustration, and Layout:
Lee Davis
Alex Mendoza
Jorge Moraga

Translation:
Shamrock Idiomas Ltda.

NESsT would like to thank The Rockefeller Foundation for its invaluable support in the preparation of Social Enterprise in Emerging Market Countries: No Free Ride.

Rockefeller Foundation
Innovation for the Next 100 Years

Acknowledgment and gratitude also goes to the following institutions for their participation in the research: Acumen Fund, Adobe Capital, Agora Partnerships, Artemisia, Aspen Institute, Avina Foundation, Banco Nacional de Desenvolvimiento Económico e Social (BNDES), BBVA Momentum Project, Brons & Salas Abogados, CAF Venturesome, Carec, Citigroup, CORFO, E+Co, Eleos Foundation, Fondo de Inversion Social, Fundes, Grassroots Business Fund, Halloran Philanthropies, Imprint Capital, Inter-American Development Bank/ Fondo Multilateral de Inversiones (FOMIN), Inter-American Development Bank/Social Entrepreneurship Program, International Development Research Centre, Inversor, Invested Development, KL Felicitas Foundation, LGT Venture Philanthropy, Mattos Filho, Veiga Filho, Marrey Jr. e Quiroga Advogados, Veiga Filho, Marrey Jr. e Quiroga Advogados, Morales & Besa, New Ventures Mexico, Njambre, Omidyar Network, Pomona Impact, Rebaza, Alcázar & De Las Casas, Romanian American Foundation, Serviço Brasileiro de Apoio às Micro e Pequenas Empresas (SEBRAE), Shell Foundation, Sistema B, Small Enterprise Assostance Funds (SEAF), Towarzystwa Inwestycji Społeczno-Ekonomicznych SA (TISE), The Ausherman Family Foundation, The Hub, The Lemelson Foundation, Toniic, Village Capital, Vox Capital, and many more who are mentioned on these pages.

Deep appreciation is extended to the following social enterprises and support organizations whose work has inspired many and shaped the ideas in this book:

Alaturi de Voi, Andar, Asociacion Grupo de Trabajo Redes, Café Kacaba, Cymdeithas Gofal Ceredigion Care Society, Fruit of Care, Fundatia Cartea Calatoare, HUB Sao Paulo, INCORES, Ingenimed, Kék Madár, KIDS, Kollyor, Magrini, MidiMusic, Motivation, Njambre, Upasol, Reciduca, RODA, Sitawai, Simón de Cirene, SociaLab, Viitor Plus, and Welldorf.

And a very strong thank you to the global NESsT team and all of the friends and family members who provided support and nourished us throughout the process. It takes a village!

1

The Opportunity for Social Enterprise in Emerging Market Countries*

Social Enterprise in Emerging Market Countries: No Free Ride comprehensively maps and assesses the existing landscape and enabling environment for social enterprise development in emerging market countries, as well as the support mechanisms and best practices needed for social enterprises to overcome barriers to development. The book particularly focuses on the case of Latin America and Central Europe, but is relevant to emerging markets overall, since the enabling environment is nowhere fully developed and social enterprises face similar challenges in other countries.[1] It is based on decades of experience, extensive research of hundreds of organizations and donors, and detailed case studies from many countries (see Appendix 1 for research methodology and scope). It provides a clear picture of the social enterprise ecosystem in emerging market countries today, where it needs to go, and how the players in the social enterprise field can get it there.

The book is organized into three parts: "Regulation and Policy" (chaps. 2 and 3); "Capacity-Support Structures and Scaling Best Practices" (chaps. 4 and 5); and "Capital for Growing Social Enterprises" (chaps. 6, 7, 8, and 9). Chapter 1 provides an overview of the social enterprise economy and summarizes the challenges and opportunities the sector faces in emerging markets. Chapter 10 concludes with highlights of the book's findings on the most urgent collective actions stakeholders must take to catalyze the impact of the social enterprise sector in emerging economy countries.

Why Social Enterprises?

Social enterprises are businesses that solve critical social problems in a sustainable manner.[2] Distinct from both traditional charities and most for-profit businesses, social enterprises create and sell products or services that improve the quality of life for low-income or disadvantaged people, while also earning financial revenues for the enterprise to sustain and grow its activities. Profits are for the most part reinvested (all profits must be reinvested when referring to nonprofit social enterprises) to grow and strengthen the enterprise for further impact. These enterprises engage in a broad spectrum of activities including community development, employment, education, conservation and environmental protection, financial services, health, sustainable income, and universal rights. They target a wide range of marginalized or excluded communities including at-risk youth and mothers, ethnic communities, people with disabilities, small producers and artisans, and low-income communities, overall.

The growth of the social enterprise economy in the past two decades is due to its success in addressing entrenched social and economic problems. The persistent problems of unemployment, poverty, social exclusion, poor social services, and environmental degradation—even in fast-growing emerging market economies—call for new, innovative solutions. Neither pure market-based nor pure public-sector approaches have effectively confronted these problems. The former has tended to approach them as a side activity usually addressed through corporate social responsibility (CSR) programs, whereas the latter has tended to create programs with an overemphasis on subsidizing services for a set number of beneficiaries rather than improving the root causes of poverty and exclusion. Table 1.1 demonstrates where social enterprises fall in the spectrum related to social and financial objectives. Social enterprises are at the center of this spectrum, where social objectives supersede financial objectives, but where financial objectives are key for long-term sustainability and growth.

Social enterprises offer a hybrid response to complex social problems. Social enterprises address the social and economic barriers that face marginalized or disadvantage communities, and attempt to tackle them using a market-based approach. They are often best positioned to respond to critical social problems, as most often they originate as community-based initiatives, close to the problems and with a stake in the outcome. They frequently introduce new products and services to the market, and build market demand by raising awareness around the issues that these are addressing. They also take these products and services to new sectors that adopt them, and in many respects, become engaged in also

Table 1.1   Social enterprise spectrum

Traditional nonprofits or charities	Nonprofits or charities with earned income strategies	Social enterprises	For-profit companies with CSR or incorporated social impact as part of their core business	For-profit companies
Social first—social objectives constitute the mission and supersede financial objectives—usually funded with donor funding.	Earned income activities usually tied to mission activities and designed to generate income for the organization.	Pursue both social and financial goals; can be nonprofit or for-profit organizations; and should be sustainable.	Financial first—financial objectives supersede social objectives—and social impact is designed through CSR programs or are tied to the value/supply chain of the company.	Purely for-profit companies that base performance on profit.

solving these problems. There are very solid examples of how social enterprises have provided concrete ways for marginalized communities to access the formal economy and a better quality of life. Boxes 1.1, 1.2, and 1.3 provide some of these examples.

Box 1.1   Kék Madár

In Hungary 90 percent of people with disabilities are unemployed, and many are socially excluded.

Kék Madár is a foundation in Hungary established to create economic and educational opportunities for people with intellectual and physical disabilities (http://www.kek-madar.hu/). In 2007, Kék Madár entered the NESsT incubation portfolio and received a start-up grant to equip a restaurant and assist with marketing and communications, pricing structure, and customer service. Kék Madár offers a restaurant skills training program, and with the exception of the chef, all of the employees at the restaurant have a disability. The social enterprise also prepares a number of trained employees for the labor force each year. In 2013, the social enterprise expanded its seating capacity from 25 to 100 (40 for a catering service) allowing Kék Madár to train and employ additional beneficiaries. Kék Madár has become a model social enterprise for other entrepreneurs that want to offer employment to marginalized communities. It plans to launch five similar restaurants in Hungary in the next five years.

Box 1.2   Ingenimed

One in three newborn babies in Peru is born with jaundice, which occurs when there are high levels of bilirubin in the blood that can become toxic and lead to other complications if left untreated or treated poorly. Because imported phototherapy equipment is expensive, many clinics in Peru opt for improvised, ineffective treatment.

In a rural clinic in southern Peru, a newborn is being treated with locally designed and manufactured Neoled phototherapy and will be home safely within 24 hours. In the coming years, this affordable Neoled technology will be sold to clinics throughout Peru by Ingenimed, an invention-based social enterprise created in Cusco by a group of engineering students and a member of the NESsT incubation portfolio (http://www.ingenimed.net/). After an initial pilot, the social enterprise is in the process of developing a laboratory that will mass-produce the equipment. It plans to manufacture three different models of the technology, including a portable version, which is more accessible, and to reach over 70,000 newborns in the next four years.

Box 1.3   Interrupcion

Creating "a system of global commerce that yields fantastic-tasting, superior-quality products; prosperous producing communities; a healthier earth; and opportunities for consumers to do good things through the purchases they choose to make." http://interrupcionfairtrade.com/site/social.php

Interrupcion is a fair-trade Argentinean social enterprise that uses social responsibility practices and citizen participation at every stage (www.interrupcionfairtrade.com). Started in 2001, today it partners with 11,000 small- and medium-sized fruit and vegetable producers in Latin America to provide premium, certified organic, and fair-trade products to North American markets. Interrupcion offers a guaranteed fair price in advance of the harvest, and if the market price is higher, the producer receives 90 percent of the higher price. In each producer community, the workers decide how to invest the "social premium"—approximately 2 percent of the sales volume, and by 2012 Interrupcion had allocated about USD 400,000 to communities. Workers have invested in community centers, computers, healthcare, recycling, and a range of other beneficial programs. Consumers benefit too—they receive healthy, high-quality fruits and vegetables that are grown by farmers practicing sustainable agriculture and receiving a fair price.

THE OPPORTUNITY FOR EMERGING MARKET COUNTRIES

Over the past two decades, the social enterprise sector has grown in more developed countries and is gaining traction in emerging economies. The social enterprise "ecosystem" in each country comprises individual enterprises and networks of enterprises, a range of intermediary or support organizations providing capacity-building and financial assistance, research and advocacy services (often civil society organizations [CSOs],[3] but can include university and government programs), philanthropists, foundations, and impact investors, and the public policies that encompass all of these entities.

The social enterprise sector is very advanced in Western Europe, particularly in the United Kingdom, and has been catalyzed for the most part by relatively strong government policy. The entire European social economy has been estimated to employ more than 11 million people, about 6 percent of the active workforce.[4] The EU views social enterprise as a model with high potential to respond to the challenges—in particular high unemployment rates—and make Europe more competitive in the world markets, as well as socially inclusive and environmentally sustainable.

The social enterprise sector is also relatively advanced in the United States. In addition to regulations designed to foster social enterprise,[5] there are numerous social enterprises and social enterprise support organizations dedicated to foster their growth. According to the results of the first Great Social Enterprise Census, an important new initiative that maps the social enterprise landscape, Ben Thornley, director of Pacific Community Ventures and co-convenor of the Impact Investing Policy Collaborative, estimates that "this is an economic sector employing over 10 million people, with revenues of $500 billion; about 3.5 percent of total US GDP."[6] The Social Enterprise Alliance, established in 1998 and focused mostly on social enterprise practitioners, has 13 chapters in 11 states and convenes its members annually to build their capacity and advocate for a stronger, enabling environment for social enterprise at a national level. Net Impact was founded over a decade ago to inspire the next generation of leaders to use their careers to tackle the world's most urgent problems. The organization has over 40,000 members and 300 volunteer led chapters, the majority based at US colleges and universities. And according to a Bridgespan Group study,[7] across all of the top MBA programs, there has been soaring interest in social enterprise in recent years and schools have expanded their offerings to meet the demand.

Since the world recession of 2008, Central and Eastern European emerging economies have struggled with high levels of unemployment, political unrest, exclusion of minorities, and decreasing levels of public financing to address these and other problems. In Latin America, many countries have fared better than Europe during the recession, and their economies have expanded overall. However, the historic inequality within these countries has continued (and in some cases increased), and the economic growth has been concentrated in the highest income sectors. Large segments of the population remain outside the formal economy.

In Chile, for example, economic growth (in constant terms) has averaged 6 percent since 2008. Per capita income is about USD 16,330 (adjusted for purchasing power parity), but more than 40 percent of all income goes to the wealthiest 10 percent of the population (the poorest 10% receive less than 2% of all income). Chile's Gini index in 2009 was the fifth worst in the world of data reported for that year.[8] The situation is similar in many countries, where despite growth there are persistently very high youth unemployment rates and poverty levels, and ethnic minorities and the disabled face discrimination and isolation.

The growth of many emerging market countries in the past two decades provides a unique opportunity to catalyze the positive impact that the social enterprise sector can have on current social and economic problems. The opportunity builds on the efforts of a group of pioneering organizations that recognized the potential of social enterprise 10–15 years ago and began to support them in these countries. Today, with this experience as a base, alongside the growth of the sector in North America and Western Europe and the inability of emerging countries to address systemic poverty and inequality, there is rapidly growing interest in this sector. The moment is ripe for emerging market countries to leverage this interest, adopt long-term and realistic approaches to social enterprise development, and to advance the entire ecosystem.

A concerted, comprehensive approach to catalyze the social enterprise sector could enable these countries to create more stable economic opportunities for marginalized communities, providing training in employment and life skills to integrate the chronically excluded members of society into the formal economy. Social enterprises can help small producers and artisans develop high-quality products and attain the volumes needed to compete in the market. They can produce innovative, affordable, and sustainable technology solutions to energy, health, and water needs, as well as to improve productive activities. At the same time, countries could reduce inequality and social and political dissention due to unfulfilled rising expectations or steadily shrinking economic opportunities.

In order to take advantage of the opportunity, and to truly leverage the potential of social enterprise, all stakeholders must take on some risks and make contributions. There is no "free ride" in the challenging road toward social enterprise development. This is particularly the case for start-up or early-stage social enterprises. NESsT defines early-stage enterprises as enterprises that are one to four years into their development and show potential to be financially self-sustainable and scalable. The enterprise may be growing or replicating its model, but it is still not ready for pure market investment. Therefore, it relies on patient capital (grants, soft loans, quasi-equity) and ongoing and tailored capacity support to get to the next phase of growth.

The recent interest in social enterprise has tended to focus on investment-ready models that are ready to grow and scale. Given the costs involved and the desire to focus on scaling impact, little has been invested to support the development of a pipeline of social enterprises. Focusing only on proven models that are ready for impact investing, could result in a very small number of social enterprises that are truly solving systemic problems and an overemphasis on technology or other models that can more easily scale.

CHALLENGES AND OPPORTUNITIES FACING THE SOCIAL ENTERPRISE SECTOR

Social Enterprise in Emerging Market Countries: No Free Ride has not only identified the challenges, but also the steps stakeholders in the social enterprise sector must take in order to address them and ultimately to significantly increase its impact on social and economic problems. Based on its extensive research and experience, NESsT has identified the most effective "opportunities for change" for stakeholders interested in taking advantage of the opportunity for this sector to address entrenched problems in emerging economies. Figures 1.1 and 1.2 show a summary of these opportunities.

Regulation and Policy

An analysis of the regulations and legislation in five Latin American countries revealed that they had no regulatory or legal framework recognizing social enterprises. For example, there was no specific legislation for either nonprofit or for-profit social enterprises. In most cases, entities are created under existing legislation for associations, corporations or foundations (in the case of

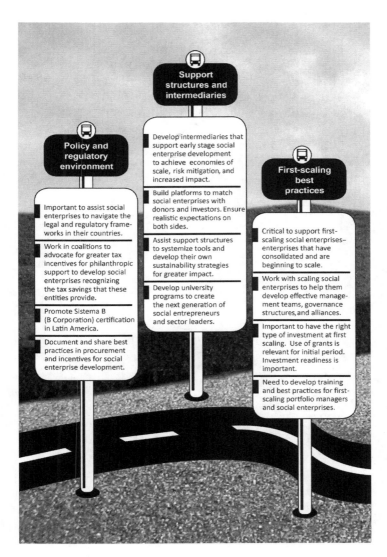

Figure 1.1   Opportunities for change 1.

nonprofits), and for-profit limited liability companies (in the case of for-profits). Nonprofit social enterprises typically are subject to value-added taxes, but do not pay income taxes as long as revenues generated go back to fulfilling the mission of the parent organization. Processes for setting up or operating "commercial activities" tend to be burdensome, confusing, and subject to local interpretation.

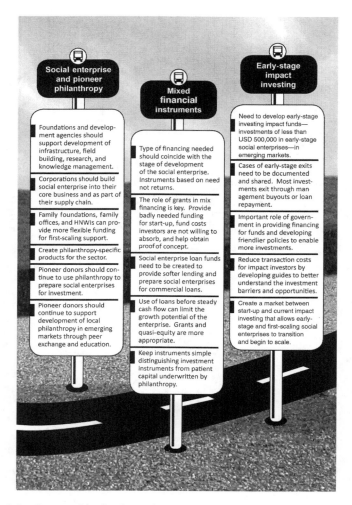

Figure 1.2   Opportunities for change 2.

Additionally, the tax or other financial benefits for philanthropic giving are very limited. There are policies and programs that provide incentives and financing, and could potentially be leveraged to develop social enterprises.

Legislative bodies and government agencies have enormous power and resources to develop the sector. Supporting legislation that simplifies the establishment, implementation, and reporting of social enterprise activity would go very far to foster their growth. Some countries in Latin America are beginning to implement "B Corporation" certification, a certification process that recognizes entities focused on social and environmental impact. Certifying social enterprises could potentially position them to leverage funding. In Central and Eastern Europe, new labeling legislation can also be adopted by social enterprises in order to attract needed capital. Additionally, agencies can use their project approval and procurement powers to support social enterprises, and also establish or subsidize financing mechanisms specifically for them. And finally, government agencies can play a leading role in nurturing networks and collaborative opportunities for all stakeholders to share experiences, learn, and advance the field.

Capacity-Support Structures and Scaling Best Practices

There is a slow but rising trend toward the development of capacity-support structures for social enterprise, both within more traditional actors such as government and universities, as well as newly emerging ones such as incubators and other intermediaries. Traditional actors such as universities have a unique opportunity to develop the next generation of social entrepreneurs and ecosystem leaders. Intermediaries tend to be divided among those that are *community driven*, and have looser and less formal initiatives to support social enterprise, and those that are more *process driven*, and provide tailored technical assistance and more structured support, often based on private sector strategies and tools. There is a need to expand the universe of intermediaries that can provide direct technical, financial, and managerial assistance, as well as links to resources such as potential clients, business partners, donors, and impact investors.

Capacity support should be tailored and respond to the specific development stage of each enterprise. This usually requires patient investment of time and money. Particular attention needs to be given to the development of early-stage and first-scaling social enterprises. First scaling of a social enterprise refers to the stage[9] of development during which the enterprise has consolidated its operations and is capable of beginning more rapid growth or replication to achieve greater social impact. Best practice tools need to be developed to ensure that leadership, management, and governance issues are addressed and that appropriate scaling business models and strategies are identified. Incubators and other intermediaries must educate donors and investors on the early costs inherent in developing social enterprises, as well as the future financial and social benefits.

Capital for Growing Social Enterprises

NESsT research of the landscape in both Central Europe and Latin America in the past five years demonstrated very few financing instruments available for social enterprises to fund their start-up, consolidation, and growth. Support for early-stage enterprise development is generally scarce and short term. Local philanthropy is not well developed, and most international donors (important exceptions will be discussed) have not yet been ready to provide the significant, multiyear investment required by early-stage enterprises.

In Latin America, despite the presence of a microfinance sector, there are few actual experiences of social enterprise lending or equity investments. Many nonprofits have become too accustomed to receiving grants, and seek the same type of financing when developing social enterprises. Social enterprises usually have few assets for collateral, and providing personal collateral for a social enterprise can be complicated. Some early-stage impact investors have established operations in Latin America, but most impact investing has been in large, late-stage enterprises, with minimum investment levels far exceeding the capacities of start-up enterprises.

Foundations and multilateral agencies should support multiyear commitments to develop the infrastructure and ecosystem of the social enterprise economy. Corporations, financial institutions, philanthropists, and impact investors can focus more directly on providing resources to early-stage social enterprises. Corporations can practice "engaged philanthropy" that leverages volunteer support for social enterprises, and can enter communities with a view to including social enterprise in their core business. Family foundations and individual philanthropists have greater flexibility to be innovative on the funding side such as underwriting patient capital. Support for field building, such as the development of metrics and research and dissemination of knowledge and practice, will go far to professionalize social enterprises and attract needed capital. The pioneering donor practices highlighted in this book must be replicated, and local resources tapped if early-stage social enterprises are to obtain capital necessary for their growth.

Financing is clearly critical for the development of the social enterprise economy in emerging markets. Lessons from NESsT's experience demonstrate that grants, loans, and equity have specific roles in the development of social enterprises, and when used wisely, can be the key driver to success. Tailored financial packages that offer flexible grants alongside softer loans or equity with returns contingent on future performance are ways to adapt to the social costs and longer growth periods needed by social enterprises. Establishing alternative loan and loan guarantee funds and mechanisms is important. Intermediaries also require financing not only to provide capacity support, but also to demonstrate models and disseminate best practices.

Generally, impact investors seek opportunities in later-stage enterprises. The recommendations in this book will accelerate the development of a pipeline of social enterprises ready for impact investments. However, emerging markets must also promote the opportunities for investors and support the development of early-stage impact-investment funds that can invest in earlier stages of social enterprise development, where financial returns do not always precede social ones. Providing tools that help investors navigate the complex policy and regulatory environments of emerging market countries is an important entry point to foster more investments.

Policies creating a supportive environment, intermediaries enabling early-stage enterprises via incubators and other programs, and a wide range of donors and private sector financial institutions creating and extending appropriate funding for social enterprises—these collective actions will create huge social and economic benefits in emerging market economies. The following chapters provide greater detail on how others have successfully taken these steps, the benefits they have achieved, and how we can successfully expand this impact.

Part I

REGULATION AND POLICY

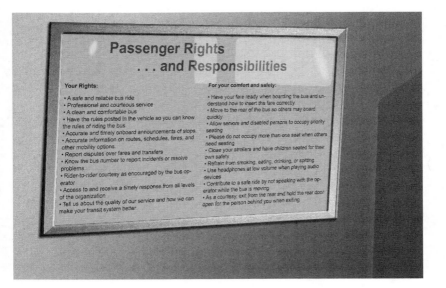

Passenger Rights
. . . and Responsibilities

Your Rights:

- A safe and reliable bus ride
- Professional and courteous service
- A clean and comfortable bus
- Have the rules posted in the vehicle so you can know the rules of riding the bus
- Accurate and timely onboard announcements of stops.
- Accurate information on routes, schedules, fares, and other mobility options.
- Report disputes over fares and transfers
- Know the bus number to report incidents or resolve problems
- Rider-to-rider courtesy as encouraged by the bus operator
- Access to and receive a timely response from all levels of the organization
- Tell us about the quality of our service and how we can make your transit system better

For your comfort and safety:

- Have your fare ready when boarding the bus and understand how to insert the fare correctly
- Move to the rear of the bus so others may board quickly
- Allow seniors and disabled persons to occupy priority seating
- Please do not occupy more than one seat when others need seating
- Close your strollers and have children seated for their own safety
- Refrain from smoking, eating, drinking, or spitting
- Use headphones at low volume when playing audio devices
- Contribute to a safe ride by not speaking with the operator while the bus is moving
- As a courtesy, exit from the rear and hold the rear door open for the person behind you when exiting

2

THE REGULATORY AND POLICY
VACUUM FOR SOCIAL ENTERPRISE
IN LATIN AMERICA*

The philanthropic tradition in Latin America has been deeply rooted in the context of social services provided by religiously affiliated charities and the government, which led to a weakened civil society sector. As many countries transitioned to democratic republics, the flow of philanthropic funds coming from foundation and multilateral agency support outside the region stopped, creating a veritable vacuum. It can be argued that social enterprise has grown in response to the many social challenges that remain and have not been addressed by the traditional sources of social giving. This chapter will briefly review some historical and cultural aspects of the development of the civil society sector in general and the social enterprise sector specifically, and analyze the current regulatory and policy environment (including government programs) for social enterprises in Argentina, Brazil, Chile, Peru, and Ecuador. It concludes with recommendations that would significantly increase the capacity of the social enterprise sector to address economic and social challenges in Latin America.

RELEVANCE OF SOCIAL ENTERPRISES IN ADDRESSING
LATIN AMERICA'S SOCIAL PROBLEMS

In Latin America, the reform coalitions that pushed and implemented the transition from oligarchic rule from 1910 to about 1950 were comprised not only of labor unions, but also of dissident factions of the oligarchy. These cross-class reform coalitions excluded rural peasants and unorganized urban workers, perpetuating their political marginalization. While postwar import substitution industrialization (ISI) strategies accommodated welfare entitlements for the organized urban working class, they largely failed to address the impoverishment of the politically excluded classes. In short, these political realignments and ISI strategies resulted in a highly skewed welfare system that benefited the middle class and upper echelons of the blue-collar working class.[1]

Social problems that plague the region stem from such issues as inequality, low pay in large informal employment sectors, and the lack of access to quality health care and education, to name a few. Investment in job creation and innovative programs to address these issues are key to the improvement of communities in the region. In more economically advanced countries, CSOs and philanthropy have been central to addressing these same social problems. Yet, the culture of giving has only recently begun showing signs of maturation in Latin America. According to the Johns Hopkins Center for Civil Society Studies, "in a ranking of 36 nations, Latin American countries—with the exception of Argentina—appeared in the bottom 10 in terms of volunteering and giving as a share of GDP."[2] Further, Richard Kiy of the International Community Foundation states that, "until recently 74 percent of average nonprofits' income came from fees for services, 15 percent from the public sector and 10 percent from private donations…and when you separate out international giving, national private philanthropy is in the single digits."[3] Giving has become a new phenomenon among the growing middle class in Latin America, but stronger institutional support is necessary to deepen the culture of giving.

KEY BARRIERS TO THE DEVELOPMENT OF SOCIAL ENTERPRISES IN LATIN AMERICA

Certainly, barriers exist for social enterprise development across the globe, and the specific barriers depend on the context. In Latin America, barriers have included a lack of entrepreneurial culture, limited access and use of information and communication technologies, growth restriction for small and expanding companies, lack of skill development, limited networks, and limited access to financing.[4] Importantly, the phrase "social enterprise" and its various definitions have only recently begun to enter the vocabulary of public actors. This, in and of itself, presents a huge challenge for social entrepreneurs, incubators, and investors who are all attempting to work within existing frameworks and simultaneously trying to expand those frameworks to benefit this new venture class.

ROLE OF LATIN AMERICAN COUNTRY POLICIES IN ADDRESSING BARRIERS

Although much debate exists over the balance needed between the role of government and the role of the private sector in reducing inequality and poverty, and increasing access to basic services, structuring public policy remains central to the ability of a nation to solve these problems in an entrepreneurial and sustainable manner.

There are interesting contradictions related to social enterprise in Latin America. There are no regulatory or legal frameworks recognizing social enterprises, and social enterprise is generally not part of any public policy debate, although this is starting to change in some countries. CSOs can sell products and services to generate income for their social purpose, but they often have to pay income tax and there is no recognition of the many positive effects brought about by their work. And there are few philanthropic incentives for donors who might want to provide charitable contributions to these entities.

Regulators are unsure of exactly how to treat social enterprises because they exist in a space between exclusively profit driven and sufficiently charitable in their purposes. There is no "in between" type of legal entity, falling between fully commercial organization and a recognized charity. And, regulations and associated bureaucracy that do exist tend to be excessive and encumbering. "The rules channel resources in a way that is not necessarily the most efficient," argues Claudio Lottenberg, president of Instituto Israelita de Responsabilidade Social Albert Einstein (IIRSAE), Brazil's largest private donor.[5] Existing laws governing corporations and charities are too restrictive. For-profit firms, it can be argued, often face pressure to abandon social goals in favor of increasing profits. Nonprofit firms and charities are needlessly restricted in their ability to raise capital when they need to grow. Arguably, this prevents socially minded organizations from pursuing their goals as efficiently as possible.[6]

There are recent efforts to try to adapt to the region (see box 2.1 on Sistema B) the US Benefit Corporation (B Corp) program, which certifies companies that meet certain social and environmental standards. However, although this will no doubt contribute to putting social enterprise on the map in the region, some fear that it could also lead to pigeonholing social enterprises, restricting them to this definition, and stifling other innovative efforts that could also encompass the dual purpose of social enterprises. Some argue that "a more ideal environment would be one that allows a multitude of organizational forms which social entrepreneurs can take advantage of depending on their own circumstance, and not bound by various constraints."[7] The issue of excluding certain types of social enterprises is also raised in chapter 3 regarding recent efforts adopted by the European Union (EU) to label social enterprises in that region.

Box 2.1 Sistema B and the Benefit Corporation

"Benefit Corporation"—usually referred to as a B Corp—creates the legal framework for socially focused enterprises to stay true to their social goals.

B Corps make up a specific class of corporation bound by law to create measureable social benefits through its existence and operations, as well as benefits to shareholders. This concept is taking hold in individual states across the United States through a combination of optimal existing legislative and judicial environments, the creation of legal frameworks to allow for third-party certification of B Corps, and market enthusiasm.

To qualify as a B Corp, a firm must have an explicit social or environmental mission, and a legally binding fiduciary responsibility to take into account the interests of workers, the community, and the environment as well as its shareholders. It must also publish independently verified reports on its social and environmental results, alongside its financial results. Other than that, it can go about business as usual.

The B Corp is a deliberate effort to change the nature of business by changing corporate law, led by B Lab, a nonprofit organization (NPO) based in Pennsylvania. B Lab has entered Latin America through Sistema B. This regional program aims to transfer the B Corp to Latin America, establishing B businesses in the region, and working with governments to recognize this type of entity within regulatory frameworks.

Sistema B has identified three main strategic areas:

- Community building for B Corp business leaders in the region.
- Promoting support systems to generate greater access to financing and capital market opportunities and positioning opportunities for exchange, knowledge management, and installation capabilities around innovation and social entrepreneurship.
- Motivating public policy and new legal forms that are aligned with B Corps and their support systems.

Sistema B plans to support and help create 500 B Corp businesses in South America by 2015, which will generate measurable social and environmental benefits. Initially, Sistema B will focus efforts on Argentina, Brazil, Chile, and Colombia to accomplish the following:

- Building a community of 150 B Corp companies by the end of 2013
- Implementation and execution of support systems
- Development of multiple strategies for awareness and communication at regional and national level
- Development of different areas of exchange and reflection
- Conduct regional investigations about the market potential for B Corps
- Development of a long-term strategic plan to raise necessary funding and building financially sustainable business models

REGIONAL, LEGAL, REGULATORY, AND TAX CONSIDERATIONS

Over the course of several years, NESsT has worked with legal advisors to complete a series of country-specific guides in Latin America focusing on the legal and regulatory framework for self-financing (activities that generate income to be used to advance the organization's mission) and social enterprise among CSOs.[8] Given that most social enterprises currently operating in the region are set up within a nonprofit structure, it is important to understand how NPOs are formed and the challenges they confront. The following is a legal and regulatory survey of Argentina, Brazil, Chile, Ecuador, and Peru. This review considers the tax systems, registration, classification, funding, and self-financing for CSOs and prospective social enterprises.

The key findings from this survey include the following:

- There is no legislation for nonprofit or for-profit social enterprise.
- Commercial activities, as stipulated by legislation, are permitted as long as revenues generated go back to mission activities.
- Tax exemption varies from no exemption, to exemption depending on legal form, to exemption tied to a specific sector (e.g., social services).
- Often regulations and/or their interpretation are at the discretion of a specific ministry, or a specific regional or local official.
- Procedures are often complex and bureaucratic.
- Benefits for philanthropic giving are very limited—no individual deductions are allowed in most countries and corporate deductions are limited to certain sectors, such as culture or education.
- There exists little appreciation for the government savings derived from social enterprises.

These findings, therefore, emphasize once again the challenges social enterprises face to establish themselves, attract capital, and operate. A summary of the findings are in box 2.2, followed by a narrative of the situation in each country.

LEGAL AND REGULATORY FRAMEWORK

In *Argentina*, the legal system does not provide specific legislation for CSOs (civil associations and foundations);[9] rather, they are primarily governed by the civil code. The current law that establishes foundations refers to the financial resources coming from donations, and does not mention self-generated income. Current legislation on commercial activities is blind to the nature of the activity in question and focuses exclusively on the final purpose of the activity's profits (destination-of-income test). However, despite the more flexible nature of the code, in practice the provisions are interpreted on a case-by-case basis by administrative and judicial judges. And given the general government distrust of NPOs and current realities that limit and pose barriers to commercial activities, particularly among foundations, many entities are faced with the dilemma of whether or not to engage in self-generated income. There are currently no bills or efforts that seek to change this situation, which restrains social enterprise development overall.

Brazil is similar to Argentina; there is a lack of legislation specific to CSOs, and they can practice commercial activities as long as profits generated are destined to the mission of the organization. However, perhaps somewhat different is the legal regulation that encourages CSOs to seek ways to generate their own revenues through self-financing or commercial activities and to decrease their reliance on public funding through contracts or subsidies. Brazilian legislation is very clear in not linking commercial activity to profit. It is perfectly possible for a NPO to carry out commercial activities, as long as it follows a list of legal requirements that attempt to guarantee that the resources will be used to further

Box 2.2 Legal and regulatory overview of social enterprises[10]

	Legal characteristics	Definition of social enterprise	Criteria to conduct commercial activities	Income tax—blanket tax	Income tax—destination of income	Income tax—source-of-income	Value added tax (VAT)
Definition	Organizations are considered NPOs as long as their objective is to provide a public benefit and uphold the principle of nondistribution.	Legislation in region refers to commercial or economic activities of NPOs. The term "social enterprise" is not used.	*Principle-purpose test:* An organization's commercial activity cannot be its principal activity. *Destination-of-Income Test:* An organization must devote all of its commercial-activity income to its not-for-profit purposes.	The organization is not limited by the level or type of activity, but is taxed on all revenues generated by these activities regardless of how the revenues are used.	The organization is not limited by the level or type of economic activity, but is not taxed on all income that is not used to further its public-benefit purposes.	The organization is taxed for all income generated from non-mission-related activity even if the income is used to support mission-related programs.	
Argentina	Civil associations, foundations, and simple associations	Civil legislation does not differentiate between commercial activities and other types of income-generating activities for CSOs, as long as	Destination of income: an organization must devote all of its income to its not-for-profit purposes— all profits must be	No	Yes	Yes	17% foundations have lost their exemption from income tax, VAT, and other taxes. Associations can, however, engage in commercial activities with some VAT

		these are considered within the objectives defined in their bylaws.	reinvested in the organizational mission.		No	restrictions depending on the particular activity. VAT implies a significant cost.
Brazil	Civil associations and foundations	As long as the commercial activity does not become the purpose of the organization, they can engage in it.	Destination of income: NPOs apply all surplus wealth to the furtherance of their purpose.	No	Yes	No	17%
Chile	Corporations and foundations	CSOs may pursue commercial activities as long as they are not principal activities, rather are incidental or supplementary or operations of the organization or assist in promoting its mission.	Destination of income: surplus income generated must be applied to the mission as described in its bylaws.	Yes (20%), except social assistance organizations that are exempted by the president.	No	No	18%. A CSO seeking to open a commercial line of business of any kind must necessarily be considered a VAT taxpayer; there are very few special exemptions.
Ecuador	Corporations and foundations	Law does not address commercial activity in relation to organizations working for the public benefit.	Destination of income: Must obtain 5%–15% of annual budget from donations.	No	Yes	No	12%

continued

Box 2.2 Continued

Legal characteristics	Definition of social enterprise	Criteria to conduct commercial activities	Income tax— blanket tax	Income tax— destination of income	Income tax— source-of-income	Value added tax (VAT)
	Though NPOs are not explicitly prohibited from engaging in commercial activities, there are no regulations.	If a surplus exists, it may not be accumulated for more than one fiscal period, and must be invested toward fulfilling the mission. Bylaws must clearly state that commercial activity will be destined to mission fulfillment.				
Peru Associations, foundations, committees, and NGO/civil associations	Legislation does not differentiate between commercial activities and other types of income-generating activities, so long as it furthers the social purpose.	Destination of income: revenue/ profit derived from activities must be destined toward its social purpose.	No	No	Yes	19%

its cause and will not be misused in any way. The key problem in Brazil is that these regulations are not widely known by authorities and are often subject to random and conflicting interpretations, contributing to confusion on the part of CSOs. There has also been corruption and abuse of the law among entities that conduct commercial activities. Although these are isolated cases, they received significant attention from the public and contributed to promoting a negative public image of CSOs.

Chile is also similar to Argentina and Brazil, in that there is no specific legal framework for CSOs; they are governed by the civil code and are considered legal entities like all others.[11] However, unlike the other countries in this chapter, the basic legal regulations governing CSO commercial activities in Chile are identical to those governing any private entity. Since CSO commercial activities, with the exception of those conducted by CSOs classified as exempt from paying income tax by the president of the republic (NPOs that practice welfare or social assistance), are uniformly regulated not only within the sector but also in line with the for-profit sector, the system is relatively simple to administer. Many business and government leaders believe that this uniform legislation is justifiably neutral and that establishing different sets of rules for CSOs and for-profit businesses would give unfair advantages to CSOs. However, the simplicity of the system underscores its problems since the uniform treatment of commercial activities conducted by CSOs and for-profit businesses fails to recognize the public benefits achieved by CSOs, the additional social costs that are incurred in conducting commercial activities by social enterprises, and the government savings that are derived from these activities.

The case of *Ecuador* is in keeping with others; CSOs (civil associations and foundations) are constituted within the civic code. Unlike the recent changes made in Chile, these entities must be approved by the president of the republic, through a presidential decree. In Ecuador, foundations and corporations may engage in commercial activities provided the profits are put toward the organizational mission and objectives. Legal recognition of this right is still implicit. For example, the Tax Regulation 40 mentions that an entity of this nature must obtain between 5 and 15 percent of its annual budget from donations, which implies that the majority of income could possibly come from self-financing activities generated by the organization itself.

Although in Ecuador there is currently no policy or specific law to regulate a CSO's commercial activities, and this gives organizations a certain level of flexibility, it also allows the authorities to make decisions based on their own interpretation or understanding of the law. And, the tax regulation authority—the SRI—evaluates if CSOs are actually putting their goods and income toward their specific purposes, and if they are doing so with all of their resources or only with a percentage of them. The diversity of forms and activities has had a negative effect on the authorities' perception of the work carried out by CSOs, which has led to tougher regulations, such as increased oversight and application of sanctions and penalties for those organizations that do not comply with the laws.

In the case of *Peru*, where CSOs (civil associations, committees, and foundations)[12] are also governed by the civil code, there are no specific legal provisions for regulating their economic activities. The development of these types of activities is contemplated and legally permissible, provided they do not threaten the nonprofit status and are related to or further the social purpose. No clear legislation has been established in Peru for promoting CSO commercial activities. Specifically, no significant tax incentives have been created that would motivate CSOs to develop economic activities. This situation is the result of the general tax administration policies over the last few years, which have been designed to increase tax collection and eliminate tax exemptions (or limit their application).

Finally, none of the countries has legislation that is specifically aimed at for-profit social enterprises, nor are they provided with particular benefits or incentives. Box 2.3 summarizes how these entities are treated by the legal and regulatory framework in Brazil.

Box 2.3   For-profit social enterprise in Brazil

Brazilian for-profit social enterprises may only be created in the form of a company or a corporation (or individual limited liability company, if there is single "quota holder") and cannot benefit from the tax exemptions and incentives that NPOs enjoy.

The limited liability company is by far the most common business form in Brazil because of its simplicity, flexibility, and low cost, plus the limited liability of its quota holders in relation to the obligations undertaken by the company. Within certain reasonable requirements, Brazilian quota holders are legally entitled to create any contractual rights and obligations in the corporate documents of the limited liability company. Therefore, social entrepreneurs may create provisions to address the needs of for-profit social enterprise.

However, quota holders enter contractual obligations without the supervision of a governmental or independent regulatory body. As a result, the quota holders may overturn such agreements, posing legal risk that the company may suddenly change from a for-profit social enterprise to a pure for-profit company, without regard to any social endeavor.

In this sense, the paramount difference between the Brazilian law and the Community Interest Company (CIC) corporate[13] model in the United Kingdom is the adoption of mandatory rules that ensure the compliance of for-profit social enterprises with the social purposes set in their respective bylaws. In addition, the CIC statute created an independent regulatory entity to approve new CICs and oversee compliance with statutory duties.

Among these duties, the limitation on the payment of dividends and rules governing the transfer of assets could be considered to create a Brazilian hybrid for-profit social enterprise. However, limitation—but not the exclusion—on the payment of dividends can be established. The Brazilian civil code includes a mandatory rule that makes null and void clauses that exclude any of the quota holders from the sharing of profits.

In order to prepare for distribution of a low percentage of net income, partners are given discretion to allocate the remaining income. Profit can be reinvested by the company and an accounting reserve for profits (up to 30% of capital) may be created. Where this limit is exceeded, the quota holders can capitalize the reserves (i.e., turn them into capital) and need not distribute them as dividends. Additionally, the distribution of profits by a limited liability company need not be made in accordance with the respective ownership interests of the shareholders and may be distributed disproportionately, provided all quota holders agree or upon resolution of the majority of the quota holders, if the articles of association allow so.

In Brazil, asset lock clauses inserted in the limitada's bylaws have not been tested before the courts and it is not possible to prevent quota holders from simply changing the articles of association to a different structure. Finally, Brazilian for-profit social enterprises would basically be subject to the authority of the Ministry of Development, Industry, and Trade, which has not enacted any particular regulation to address social enterprise needs. Therefore, the enactment of a new federal law to amend the civil code, or the creation of legislation to support the hybrid model of for-profit enterprises would be crucial.

TAXATION SYSTEM AND INCENTIVES

In *Argentina*, CSO commercial activity is not taxed as long as the revenues generated are designated to the organization's mission (destination of income) and the source of the income comes from mission-related activities (source of income). However, due to a series of contradictory laws, foundations[14] today are reluctant to pursue commercial activities. There are also limitations regarding tax benefits for philanthropic donations. The Income Tax Law (article 81, clause c) allows contributors to claim donations as tax deductible, but only when these are made to tax-exempt entities whose primary purpose or mission falls within any of the following areas: (1) medical aid (nonprivate sector); (2) scientific and technological research; (3) scientific research on economic, political, and social issues related to political party development; and (4) early education and higher education, and degrees bestowed officially by the National Ministry of Culture and Education. Where applicable, the benefit specifically involves the following:

1. The donation is considered to be an expense that is deductible from the taxable base. In practice, the savings consist of the tax rate applied to the

donation, which varies based on the different contributor categories (between 6% and 35%).
2. The deduction cannot exceed 5 percent of the donor's net profits for the fiscal year in which the donation is made.[15]

In *Brazil*, foundations and associations are not taxed for commercial activities as long as the income is designated to the social purpose of the organization. For nonprofit entities, the conditions for constitutional immunity[16] or exemption are broad, such that NPOs are rarely taxed, even for commercial activity. Immunity is only granted to CSOs dedicated to education or social assistance. Exemption can apply to the following: "Philanthropic, recreational, cultural, scientific, and civic organizations that offer the services they were created to offer to the individuals for whom they are intended, without profit as a motive."[17] Exemption is much more broadly applied than immunity, reaching entities dedicated to many activities, as long as they are NPOs. The inclusion of the term "philanthropic" means that the majority of CSOs are exempt as long as they do not distribute their profits. To earn immunity or exemption from income tax, a series of requirements must be met that are related to good governance and transparency.[18] The application of Brazil's other taxes applied to commercial activities (sale of event tickets, sale of products, services, royalties, etc.) differs for CSOs in education and social assistance versus those focusing on other areas. It should be noted that the tax code, in particular, is even more difficult to comprehend because of the division of responsibility for taxation. Each state and municipality has its own rules and regulations with their own specificities.

With regard to philanthropic donations, Federal Statute No. 9,249/95 provides that all donations from corporations to NPOs meeting certain requirements provided by law (qualified as "public interest" organizations) are deductible from the corporate entity's operating income, limited to 2 percent of the amount of such operating income. The donations are accounted for as expenses. As a result, donors benefit by reducing the amount of their operating income, which is the basis for calculation of their income tax and social contribution obligations. This deductibility generally provides the donor with a 34 percent return on the amount donated in the form of a reduction in the donor's income tax and social contribution obligations, meaning that for each BRL 100.00 donated, the donor has a reduction of approximately BRL 34.00 in its income tax and social contribution obligation. Tax incentives are also provided for donations for specific projects tied to specific laws including the Cultural Promotion Law or Rouanet Law (cultural projects), the Audiovisual Law, the Sports Promotion Law, and those linked to the Fund for Childhood and Adolescence. Amounts allowed for deductions depend on the project and can vary from 1 to 80 percent of income, which also varies between individuals and legal entities. There are also benefits for donations given for certain state- or city-level activities.[19]

The *Chilean* tax system is perhaps the least favorable toward CSO commercial activities because there is little differentiation made between nonprofit and for-profit entities—there is a blanket income tax. The majority of entities must pay first category income tax, at a rate of 17 to 20 percent. The only exception is for welfare organizations that have been granted exemption by the president, and it can be applied only when those activities are mission related.[20] To be eligible, these organizations are subject to a rigorous application process with the Ministry of Hacienda (Interior) and the actual tax exemption is granted and monitored by the Internal Tax Service (Servicio de Impuestos Internos). Generally speaking, the system tends to exclude community-based organizations, as well as those focusing on health, education, culture, human rights, and the environment even if they are working with low-income communities. There are very few philanthropic tax incentives in Chile, and those that exist only apply to companies, not to private individuals. Donations (up to 10% of a company's earnings) made for approved cultural and educational activities can be considered as expenses and deducted from earnings, which reduces the overall tax amount.

Ecuador exempts CSOs from paying income tax as long as they meet all of the requirements, including declarations and third-party withholding. Even when there have been no business transactions or the organization is not operating, it must make the respective declaration. The Internal Income Tax Law has not focused on the origin or source of income (specifically for income originating from commercial activities). Rather, it generally establishes the tax exemption for CSOs and those working for the public benefit whose profits have been destined toward specific and exclusive purposes in the country, provided that this income is not distributed among partners (nonprofit purpose). However, income generated from commercial activities must be reinvested within one year; failing that, the organization must pay income tax on any accumulated interest. A good tax reform measure would be to allow NPOs to maintain a certain percentage of reserve funds without having to pay taxes.

Although for many years, donations from within Ecuador and abroad were tax deductible, they were used by some as a way to evade taxes. The tax authority (SRI, or Servicio de Rentas Internas), in an effort to increase efficiency and control, chose to limit the deductibility of these contributions, applying a progressive elimination of tax shields (caused by legal gaps) to avoid a drastic reduction in tax collection. The percentage of tax deductions varied for the next few years until they were completely eliminated in 1996, leaving only the possibility of deducting donations made to universities. Currently, donations may not be deducted from the donor's income tax, but they are exempt from paying VAT when donated to public sector entities and private institutions and associations that are legally constituted and dedicated to charity, culture, education, research, health, or sports.[21]

In *Peru*, CSO commercial activity is also tax exempt. However, the exemption is not across the board, but rather tied to the specific purpose of the entity, determined by law and applied by the National Tax Authority (Superintendencia Nacional de Administración Tributaria, or SUNAT) when a CSO applies to the corresponding administrative registry. Income tax exemption has been established for associations and foundations, but not for committees (see endnote 12 for definition). The law provides exemptions for income generated by foundations and nonprofit associations whose corporate charter exclusively comprises the following purposes: charity, social assistance, education, culture, science, art, literature, athletics, politics, unions, and housing. Their profits must be destined toward their specific purposes in the country, and cannot be distributed directly or indirectly among members; the bylaws must establish that in the case of dissolution, assets will be destined toward any of the purposes contemplated in the law.[22] Interestingly, the law also stipulates that income from business operations of foundations and nonprofit associations, other than purposes established in the bylaws, will not be exempt from this tax. However, in practice, several court rulings indicate that the government is less concerned about compliance with the bylaws and tends to exempt commercial income as long as it is destined for social purpose.

In terms of philanthropic donations, the law stipulates they are tax deductible if made by businesses to charity, social assistance or public benefit, education, culture, science, art, literature, athletics, health, historical heritage, indigenous culture, or other similar areas. The deduction may not exceed 10 percent of the business net profit after compensation for losses. To receive these donations, the CSO must previously qualify as a donation recipient by the Department of Economy and Finance through ministerial resolution. There are no tax-deduction benefits for individuals.

VAT

In all of the countries researched, CSOs are subject to a VAT ranging from 12 percent in the case of Ecuador to 20 percent in the case of Chile. There are very few exceptions to this; probably the most generous is Brazil, where CSOs can be exempted from charging VAT if the activity is not ongoing, or for certain products made by them. There are also state-by-state provisions that allow CSOs not to pay VAT for purchases. In Argentina, there are VAT exemptions for the sale of services related to the mission of the CSO, and there are also exemptions for sale of large volumes of products. There are also exemptions for purchases of certain products no matter the legal entity. In Chile, there are very few exceptions to VAT payments, even for those organizations that have been designated welfare institutions by the president. The exceptions are VAT on tickets to cultural events or events sponsoring the construction of buildings for certain causes, some educational activities, including CSO capacity-building trainings. In the case of Ecuador, all commercial activity is subject to VAT unless the activity is related to a product that is VAT exempt. There are also VAT exemptions for exported products such as fair trade. And, similar to the case with Peru, products and services paid for by international development assistance are exempt from VAT. Lastly, in Peru, CSO commercial activity that is ongoing is not VAT exempt. There are some exemptions for educational activities, activities determined by presidential decree for cultural and athletic institutions, and income derived from lending activities (interest payments), which is also applicable to for-profit entities.

GOVERNMENT POLICIES AND PROGRAMS

The lack of recognition of social enterprise in legislation in Latin America makes assessing incentive policies and programs[23] for social enterprise quite difficult. A high-level assessment reveals that there are a number of important initiatives that provide incentives and infrastructure to foster entrepreneurial solutions to social problems, some of which are directly related to social enterprise. These programs and incentives can be categorized as focusing on job creation and income assistance for the very poor; cooperative or other types of collective-action assistance, including the development of labels; and capacity-building activities, including microfinance.[24] The following programs in Argentina, Brazil, Chile, and Peru can help social entrepreneurs organize themselves and solicit much needed seed capital and technical assistance.[25]

ARGENTINA

Regional Social Enterprise Network Program (Programa REDES)

This Ministry of Social Development program promotes economic and productive activities to improve the livelihood of low-income and vulnerable communities. It fosters and supports cooperation among government and civil society around a specific productive activity. It provides funding, technical assistance, and capacity building, and it recycles part of the funding to reassign to new productive activities.

Enterprises That Share a Collective Label (Emprendimiento de Marca Colectiva)

This is a program developed by the Ministry of the Republic of Argentina. A collective label is a distinctive sign to identify common products produced and/or services provided by groups of entrepreneurs in the social economy.[26] The label represents the values of partnership working, local identity, common production methods, and shared standards for each of the products.

The main purpose of this tool is to strengthen the production and marketing of the labeled products, providing value addition and giving them greater visibility, while ensuring their quality. At the same time, the label fosters social engagement, fair trade, and responsible consumption. The Ministry of Social Development supports entrepreneurs in building their brands, accompanies them in their design and image, and provides advice with regard to the procedures required to register with the National Institute of Industrial Property (INPI).

National Commission of Microcredit (CONAMI)

The commission was established by Law No. 26,117 to implement microcredit to organizations that comprise the country's social economy. It provides support and assistance to entrepreneurs and enterprising and grassroots organizations and builds bonds of trust and solidarity between workers and social organizations. More than 1,500 organizations (microfinance institutions) work together with the national government and other provincial and municipal agencies receive training, support, and funds for microcredit.

Socioproductive Projects "Get to Work" (Proyecto Socioproductivos "Manos a la Obra")

This program promotes the development of different localities and regions by supporting productive activities that lead to self-employment and offer goods and services that are of high quality and at fair prices. The support offered by this initiative includes the financing of machinery, tools and supplies for productive enterprises, and, ongoing technical assistance (training, organization and monitoring) to strengthen and optimize operations.

The implementation is done in conjunction with municipal, governmental, and social organizations that act as executing agencies. It promotes the formation of networks by putting entrepreneurs in touch with other organizations of the social economy, so they can share their experiences and replicate their successes.

National Institute of Cooperatives and Social Economy (INAES)

This decentralized agency exercises functions in the promotion, development, and oversight of cooperatives and social enterprises. It supports training, development, and promotion of the social economy as well as develops policies aimed at the promotion and consolidation of cooperation.

BRAZIL

National Economic and Social Development Bank (Banco Nacional de Desenvolvimiento Económico e Social—BNDES)

BNDES offers support for projects in the social and environmental development areas. BNDES incentivizes undertakings that encourage social environmental development or improve living conditions for people. The bank seeks to maximize the positive social impact of projects it finances, such as creating jobs and increasing local development. The most common types of financial support include lines of credit that are permanent in nature and that can be granted at any time, programs that have resource allocation and/or expiration dates, and funds managed by the BNDES.

Described below are six BNDES programs. Each is valid only for a specific period and may or may not be renewed by the BNDES.

Corporate Social Investments

"Corporate social investment" provides financing for the implementation, expansion, and consolidation of social investment programs and projects carried out by companies or in partnership with public institutions or NPOs.

Environmental Sanitation and Water Resources

"Environmental sanitation and water resources" programs increase access to basic sanitation services. Public- or private-sector players can participate in this program, thereby encouraging businesses to develop projects with these purposes.

Innovation

BNDES has an "Innovation" program designed to improve the competitive position of businesses. Innovation contributes to the creation of better-quality jobs, increased productivity, environmental sustainability, and the sustainable growth of the country. In order to effectively support innovation, BNDES acts in conjunction with existing public policies and in a manner that is complementary to other institutions, working in all sectors of the economy, including those of low and medium technology that are deemed more traditional.

Sustainable Businesses in the Amazon

The "BNDES Sustainable Businesses in the Amazon" program supports, by means of an investment fund, investment opportunities in the Amazon that generate financial returns and positive social and environmental results.

Microcredit

Microcredit is defined as small-value lending to formal and informal microentrepreneurs who would otherwise be without access to affordable credit. The BNDES Microcredit program promotes small businesses by providing microcredit to individual and corporate-oriented entrepreneurs. The program seeks to encourage employment, income growth, and social inclusion. Microentrepreneurial legal entities (defined as those having annual turnover less than or equal to BRL 360,000 or USD 180,000) are entitled to obtain resources from BNDES. This program is a reflection of an important trend in the Brazilian regulatory environment, specifically, to promote microcredit for its impact on the foundation of the economy, which is so important for social enterprises.

Innovation Fund for the Environment

The "BNDES Innovation Fund for the Environment" is a program that supports entrepreneurship and explores investment opportunities in innovative companies to promote the development of clean technologies. Clean technologies are those that, compared with conventional alternatives, minimize impact to the environment through actions such as reducing carbon emissions and other solid and liquid waste, waste treatment, and the more efficient use of resources (energy and other resources).

National Entrepreneurship Policy

Brazil's federal government has initiated a program denominated the "National Entrepreneurship Policy" to establish a legal framework for the treatment of issues relating to entrepreneurship and the promotion of a favorable business environment.

In its current iteration, we are unable to make any prediction relating to the policy's impact on social entrepreneurship. However, it is possible that this initiative will lead to meaningful discussions of a government agenda to promote entrepreneurship and ventures having positive social and environmental attributes.

The Brazilian Service of Support for Micro and Small Enterprises (Agência de Apoio ao Empreendedor e Pequeno Empresário—SEBRAE)

Founded in 1973, SEBRAE is a private entity of public interest funded primarily by Brazilian business taxes. SEBRAE works in rural and urban environments in all 27 Brazilian states and practically every economic sector. Its main mission is to support entrepreneurship and promote the competitive and sustainable development of Brazil's micro and small enterprises—a huge segment of all Brazilian businesses—thus contributing to the country's development agenda of income generation and job creation.

SEBRAE also encourages these micro and small enterprises to organize themselves in associations, cooperatives, local productive arrangements, and consortia to strengthen their competitiveness. SEBRAE provides them customized services based on collective projects and initiatives of common interest. SEBRAE's main services to micro and small enterprises cover opening markets, accessing technology, innovation, and financial services, and strengthening management practices and businesses processes.

In recognition of the importance of Brazil's social enterprise movement, SEBRAE is currently interested in developing a strategy to incorporate social businesses into the agency's services to micro and small enterprises. This topic has gained well-deserved attention at SEBRAE National, headquartered in Brasília and responsible for designing nationwide programs. In addition to SEBRAE's involvement with the 2012 Social Enterprise World Forum, held for the first time in Latin America (in Rio de Janeiro), the agency has been reaching out to organizations to jointly focus on mapping best regional and international practices, assessing its own portfolio, and promoting internal capacity building. These activities most likely will be followed by initiatives centered on developing methodologies, tools, tailored services, and metrics to capture and measure the social impact of Brazilian social enterprises.

Box 2.4 demonstrates how a social enterprise has been able to leverage a public policy that encourages the training and hiring of apprentices, and used it as a way to provide access to employment to a vulnerable community who would otherwise encounter many barriers to labor inclusion.

CHILE

The government of Chile has incorporated strategies for overcoming poverty and programs to encourage individual entrepreneurship. Such initiatives can open up certain sectors in the Chilean economy, and provide opportunities for investment.

Box 2.4   INCORES

INCORES[27] was created in 2010 (http://www.incores.org.br/), after its predecessor organization exited Brazil upon termination of its US Agency for International Development grant. The organization had trained Brazilian youth for eight years, and Tanya Andrade was determined not to let that accomplishment disappear. She worked with her small team day and night on a volunteer basis to establish the organization, raise funds, and complete a business plan for a social enterprise. The enterprise takes advantage of a legal requirement in Brazil for private companies (with eight or more employees) to have 5–15 percent of their workforce in apprenticeships trained by a certified training agency. The companies must pay for the training and mentoring of these apprentices. INCORES became a certified agency, and in less than 2 years has placed over 300 disadvantaged youth with local companies and is 96 percent self-sufficient. The enterprise's 2-year training program offers 1,840 hours of hands-on training and 460 hours of classroom learning. This careful training and mentoring prepares the youth for labor inclusion and ensures that they are able to meet the day-to-day demands of their employers while also preparing them for future employment. The law on apprentices drives the demand for this service since companies are required to work through a certified training agency. This procurement regulation provides a tremendous growth opportunity for INCORES whose high-quality services and proven track record demonstrate a strong scaling potential. The social enterprise has client contracts to place one thousand youth this year.

In a country with huge unemployment challenges for youth in poor communities, INCORES literally has life-changing impact on the youth, their families, and even other young people who see them as role models. The program's social impact has tremendous implications for overcoming poverty in Brazil.

Solidarity and Social Investment Fund (Fondo de Solidaridad e Inversión Social—FOSIS)

FOSIS's main purpose is to help finance, support, and develop programs, plans, projects, and activities that produce social development. FOSIS seeks to eradicate poverty and reduce vulnerability in Chile, and develops programs in three main areas: entrepreneurship, work skills, and social empowerment.

Institute of Agricultural Development (Instituto de Desarrollo Agropecuario—Indap)

Indap's main purpose is to support the development of small farmers or land workers through activities destined to promote production, strengthen human capital, and develop financial incentives in order to contribute to poverty alleviation, sustainability, and competitiveness of domestic agriculture. Among other actions, Indap provides credit assistance to organizations that develop programs providing direct benefit to rural areas. Indap administers grants or credit lines to contract such services directly from the private sector.

Technical Cooperation Service (Servicio de Cooperación Técnica—Sercotec)

Sercotec's main mission consists of promoting and supporting initiatives to improve the competitiveness of micro and small enterprises and to strengthen their ability to manage business. Among Sercotec's various entrepreneurship programs, "Seed Venture Capital" (Capital Semilla de Emprendimiento) is of particular interest. This program provides a line of credit that is meant to accommodate and support, both financially and technically, the best initiatives of entrepreneurs from all over Chile.

PERU

There are no established tax incentives in the current tax legislation that are specific to social enterprises. However, there are special tax regimes that promote the development of activities in certain geographical areas and sensitive sectors:

- *Jungle and Amazon Region*: The government supports the sustainable development of the Amazon by promoting conservation of biological diversity and natural protected areas. The Amazon region receives income tax benefits for the following activities: livestock and agriculture, agricultural production, aquaculture, fishing, extractive forestry, and so on.
- *High Andean regions*: This sector has tax exemptions in several areas in order to promote and support the development of production and services that add value, generate employment, and alleviate poverty in the High Andean regions. To qualify for these exemptions, beneficiaries must live 3,200 meters (10,500 feet) above sea level and must engage in the following activities: aquaculture, meat processing, forestry for commercial or industrial purposes, agro-industry, handicrafts, textiles, and so on.
- *CETICOS* (Centros de Exportación, Transformación, Industria, Comercialización y Servicios): These export, transformation, industry, sales, and services areas are clear geographic areas near the border defined as primary zones. Primary zones are part of the customs territory that includes customs buildings and structures, which are used for the purposes of land or sea disembarkation, embarkation, transport, or storage of goods. These areas have a series of tax exemptions for the purpose of converting them into development nodes.
- *Agricultural sector*: This sector provides tax benefits for individuals and businesses engaging primarily in crop or breeding activities (with the exception of

forestry). Tax benefits also apply to agro-industrial activities that primarily use fishing and livestock products outside the province of Lima and the constitutional province of Callao.

- *Aquaculture*: There are tax benefits for individuals and companies that develop aquaculture activities, such as breeding hydrobiological species. Tax benefits apply to research and primary processing of direct products.

OVERALL ANALYSIS AND RECOMMENDATIONS

An analysis of the legal and regulatory frameworks and tax systems for CSO commercial activity in these five countries reflects an inconsistency in allowing commercial activity and income tax exemptions. It might depend on the type of legal entity (i.e., in Argentina) and it most often depends on the particular social purpose of the entity, with greater benefits given to more traditional activities such as culture, education, and social assistance. The blanket tax applied in Chile is particularly worrisome given the large income inequality that exists in the country.

A second common denominator is that in many cases the laws and regulations are left to the interpretation of the tax authority officials and can often vary within countries based on city or state laws. Not only does this create certain inequities in the application of the laws and regulations, but it is also very confusing for entities that often do not have access to low-cost legal or tax advice. Trying to navigate the multiple regulations is extremely time consuming and discourages many CSOs from undertaking commercial activity. The regulations and procedures remain either unclear or unknown to social enterprise practitioners, tax and legal professionals, and the authorities who control and monitor CSO activities in the country.

Across the board, there are not many incentives for donations, particularly individual donations. Although there are tax deductions in all of the countries, they are mostly provided only for business income and given to philanthropists for donations made to specific activities. Again, there is an overemphasis on providing deductions for donations to cultural, educational, and welfare activities, and very few for social enterprises engaged in community development, the environment, health, and human rights. And the percentage of income that is tax deductible tends to be quite low, less than 10 percent in all of the countries. Given the level of accumulated wealth among the upper-economic tier in these countries,[28] the need to offer very strong philanthropic incentives becomes even more pertinent.

The overall framework seems to be based on mistrust and on the legacy of some organizations and companies that took advantage of tax incentives and benefits through questionable or illegal methods. A more uniform, friendly, transparent, and efficient enabling environment is needed. The visibility and transparency of CSOs must be strengthened, with clear guidelines on structure and governance, as well as ethical and responsible practices. CSO commercial activity should be monitored, but it should be recognized as addressing social problems that are often not being addressed by the private or public sectors.

Education and dissemination of existing policies is critical. Special attention should be placed on training government officials responsible for application of the legislation. CSOs need support and specialized technical assistance to help them comply with the requirements imposed by the tax regulations. The best solution would be for CSOs, intermediaries, legislators, and regulators to work together to achieve a better consensus on fostering the development of social enterprises. Self-regulation methods should be discussed, as well as serious policy incentives for the sector and a reduction in excessive government processes, layers, and regulations.

These recommendations become even more critical when considering the needs of early-stage social enterprises, where access to tax benefits and philanthropy, even in the form of patient investment capital, is even more necessary. Decreasing the social costs of enterprise activities makes these incentives key drivers of success. Claims of unfair competition seem to bear little weight when one considers that similar claims in countries such as the United States and the United Kingdom have not been substantiated given the costs associated with running these enterprises. And the government savings associated should also be recognized and compensated.

High-level policy discussions on the social enterprise sector are needed. Recognition of a class of corporations through Sistema B would be positive for the region in that it would put hybrid socially enterprise-focused entities on the map. However, this could exclude many entities and potentially provide an opportunity for political interests to do away with this certification process.

The policy environment in Latin America has yet to reach a maturation level that best serves the growing number of CSOs that are in need of self-financing activities, or that look to create social enterprises for their sustainability and to further a social mission. In sum, these country-specific summaries highlight that there is a need to have more uniform legislation, to recognize the value of these entities, and to increase the tax incentives and benefits for these enterprises and the donors that support them.

3

TRADE-OFFS BETWEEN REGULATION AND FOSTERING OF SOCIAL ENTERPRISE: THE CASE OF EUROPEAN UNION POLICIES*

INTRODUCTION

Social enterprise[1] has recently been propelled to the agenda of the European Commission (EC) and has become a top discussion item of policy makers, social enterprise practitioners and support organizations, social innovation groups, and social investors. In the midst of a major economic recession, Europe needs new approaches that address the current ills in an innovative and sustainable manner. The EC views social enterprise as a model with high potential to respond to these challenges and make Europe more market competitive, socially inclusive, and environmentally sustainable. Expectations are high for social enterprise to deliver, and the commission seems determined to do everything it can to provide the support mechanisms and regulatory framework to make this happen.

In April 2011, social entrepreneurship was included in the Single Market Act[2] as one of 12 levers to boost growth and strengthen confidence in the European economies. It envisaged the creation of more and better financing, enabling legislation, and a set of measures under the Social Business Initiative (SBI). The SBI was launched in November 2011[3] following several rounds of consultations with stakeholders, experts, and the public. The implementation of the SBI is underway; the legislative machinery has been set in motion, tripartite conversations are being held among the commission, the European Parliament, and the European Council, and further experts are involved in detailed consultations. A permanent consultative group, Groupe d'experts de la Commission sur l'entrepreneuriat social (GECES),[4] was set up in May 2012, whose mandate is to assist the relevant directorate generals of the commission (Internal Market and Services; Employment, Social Affairs and Inclusion; Enterprise and Industry), in the next three years, with the implementation of the SBI and with the design of future measures.

This chapter is an assessment and evaluation of EU policies for social enterprise development, looking at how the policies affected organizations and, in particular,

NESsT's work in the past 15 years in Central Europe. This assessment includes a variety of measures initiated and implemented in Brussels, as well as the translation of EU policies into action at the member states level. The acceleration of the new EU initiatives in 2011–2012 provided new information almost on a daily basis. This presents a challenging stage for analysis, much like shooting at a moving target. However, there is a compelling case to show how accomplishments and mistakes from the past can influence the building of a new, more effective, and powerful set of policies for social enterprise development in the EU.

DEFINING AND LABELING SOCIAL ENTERPRISES IN EUROPE

Social enterprise is not a new concept; it has existed in varying shapes and forms in European countries for over two decades and it has been called and defined as many different things. The wide variety of official and nonofficial definitions demonstrates different approaches and creates a lot of confusion even today. The terminology itself is very colorful, listing social business, social enterprise, social economy organization, social service provider, social firm, and social entrepreneurship among others. These terms often rely on common basic characteristics, while emphasizing specific features that they deem especially important. Social firms, for example, are market-led enterprises set up to create good-quality jobs for people disadvantaged in the labor market.[5]

Often the same term is borrowed and used with a very different meaning, or various terms are used (often within the same document) to mean the same thing. This has caused confusion among social enterprises themselves, which often are not sure which term to use. It also generates resistance among other potential partners, such as the public or the business sectors that have not found their way in the terminology jungle and have thus preferred to ignore social enterprises altogether. In some cases, partners took a term and created their own definition so that they had something to operate with.

There was no EU-wide agreed definition, so practices in EU member states varied a great deal. In the United Kingdom, which is the EU country with the most developed social enterprise sector, the definition is very broad and inclusive: "Social enterprise is a business driven by social and/or environmental purpose. They are trading organizations (their main income streams are revenues for goods and services provided, not grants or donations). Successful social enterprises generate surpluses or profits, which are reinvested towards achieving their social mission. Their assets are often locked for community purpose."[6]

Other European countries created legal definitions of social enterprise and enshrined them in specific laws. Either they created a new legal form (e.g., The Social Enterprise Act in Slovenia[7]) or they defined which of the existing legal forms can qualify as social enterprise and which ones cannot. In Slovenia, social enterprises can be of various nonprofit legal forms, (association, fund, foundation, cooperative, organization for people with disability) and of different types, classified on their field of activity: type A (products and services of public benefit) or B (employing marginalized people). By law they must have a defined social purpose, a market orientation, and be privately founded. Organizations that wish to obtain the social enterprise status have to register with the government.

In Slovakia, as described in box 3.1, the legal forms allowed for social enterprises cross the boundaries of private and public entities. Municipalities are allowed and encouraged to set up and register social enterprises, which is quite unique in the European context. In most countries, social enterprises are non-state entities, and according to Social Enterprise UK, even if they are some sort of spin out from the public sector, the involvement of the government is recommended to be transitional.[8]

Box 3.1   Social enterprise in Slovakia

In Slovakia, social enterprise is legally defined by the Employment Services Act, whose corresponding amendments entered into force in 2008. A social enterprise[9]

1. employs persons, who were disadvantaged job seekers prior to taking up the employment, as defined by the Employment Services Act (the share of such employees must be at least 30%);
2. must provide support and assistance to employees, who prior to taking up employment were disadvantaged job seekers, to find employment in the open labor market;
3. derives at least 30 percent of its funds from income from business activities; and
4. must be registered in the register of social enterprises (this is available at the Central Office of Labor, Social Affairs and Family).

Due to this definition in the Employment Services Act, the social economy in Slovakia is perceived predominantly as an employment policy tool, with the agenda dictated by the Ministry of Labor, Social Affairs and Family.[10] This can limit social enterprise work in other fields that are also creating social impact.

Another debated element of the Slovak definition is that it includes municipal companies in the social enterprise category. This is partly explained by the fact that one of the main tasks of municipalities in Slovakia is to help people obtain or create jobs. Successful municipal companies, enterprises created by municipal governments, try to put formal employment generation programs on sustainable footing by setting up businesses. This way they are able to generate social impact, providing opportunities for disadvantaged communities, as is the case of the Roma in Slovakia. NESsT's practical experience with municipal companies confirms that they focus on employment models: work integration for long-term unemployed or income generation (rural communities, small farmers). The revenues they generate may cover the costs of the company, while profits, if any, could go back to the social enterprise (further development) or to the municipality to finance solutions to problematic issues related to the beneficiaries of the social enterprise (e.g., improvement of the living conditions of the Roma minority).

Municipal social enterprises potentially create problems, however, when one takes into account that social enterprises as defined by the Slovak Employment Act are eligible for government subsidies for the creation and retention of jobs. Municipal social enterprises could thus crowd out other social enterprises, which are privately founded and have less or no access to government subsidies. Critiques of municipal social enterprises mention that they tend to be nonentrepreneurial in nature, given the reverse incentive system (no profit generation) typical of state-owned entities, so they don't meet a key criterion of social enterprise. There is also the problem of municipal companies being their own clients, carrying out activities with government financial support that would be their task, but which they don't have the budget to finance.[11]

Legislation in some countries was more functionalist in nature and focused on the social problems that social enterprises aimed to tackle and their targeted beneficiaries. They defined social enterprises as businesses that provide social services or help with the integration of unemployed people, poor communities, elderly, or children into the economy. In Slovakia, for example, social enterprise is defined within the Act of Employment Services.[12] This approach runs the risk of social enterprise being understood very narrowly, limited to a few fields of activity (or industry) that social enterprises are active in. It does not take into account the fact that social enterprises actually often challenge the existing systems/paradigms and aim to go back to the root causes of social problems. There are many other forms of business, however, that operate in the above industries and cannot be classified as social enterprises (e.g., private homes for elderly people that are for-profit companies).

In Poland, social enterprise is not defined officially, which allows for all types of legal entities (associations, foundations, and cooperatives) to launch social enterprise activities. In fact, Polish social enterprises were largely seen as a response to massive unemployment and the widening welfare gap, which followed the political and economic transition at the end of the 1980s.[13] This led to the rise and dominance of work integration social enterprises (WISEs) that took different shapes and forms. The emphasis on employment was further strengthened by the introduction in 2006 of a special legal form, the social cooperative. The act on social cooperatives encourages various disadvantaged groups to set up social cooperatives and thus provide employment for themselves, often by obtaining public contracts or performing public tasks. The government designated substantial amounts of funding to support the foundation of social cooperatives and created "Support Centers for Social Cooperatives" throughout the country.[14]

The social cooperatives were later copied by other Central European countries, including Hungary. There is now a lively debate and exchange of experiences between and within the two countries about the effectiveness and potential of social cooperatives.

Due to these laws, people began to interchange the concepts—social enterprise and social cooperative. This definitional confusion was especially problematic in Central European countries with little or no tradition of social economy and no examples of social enterprises. It made it difficult for social enterprises to identify themselves, and difficult or impossible to involve other stakeholders to work with them. It also caused mislabeling or the incorrect adoption of the term and ultimately resulted in the wrong allocation and utilization of resources (financial and others) that had been intended for social enterprise development.

NESsT uses and supports an inclusive, broad definition: "Social enterprise is a business created to further a social purpose in a financially sustainable way." Motivation and intent of purpose are the most important elements to assess whether or not an entity is a social enterprise. In other words, does it practice what it preaches? Does it try to balance the social, financial, and environmental bottom line in its everyday running of the business in order to solve a critical social issue? A broad definition such as this can be especially helpful in countries where the sector is only nascent or still very small, as it provides the space for the sector to grow and include many different models if they subscribe to the basics. At this stage, definition and regulations should focus on building and strengthening the social enterprise community. The new European social enterprise definition proposed in the SBI is lengthier, but contains most necessary elements without being too restrictive:

> Social enterprises seek to serve the community's interest (social, societal, environmental objectives) rather than profit maximization. They often have an innovative nature, through the goods or services they offer, and through the organization or production methods they resort to. They often employ society's most fragile members (socially excluded persons). They thus contribute to social cohesion, employment and the reduction of inequalities.[15]

Certainly, such a definition can be accepted by practitioners in the market, but more emphasis should be placed on the enterprise side—in other words, that social enterprises are market-oriented businesses, which need to be successful in a market environment in order to become sustainable. This is not a final definition and serious debates are taking place in the European Parliament, the European Economic and Social Committee, and other organs that are proposing amendments to the SBI definition. The final outcome may be more restrictive than the above, introducing, for example, the asset lock criteria, which is a key element in community-based social enterprises. It expresses the motivation of the founders very clearly: they are not interested in private gain or in getting their initial investment back. The UK Community Interest Company (CIC) Act[16] defines asset lock as "a general term used to cover all the provisions designed to ensure that the assets of the CIC (including any profits or other surpluses generated by its activities) are used for the benefit of the community."[17] The assets of the CIC must be retained within the CIC or can be transferred to another asset-blocked body or made available for the benefit of the community. "With only very limited exceptions such as the payment of dividends and the return of paid up capital on liquidation, a CIC's assets cannot be returned to its members unless they are themselves asset locked bodies."[18] Dividend payments are capped, however, if it is not an asset-locked company. According to the guidance of the UK CIC regulator, "the Dividend Cap strikes a balance between encouraging people to invest in CICs and the principle that the assets and profits of a CIC should be devoted to the benefit of the community." Not all social enterprises are community based, however, and a blanket application of the asset-lock requirement may reduce their chances to raise external capital, and may hinder the development of a social investment market.

Collective ownership is another debated element, which originates in the cooperative movements that make up the bulk of the social economy in some of the older EU member states, such as France or Italy. The appearance of new types of enterprises focusing on social causes (e.g., in many countries, nonprofit organizations [NPOs], small and medium enterprises [SMEs], or other) has moved the thinking away from collective ownership toward stakeholder engagement or beneficiary support. The latter concepts still express the commitment to community engagement and participation, while at the same time they do not require formal ownership of all stakeholders in the social enterprise, and are thus more inclusive.

It will be a huge step forward to have a commonly agreed definition for the EU, as it would help promote social enterprise in various sectors and at various levels, while also helping social enterprises access resources they have not had access to in the past. A final, inclusive decision will benefit both practitioners as well as enterprises, and will allow for diversity, a key strength of the sector.

LABELING

A commonly agreed upon definition could lead to a European social enterprise label to orient investors, public agencies (potential clients, procurement), and the general public. The labeling discussion is underway, so it is uncertain what final form it will take, if any.

While labels can be very useful in raising the visibility and promoting the concept and models of social enterprise, labels should be demanded and appreciated by customers. Such consciousness and demand from the market does not seem to exist in most of Europe yet (certainly not in Central Europe), therefore obtaining the label might not bring market advantage and differentiation to social enterprises currently. The public sector is one of the potential markets, of course, and as such could offer significant rewards to those social enterprises that obtain the label. But what would happen to other social enterprises whose customers are not in the public sector, and therefore would not want to go through the certification process, as it would not be beneficial to them? Would they lose the right to use the name "social enterprise"?

Another issue is the difficulty to participate in public procurement. At the moment, there are few social enterprises that are able to do so in Central Europe, as public authorities are unreliable clients and they often do not have the public procurement procedures that would open bidding processes to organizations, including social enterprises. So in this sense, the labeling effort would need to be strengthened by the reform of public procurement procedures (see action item of SBI later in this section), which could in the future give preference to labeled social enterprises in some industries. This could be attractive and useful even in Central Europe in the future. Many believe the commission will push for simplification, inclusion of social enterprise, and universal use of new procedures across Europe. Best practices in Sweden and Belgium give preference to social enterprises in certain public contracting cases. They reserve some contracts, take social impact into account when selecting among bidders, or encourage social enterprises to establish partnerships with other bidders, allowing them easier access to public contracts.

Discussions are still ongoing, and much of the outcome will depend on what the certification criteria are, how enterprises are expected to be monitored, who will grant the label, how often it needs to be renewed, and what benefits it provides to those that obtain it. Public authorities need help to improve their understanding of and engagement with social enterprise and a label could be a good way to assist them, but careful consideration should be given to where and when (in what phases) the certification procedure is introduced. Public authorities could be assisted by awareness-raising programs and training, which in turn would need to be preceded by clear definitions (still in discussion) and clarification of the social performance of social enterprises. The latter is a huge topic of debate in the field: what is considered social impact, what indicators to use, and how to monitor that impact. If social impact can be achieved only in the long run, it could be extremely difficult to determine compliance beforehand. If obtaining a label is connected to achievement of social impact, the field might have to contend with shorter-term outputs or outcomes. In some countries, where the concept of and law on public benefit exists, that law could be used and modified to facilitate capturing and monitoring social impact.

An independent agency could also be in charge of the labeling. It would not have to be a public authority; a credible European organization could be tapped to do this. If the certification remains at the national level, then the EU would need to find credible national agencies to grant the label, which would then need to be monitored to ensure the quality of the label. This is not impossible and lessons could be drawn from the fair trade or organic certification movements or other environmentally driven labels.

Finally, it is not certain that a label by itself would solve the issue of lack of investment capital. Investors would still do their own due diligence before making an investment and would need to have a basic understanding of what social enterprise is, before they would just "blindly" trust the label.

The best-known attempt for creating a social enterprise label so far has been that of the Social Enterprise Mark in the United Kingdom.[19] It was launched in 2010 by a CIC founded by the RISE Legacy Trust, aiming at customers and consumers with the goal of "establishing social enterprise as the business choice of everyone."[20] No official evaluation has been done, but the Mark has had limited success even in a country with such a developed social enterprise sector, due to the high costs of certification and for many of the reasons mentioned above.

No doubt, that much work remains to be done before a label can be introduced in Europe. If a label is introduced when conditions are ripe to promote social enterprises and help them gain better access to markets and capital, the timing and benefits should match the markets where the label is introduced. Introducing a label should proceed according to the following steps:

1. Continued awareness raising of social enterprise
2. Agree on the basic definition of social enterprise
3. Agree on social impact measurement and monitoring
4. Build capacity of actors (e.g., public sector)
5. Reform of public procurement (see further details later in this chapter)
6. Introduce label

THE RELEVANCE OF SOCIAL ENTERPRISE IN ADDRESSING EUROPE'S SOCIAL PROBLEMS

European countries are struggling with major economic and societal challenges and have not been able to respond to them using conventional methods and models. New and innovative solutions are called for to respond to persistent and recently emerged problems of unemployment, poverty, social exclusion, ageing, deteriorating social services, and environmental disasters. Social enterprises are best positioned to respond to critical social problems and provide innovative solutions, as most often they originate as community-based initiatives, close to the root causes of the problems. They have a thorough understanding of the issue, the people affected, the constraints, and the possible solutions as well. Social enterprises often fill the gap (e.g., in social service provision) and even more often they set out to provide a systemic solution to the problem, for example, to raise awareness, educate, change societal attitudes and behavior, initiate new legislation, and affect policy. Box 3.2 describes an example of a social enterprise that provides a key social service to the homeless in Wales while promoting policies that will address the causes of the problem in the long run.

> **Box 3.2   Cymdeithas Gofal Ceredigion Care Society, Ceredigion, Midwest Wales**[21]
>
> *Cymdeithas Gofal Ceredigion Care Society*'s mission is the alleviation of homelessness in Ceredigion, Wales. The society provides a range of housing services to the most vulnerable and excluded, knowing that homelessness is a complex problem.

The society is contracted by the local government to provide shelter and support services to homeless people and people in inadequate housing. It manages various emergency accommodation units for the local authority. In 2010, the enterprise also established a Social Enterprise Maintenance Scheme, which offers "affordable, professional and accessible property maintenance and removal services, and took on the management of storage facilities in the center of Aberystwyth."[22]

In 2010, 92 clients accessed the night shelter, with 63 resettled into accommodation. Two hundred and thirty tenancies were secured through bonds and rental units, and over one thousand individuals and families received support and advice. Bringing people into homes and off the streets offers considerable local benefits. The society works closely with the council and the Welsh Assembly government on homelessness issues.

According to some studies, the European social economy sector currently employs over 11 million people and thus accounts for 6 percent of the active workforce.[23] This figure varies from country to country, but the total number shows that this is a growing, significant sector. Social enterprises vary in legal form, size, field of activity, and experience (age) across the EU, but what they have in common is the desire to provide sustainable entrepreneurial solutions to social problems. According to the findings of a recent report by Social Enterprise UK, "Fightback Britain," 39 percent of social enterprises are based and working in the most deprived communities in the United Kingdom, compared to 13 percent of all SMEs, and social enterprises have higher public confidence rating than mainstream businesses and are twice as likely to have reported growth in the last year.[24] This is proof of the effectiveness, persistence, and potential for social change that a social enterprise can achieve even in uncertain economic conditions and extremely risky environments. Box 3.3 provides an example of a social enterprise that provides employment to a community that finds great difficulty in accessing the labor market.

The Role of EU Policies and Funding in Addressing Key Barriers to the Development of Social Enterprises in Central Europe

What follows are the key barriers restricting social enterprises in Central Europe.

Low Level of Awareness of Social Enterprises and the Model

A generally low level of awareness and understanding of social enterprise in all sectors is still a major obstacle in the development of a more robust social enterprise

> ## Box 3.3 NESsT portfolio—Café Kacaba
>
> *Cafe and Tearoom Kacaba* was opened in Plzen to employ intellectually disabled persons. It is operated by a Czech civic association, Moznosti tu jsou, whose mission is to create conditions for securing social services for intellectually disabled people and people in a difficult life situation, including day care programs and housing. In the Czech Republic, it is estimated that 40 percent of intellectually disabled adults are unemployed, compared to 10 percent of the overall population. Nearly 60 percent of the intellectually disabled unemployed are long-term unemployed, which results in loss of skills and difficulty with integration. Since its launch in 2005, the café expanded to provide restaurant services as well, thus increasing its capacity to employ more of its beneficiaries. In 2011, Kacaba trained and employed 29 people with intellectual disabilities and successfully placed 7 in the open job market. The cafe offers a social space, where disabled and nondisabled people meet on a regular basis. Kacaba has a strong market-driven approach and in 2011 it is estimated to have generated revenue to cover more than 50 percent of its costs.[25]

sector. Despite NESsT's many years of working to build successful and credible social enterprises in the region, there is still no critical mass to make social enterprise visible to the public eye. Lack of an enabling environment, funding, and incentives for the development of social enterprises make it very difficult to grow the sector. In addition, NESsT's assessment of the state of social enterprise in Hungary in 2011 showed a persistent tendency to totally separate the nonprofit sector from the business sector. Traditional thinking is that the former is supposed to alleviate social problems, while the latter should satisfy market demand and generate profit. Unfortunately, this sectoral separation misses opportunities that are presented by closer cooperation and by hybrid forms that frequently bring social and economic goals in line.

Lack of Business Management Know-How and Experience

In Central Europe, most social enterprises have been launched by civil society organizations (CSOs) that approached this model as a practical and sustainable way to respond to a critical social problem. These social enterprises and their leaders have varying backgrounds, but more often than not lack business and management experience and skills. These are essential for launching and operating a business. The leaders may be very entrepreneurial, innovative, and resilient in terms of their social vision, but may not know how to write a business plan or convince potential customers and investors about their idea.

Very few donors or support organizations in Central Europe have been willing to invest in long-term business training and capacity building to benefit social enterprises and their leaders. In NESsT's experience, leaders consistently value this type of support higher than financing. It would be very important for the development of the sector not only to have many well-planned and successful social enterprises, but also to see them investment ready, able to absorb the external financing necessary for start-up or expansion. If there is no "investable pipeline," potential donors and investors go away disappointed. In Central Europe, little investment is going into capacity-building support and this pipeline.

Lack of Access to Finance

Social enterprises are in the intersection of business and socially focused charitable activities, but they have not benefited from financing from either sector. Lack of financing means lack of appropriate amounts as well as types of funding. Both have presented significant barriers to fledgling social enterprises in Central Europe.

The low level of awareness, understanding, and interest have prevented most donors from devoting funding to social enterprise programs, with the exception of a few foreign donors. Grants for social programs could be considered the riskiest form of financing, as the donor never gets his/her money back, but social enterprises as businesses apparently seemed riskier to most potential funders. Even those that were willing to give grants to social enterprises often provided insufficient amounts, perhaps enough for start-up but too little for expansion. There is no practice to pool resources to create larger accessible funds for infrastructure investment, for example. EU funding has been a viable option in most cases, as it offered substantial amounts of money, even considering its limitations (see more detail on those below). Donors are also unprepared to provide tailored forms of financing that take into account the special needs of social enterprises: grants combined with loans or equity, convertible loans, or loans with soft conditions to take into account cash-flow variations or social costs[26] are not offered.

At the same time, project financiers or commercial lenders for the most part exclude social enterprises from their clientele, as they do not have the knowledge and experience with this type of investee or borrower. Social enterprises are not purely commercial enterprises and they often do not fit in the existing risk assessment frameworks. Thus, financing instruments other than grants are often also very difficult to find. NESsT's 2007–2008 research on lending to social enterprise and NPOs in Central Europe showed that there were no banks in the region that were willing to provide loans to finance a social business proposal or a functioning social enterprise, unless it was with special conditions, usually relying on the personal creditworthiness of the executive director. These loans were offered at market rates and conditions. Softer lending and equity-mixed packages of funding for different levels of development, which take into account the social costs of social enterprises were and are still unheard of. Guarantees provided by government schemes covered only regular businesses and there were no special schemes devised for social enterprises.

Lack of Enabling Regulatory and Market Environment

The economic and regulatory environment in Central Europe is not enterprise and small-business friendly. Taxes are high, access to finance is difficult, procedures are cumbersome, and support mechanisms are rare and underfunded. These circumstances affect social enterprises as well, which enter into a sector characterized by the above. Very often, the fact that they originate in the non-profit sector gives them some initial advantages, but as they grow, they soon run into limitations as NPOs and have to confront the same challenges that micro and small enterprises face. Social enterprises still do not have a level playing field: as mentioned above, they are excluded from a number of financing options and government schemes and cannot tap into commercial finance either.

Market access is a major challenge both in the open market and in publicly procured products or services. Social costs often make social enterprise proposals more expensive than competitors, so if price is the only consideration, they tend to lose. Public procurement procedures are unclear or not implemented properly, and exclude social enterprises even when they could provide a cost-effective and valuable service.

Role of Government in the Past and Present; Interpretation of Policies and Use of Funds in Member States

Most Central European countries do not have a social enterprise strategy; some experimentation has taken place in the form of ad hoc funding initiatives. Certain measures designed to address social issues directly ended up helping social enterprises too. In Slovakia and Romania, for example, regulations provide incentives to corporations to purchase goods and services from businesses (including social enterprises) that employ people with disabilities; there have also been guarantee schemes provided by government, which can help unlock private funding.

The National Employment Foundation (public body) in Hungary ran a promising training and awareness-raising program about social enterprise a few years ago, but there was no follow up and short-term thinking prevented the concept from taking hold and for social businesses to survive. The social cooperative program in Hungary was a good initiative too, but the compulsory indicators and the conditions that applicants had to meet were impossible and forced them to cheat. Expectations were not harmonized and contradicted previous program elements (e.g., from the social enterprise training program), so the two programs did not strengthen each other.

Policy makers tried to regulate and certify social enterprises before allowing the development and diversification of the sector (and of the market), which in several cases meant limitations, rather than development. A very telling example is the Slovenian case, where not a single social enterprise as defined by law has been registered since the social enterprise law and the new legal form was introduced in January 2011. Policy should allow experimentation of the different forms and approaches first and then help spread best practices. Some governments in Central Europe have tried to hijack social enterprise and use it for their own purpose, which has caused a great deal of damage. Including the public sector in the social enterprise definition and universe can be very damaging as well (see the Slovak example), as it deprives social enterprises of societal recognition and further support (from the private sector).

EU social enterprise policy initiatives have not made it across borders to Central Europe. They have been largely ignored by governments or shaped to fit their own policy priorities, which has diluted useful initiatives. Innovative approaches have often been called for, but social enterprise was not considered an innovative approach. The use of European Social Fund (ESF) funding also followed government priorities and thus often became the victim of national politics. ESF tenders were suspended in Hungary and Romania on several occasions, causing insurmountable cash-flow problems and bankruptcy in many organizations and social enterprises. This kind of ignorance and hostile attitude added to the above-mentioned barriers and resulted in slow growth and the small current universe of social enterprises.

ESF—Addressing the Barriers to Social Enterprise

The ESF is one of the EU's structural funds, set up to reduce differences in prosperity and living standards across EU member states and regions, and therefore promoting economic and social cohesion.[27] The structural funds are the EU's main financing instruments to support its regional policy, with the aim to reduce disparities in terms of income, wealth, and opportunities. Europe's poorer regions and countries receive most of the funding, but all member states are eligible under the various funding programs. Other elements of the structural funds include the European Regional Development Fund (ERDF), the Cohesion Fund, the European Agricultural Fund for Rural Development (EAFRD), and the European Fisheries Fund (EFF).

The ESF is devoted to promoting employment in the EU. It helps member states make Europe's workforce and companies better equipped to face new, global challenges. As with other EU funds, the ESF finances priorities established by each member state within its overall goals, such as higher education, lifelong learning, equal access to the labor market, employment services, and so on. This can lead to significant differences in the use of ESF funds in different countries. ESF sources are channeled through national structures, usually ministries and a national managing authority specifically set up for ESF operational programs. The ESF requires cofinancing from governments, so goal setting and implementation may depend on the availability of local sources. In line with its overall objective to promote employment, ESF grants have been received by a variety of actors: public sector bodies, private sector organizations, and civil society. Millions of people of both genders, of varying ages and educational levels have benefited from operational programs funded by the ESF in over 20 years of its existence.

The ESF is a key element of the EU's 2020 Strategy for Growth and Jobs targeted at improving the lives of EU citizens by giving them better skills and better job prospects. Over the period 2007–2013, some EUR 75 billion is expected to be distributed to the EU member states and regions to achieve these goals.[28] The ESF has brought a huge flow of EU funding into Europe in the past two budgeting periods, and particularly in 2007–2013. The funding was meant to support social enterprise and the creation of support mechanisms with significant amounts of money and required member states to match ESF funding with local resources. In countries where social enterprise was more advanced, this resulted in substantial resources flowing into the sector. In Central Europe, where social enterprise is small and lacks visibility, and where government priorities focus on more direct interventions to solve social problems, the ESF funding has hardly been used to support social enterprises. Instead, the fund was designed to support employment programs, which meant that eligibility criteria and deliverables were often contrary to the social enterprise logic. This had a distortionary effect, as it pushed organizations to want to meet those conditions, rather than build sustainable businesses. Creative organizations with long-term vision and strategic thinking were able to win and use ESF and ERDF funds to set up social enterprises and thus lay the foundations of sustainable operations, "wrapped" in other program priorities such as employment services or the development of the tourism sector. In a few countries, such as Romania, part of the ESF resources were allocated to the development of a social economy sector, which created a buzz and certainly a window of opportunity for social enterprises, but implementation was poor and thus the desired impact was not achieved. (See more reasons below and in the example of Alaturi de Voi in box 3.4.)

Box 3.4   Alaturi de Voi (ADV)

ADV is a Romanian foundation set up in 2002 in Iasi, whose mission is to ensure that people living with HIV/AIDS in Romania have access to the key services and support they need to improve their quality of life. With NESsT's support in 2007, ADV launched a social enterprise to train and employ youth infected with HIV/AIDS in Util Deco, a sheltered workshop that provides business support services, such as photocopying and binding, and creates and sells quality handmade products, such as textiles, paintings, glassworks, postcards, agendas, and calendars to meet local-market demand. By 2011, Util Deco has employed 16 beneficiaries and placed another 10 in the job market.

ADV's use of ESF funding:

ADV has won a total of EUR 5.29 million in grants so far for two strategic projects for the development of the social economy. The first three-year project was completed by October 2011, while the second will finish in June 2013. The goals were to develop the two social economy components of the foundation: authorized sheltered workshop units in Iasi, Constanta, and Targu Mures, and to contribute to the development of the social economy sector in general.

As a result of these two projects, the ADV's production capacity and range of services has increased significantly, through buying additional equipment for the workshops, replicating the tailoring workshop from Constanta to lasi and the binding-printing workshop from lasi to Constanta and Targu Mures. A social economy department has been created in the foundation to coordinate the activities of the now 11 sheltered workshops owned in lasi, Constanta, and Targu Mures. A sales and a communication and development department have been set up, including the online shop www.utildeco.ro. Within the same project, an 870 square meter Social Economy Center was built in lasi, hosting the logistic offices, painting, handicraft, binding, copying, printing, tailor workshops, IT, production unit, repository for raw materials and the Youth Club.

In the first project, 40 jobs were created, of which 24 were jobs for people with HIV/AIDS (considered disabled in Romania). In the second ongoing project, ADV maintained the jobs created in the first project, and created an additional 20 new jobs. ADV's social enterprise units employ 73 percent of the total number of employees of the foundation. After creating the sales department in May 2011, the foundation generated a EUR 40,000 profit for the first time from its business activities. The two projects increased the foundation's capacity to train, support, and offer guidance to youth with disabilities and exposed to the risk of exclusion. In addition, the organization was professionalized and positioned at the national level as an important promoter of social economy. In lasi, the foundation's infrastructure was developed, by building a social economy center accessible for people with disabilities and modern working conditions.

At the sectorial level, the foundation organized two National Fairs for Sheltered Workshops, delivered a series of training sessions, created the first edition of the Romanian Sheltered Workshops Catalogue, carried out research, and developed resource websites.

In Romania, ESF was implemented and managed by a national authority called the Management Authority for the Operational Programme for Human Resources Development (AMPOSDRU). The most important challenges that ADV faced during the implementation of the two projects were related to AMPOSDRU rules and operations:

- Changes of the implementation regulations during the project implementation period without consulting the grant recipients.
- The contracting authority did not keep the reimbursement term of 45 days and delayed the reimbursement up to 130 days. In the contract there are no penalties stipulated for these delays.
- Unclear procedures for value added tax (VAT) reimbursement and delays in reimbursement of more than one year.

- Difficulties in ensuring the necessary cash flow for the project due to the delays in the reimbursement. Nongovernmental organizations (NGOs) in Romania do not have access to bank loans, so bridging the cash-poor periods was not possible that way. ADV managed to take a EUR 100,000 bridge loan from a third-party lender with a guarantee provided by NESsT in order to cover VAT costs in the project.
- Abusive provisions in the financing contract such as the fact that the state reserves the right not to reimburse the whole amount spent on the project, if the state budget has financial difficulties.
- Exaggerated bureaucracy to meet the monitoring requirements, which often contradict the original conditions stipulated in the contract or the guidelines.
- Unclear financing guidelines, especially on social economy: lack of definition of social economy/social enterprise, unclear rules for deduction of costs/use of subsidies, illogical restrictions, such as not permitting the training of own staff.
- Lack of monitoring of the quality in project implementation, impact on the market and sustainability of the investment.

RESPONSE TO CHALLENGES

The above challenges caused serious cash-flow problems for ADV, which encouraged them to take action. They were joined by other organizations that were brought to the brink of bankruptcy by the ESF grant management process.

In April 2010, ADV was the first organization in Romania to go public about the existing problems with the implementation of ESF projects and forced the national authorities to publicly admit that the EU suspended payment to Romania due to issues of transparency and fund management. The foundation started a campaign to gather signatures requesting a solution to the situation (in the first three days over 700 beneficiaries signed the foundation's petition) and organized a street protest Iasi to draw the attention of visiting government officials. ADV also created the NGO Coalition for Structural Funds aiming to implement lobby and advocacy campaigns to regulate the field.

What are some of the lessons that can be learnt from this example?

- Structural fund projects can be useful for a designated purpose and period of time, because they allow social enterprises to develop infrastructure and create capacity for job creation. ADV was thinking strategically about the utilization and investment of a large proportion of ESF grants, so it managed to build its physical as well as human infrastructure for it social enterprises. ESF projects are only suitable for large organizations, which have the capacity to administer them, are able to generate and rigorously manage the necessary cash flow, and can carry out lobbying and advocacy in the field. ADV is a large organization (over 80 employees and a significant annual budget), so it was able to devote the capacity to take on ESF-funded projects. It was also able to obtain a bridge loan thanks to its networks and track record, which is not possible for most organizations in Romania.

- ESF projects pose significant risks and social enterprises should weigh carefully prior to applying for them and ensure that they do not include activities that could be difficult to implement or account for later.

ADV's recommendations for improving the effective use of ESF funds are as follows:

- Accrediting/authorizing private management authorities, and not only government ones.
- Creating a guarantee fund for NGOs, so that they can take bank credit to cover cofinancing and cash-flow needs of projects.
- Financing contracts must have penalties stipulated for late payments from the management authorities.
- Funding of projects that also increase job creation, and do not focus strictly on short-term training activities.

CRITIQUE OF THE ESF MECHANISM FROM THE CENTRAL EUROPEAN SOCIAL ENTERPRISE SECTOR'S POINT OF VIEW

The ESF mechanism has been mostly ineffective so far in helping to foster the social enterprise sector in Central Europe. It has not reached this target group and has mostly benefited large organizations. Many in the civil sector thought of the ESF as a silver bullet, but its specific conditions and mechanisms made its funding very hard to access for smaller or start-up social enterprises. The mechanism had unrealistic cofinancing requirements, grant sizes that were too large to manage, and heavy administrative burdens. While the money could often be used for social enterprise development, most of it was meant to support beneficiaries and create new social programs that serve disadvantaged populations, and for administrative costs associated with these programs (i.e., salary of additional program coordinator, etc.), rather than to develop the business and sustainability aspects of the enterprise. . It also targeted mostly CSOs, and thus excluded other forms of social enterprise.

The ESF increased grant dependence and the timing of the funding often hindered the development of a sustainable sector. With the departure of many

US donors after the transition to democracy, a lot of active and innovative organizations were already in the process of financial diversification. Consideration of social enterprise as an alternative model started in the mid-2000s, when the ESF funding opportunities began. The influx of large sums of money stalled these diversification efforts and oriented these organizations toward a single source— ESF funding channeled through national government mechanisms. This actually set them back several years in terms of achieving financial independence and sustainability, as they were once again dependent on grants (albeit from a different source than before).

Additionally, ESF funding was channeled through national mechanisms that were slow, bureaucratic, and exploitative of the weaker position of grantees. Contracts and funds have been withheld, causing several bankruptcies. Tenders have been canceled with short notice, destroying annual plans, and sometimes were announced in "flash floods" driven by the need to disburse funds by a certain deadline. This made the grants very unpredictable, led to weak or unprofessional projects winning, and ultimately wasted large amounts of resources on unsustainable activities. ESF tenders, mostly viewed as social programs in member states, were published with unrealistic, distorted, and risk-averse conditions, counter to the logic of entrepreneurship. They did not allow or encourage obtaining high revenues and profits, and often penalized social enterprises that produced a surplus.

The managing authorities of ESF funding were often housed within or closely linked to ministries of labor and/or social affairs, which proved to be a hindrance, as these ministries did not have the entrepreneurial approach, drive, and skills to evaluate and manage social enterprise development projects. Their risk-averse nature motivated them to use indicators and monitoring processes that focused on formalities, rather than real results and social impact. They typically financed projects with little experimentation, even as tenders called for more innovative approaches. Pilots and incubation type projects were not even funded until recently, and only projects that could demonstrate final numbers—even if they were not targeted to those most in need—than actual impact were accepted. At the same time, business plans that could reduce risk were never required in the tender documentation.

ESF tenders also took a short-term view and did not support long-term business development goals to create sustainable social enterprises. Allocations for asset and infrastructure development have often been capped, which meant that investment in social enterprise assets was limited. Most of the funding had to go toward covering operating expenses and paying beneficiaries directly. Unfortunately, this diverted many organizations away from their original long-term plans, as they were in search of funding opportunities and sacrificed sustainability for short-term gains. This also meant that grant dependency increased, rather than a philosophy of investing in a diversified and sustainable financing structure.

In Central Europe, ESF barely funded any support organizations or social enterprise infrastructure; today these exist in only a few countries in the region. Social enterprise regional support centers have recently been opened in Poland, but in other countries support usually did not go beyond financing a short-lived

Internet portal for social enterprises. Capacity building for start-ups and social enterprise expansion were lacking, which limited the growth potential and social impact. Awareness raising and promotion of social enterprise models was thus left to other actors and financiers, while ESF-funded projects often produced theoretical publications that were of little use and did not reach a large target audience.

Finally, the ESF and other sources have not been involved at all in the creation of an enabling legal and market context for social enterprise. There were no programs focused on the public sector or policymakers, so innovative and successful social enterprises would often run into outdated and slow-moving local procurement processes and systems.

In sum, there were significant problems with the ESF-grant logic overall, as well as its implementation at the national level regarding social enterprise development in Central Europe. Some of the very positive intentions of the ESF were unfortunately diluted, misunderstood, or sabotaged at the national level. This calls for a rethinking of ESF mechanisms for the next budgeting period (2014–2020).

New Policy Initiatives at EU Level—SBI and European Social Entrepreneurship Funds (EUSEF)

The SBI is the single most important initiative targeting the social enterprise sector in the history of the EU. It was launched in October 2011 by the EC with the aim of creating a favorable climate for social enterprises and key stakeholders in the social economy, as well as for innovation.[29] The commission saw the potential in social enterprises and therefore "seeks to support the development of social enterprises and to learn from their experiences in support of the whole of the economy." This is very important, as it treats the social enterprise sector as an integral part of the economy and not as an isolated experimental field.

It is the intention of the SBI to respond to the challenges that have inhibited European social enterprises from realizing their full potential. During the design and implementation phases, key stakeholders from all over the EU have been consulted in several rounds in order to base the planned measures in the European reality and to learn from past mistakes. It strives to better integrate existing facilities and programs, while also specifically putting ESF reform on the agenda. This attitude is a major departure from previous practices and was welcomed by stakeholders, who wanted to see coordinated policies and benefits in all parts of Europe. The SBI has three areas of focus, each with a series of detailed recommended measures.[30]

Financing

The SBI will increase funding for social enterprises via a EUR 90 million fund to leverage private capital. It will be used to invest or coinvest with financial intermediaries in various types of financial instruments, such as equity, quasi-equity, and debt instruments, plus portfolio guarantees. In order to attract private capital, the facility plans to provide a first-loss provision and therefore make investments (deals below EUR 0.5 million) possible in start-up or scaling social enterprises that have an annual turnover or balance sheet not exceeding EUR 30 million.[31]

There are several proposals on the table with regard to the structure and operation of this fund. The common thread seems to be that it would be invested through financial intermediaries, using the experience of previously successful microfinance and other schemes funded by the EU. Social enterprises in the ESFs and ERDF facilities should be prioritized. This would result in targeted calls for proposals and earmarked funds for social enterprise development and facilitate building an ecosystem.

The SBI launched a EUSEF label,[32] so that certified funds are created that would attract more private capital to invest in social enterprises. The legislation includes a passport mechanism for funds targeting social enterprises so that they can more easily be distributed across the EU; cross-border fund raising is also facilitated. The funds are planned to be open to professional and semiprofessional investors only. EUSEFs will be registered by and regulated in each member state by the competent authority supervising investment funds, while those in turn will be coordinated and supervised by the European Securities Market Authority, ESMA. ESMA has been entrusted to develop detailed technical implementation procedures for the national supervisory authorities. ESMA will also maintain a central database of EUSEF managers. The EUSEF is not permitted to invest more than 30 percent of its aggregate capital contributions and uncalled committed capital in assets other than qualifying investments. These are social undertakings, which the legislation defines.

EUSEF is generally seen as a positive development, and the expectation is that more private capital will be invested if the investors know what to expect from the label. Promoters of the label believe that there are two main benefits of the EUSEF label: first, it provides an opportunity for Europe-wide marketing *to* investors; and second, it provides a Europe-wide license that allows a fund to invest in social enterprises located anywhere in Europe. While certification does provide a seal of quality that can indeed encourage investors, there are shared concerns among stakeholders that involving private capital may not be that simple. The label will need to gain credibility for it to be effective; it will have to be granted and monitored by ESMA and the national supervisory authorities. This could be challenging, as they first need to become familiar with the concept of social investment and EUSEFs, and then be able to create appropriate procedures that take into account the special nature of these funds and will not strangle them with unnecessary regulation. Investors will probably still perform their own due diligence on EUSEF-labeled entities. There is a danger that this label becomes more exclusive, rather than inclusive, which could be a problem when starting new funds. But of course, if access to public (EU and national government) funds become conditional upon the EUSEF label, it is most likely that most funds will try to successfully go through the certification process. In this case, the label will indeed serve as a seal of quality for the investment of public funds.

An additional area of concern is the level of restrictions that will be placed on funds created to support social enterprises. If these are as strict as the ones applied to regular investment funds (venture capital, private equity, hedge funds, etc.), it will make it very difficult and expensive for them to operate. This could reduce or hamper their ability to make social investments, in which case the overall use of the EUSEF label might also be threatened. Thus, ESMA and the national supervisory authorities have a high level of responsibility and need to create adequate registration and monitoring procedures, allowing operations but not abuse.

It is also important to foster the development of microcredit and make it available to social enterprises. This idea has been suggested by many on several occasions and could solve the access to finance problem of many social enterprises, if the credit conditions take into account the special circumstances of social enterprises, for example, their increased social costs. The usual microfinance loan amounts, interest rates, and group guarantees may not work well in this sector, but modifying the conditions to make them suitable for social enterprise could result in more financing.

Awareness

The SBI recognizes that the awareness of social enterprises needs to increase, in general and in the public sector specifically. This would involve supporting a comprehensive mapping of social enterprise through research to identify best practices and collect data systematically. Research could enhance the understanding of the dimensions and potential of the social enterprise sector across Europe, and highlight best practices in social enterprise as well as in support policies. Several studies have been completed (e.g., Social Entrepreneurs as Lead Users of Social Innovation [SELUSI]), which surveyed the European social enterprise landscape. Research commissioned could build on these results and recommendations. New research is also being requested under the SBI to provide more information about the sector.

Another component of SBI is to create a public database of existing European labels and certification to improve visibility and make comparisons possible, and promote mutual learning and capacity building of national and regional administrations (ESF authorities and others). This is a very important element to success in countries where social enterprise is unknown, but where it has potential in public sector contracting of employment and social services. As described above, lack of knowledge and understanding on behalf of public authorities (national and local) creates a barrier to social enterprise development, so measures and programs to remedy the situation are long overdue. Existing social enterprise support organizations, successful social enterprises, and universities could be appropriate partners in this capacity-building process.

As suggested by the commission, a single multilingual information and exchange platform (online) for social enterprises and their partners is another potentially valuable service that is being included in SBI. There is an information gap that needs to be filled and a portal could be a very good way to share information: research, case studies, best practices, models, methodologies, events, available training and capacity building, scholarships, competitions, and so on. This platform could have a section where people and social enterprises could upload news and information.

Experience and learning from existing portals, such as the Social Innovation Europe, could be taken into account in order to make this a truly useful portal, which does not duplicate what many national sites already provide (e.g., websites of social enterprise coalitions), but rather provides additional information including investment opportunities. The portal should probably signpost visitors to other useful sites, where they can find further or country-specific information.

Legislation

Finally, legislation and regulation to create a stronger enabling environment for social enterprises across Europe must be introduced. One important measure is a European foundation statute that would facilitate the cross-border activities of European foundations (already approved by the European Parliament). It is also necessary to reform public procurement procedures at both the EU and national level in order to provide better chances for social enterprises to participate and successfully bid for contracts. Finally, simplifying the rules of state aid to enhance government support for social enterprise would make a great deal of sense, as it would address the overly bureaucratic processes of the past and foster support for social enterprise. This is already underway; the commission is proposing new rules that also comply with competition regulations of the Single Market. At the same time, existing possibilities offered by the current public procurement rules need to be better understood and exploited by countries. Social enterprises suffer from the lack of understanding on behalf of their local authorities of the existing EU procurement guidelines. Best practices from more advanced countries such as Sweden or Belgium should be closely reviewed.

The SBI is a very comprehensive initiative, as it approaches social enterprise development from all of the important angles that the commission can possibly influence, including definition, financing, promotion, and legislation. Having an inclusive common definition for all 27 EU member states is a major achievement already. The commission seems very committed to push all proposed measures through, focusing on the most important ones first. Discussions have already started about all of the financing measures and proposals to reform the ESF based on stakeholder feedback. In 2014, a new ESF mechanism is expected to be launched that is more flexible and deliberate in its support for social enterprises and for building an ecosystem and support infrastructure.

The challenge is to obtain the support of other key European bodies such as the European Parliament and the European Council, both of which play key roles in turning the proposals into actual law or operating facilities. Another huge task is to convince member states to adopt and implement measures proposed by the SBI. This will certainly be easier in places where the social enterprise sector is more advanced (UK, France, and Scandinavia) and more challenging in places like Central Europe, where governments are much less knowledgeable about and supportive of social enterprises.

How EU Policies Can Assist Building Successful Social Enterprises and a Strong Sector with a Supporting Ecosystem

The SBI is a new roadmap to build stronger social enterprises across the EU. Many of its measures are already being discussed, some have been approved and implementation is underway. Accordingly, the following points can be considered during this process.

First, support needs to be concentrated on enterprises that focus on social return and that may not generate financial return. This will supply a pipeline of social enterprises for social investors. However, caution is required when setting return expectations. Financial returns are hard to predict, as there are no available industry benchmarks. Financial return expectations should be adjusted to this nascent industry, while social return expectations should be clearly articulated, measured, and monitored.

Social enterprises and intermediaries need appropriate financing in terms of the amounts and type. Patient capital is necessary to build the social enterprise pipeline and absorb the higher financial risk in early stages, and social investors should offer capacity building along with financing. Market actors/social investors should be provided with incentives to invest in social enterprises that emphasize social return. The ESF is an extremely powerful mechanism to finance social enterprises directly. It should support sustainable efforts instead of subsidizing program costs and beneficiaries, by providing basic and advanced capacity building, financing for intermediary organizations, sharing best practices, and building the capacity of local and national administrations. The ESF can also make a big difference by supporting awareness-raising programs, such as Social Enterprise Days, throughout the member states.

Facilities and programs targeting SMEs should also be available to social enterprises, and additional capacity-building programs need to be funded and operated. ESF requirements should also be adjusted to accommodate the logic of social enterprise. For example, a business plan showing a sustainable concept should be a basic requirement. Requirements for social enterprises should not penalize profit, as it is one important measure of success of a social enterprise (this is especially true if profit is reinvested in the business and the social goal of the company, thus saving public resources). However, incentives should be long term, encouraging sustainability as well as profit.

Legislative reform is also necessary, which should provide an enabling framework in all member states. Policymakers should consider the special needs of the social enterprise sector and of social investors, and harmonize their efforts with existing legislation (e.g., state aid rules, procurement guidelines). Investors and incubators need to push national governments to enact social enterprise-friendly legislation and policies.

Part II

CAPACITY-SUPPORT STRUCTURES AND SCALING BEST PRACTICES

4

THE EMERGENCE AND EVOLUTION
OF SOCIAL ENTERPRISE SUPPORT
STRUCTURES*

INTRODUCTION

In this chapter, we provide a framework for understanding the development of the social enterprise ecosystem in Latin America, and particularly the support structures that focus on developing social enterprises. The framework demonstrates that traditional sectors—university, government, and industry—are beginning to develop initiatives that support the development of the social enterprise sector. There is also an incipient and emerging nontraditional or fourth sector where new hybrid organizations are emerging that specifically focus on economic, social, and environmental goals. Within this fourth sector are social enterprises as well as support organizations whose mission is to develop and strengthen social enterprises and the environment in which they operate. Traditional and nontraditional actors are converging and providing opportunities to recognize and develop social enterprises that respond to the region's economic, environmental, and social challenges.

We then delve into the emergent and diverse world of support structures and intermediary organizations that focus on building the capacity and overall impact of social enterprises. We examine the following dimensions of these organizations: mission and theory of change; governance; approach, tools, and methodology; key drivers for achieving impact; and the stage of support that they provide to the social enterprise. These dimensions are illustrated assessing the following organizations in Latin America: The HUB, SociaLab, Simón de Cirene, Njambre, and NESsT. The analysis differentiates between two complementary types of support organizations. First, there are *management driven* structures, which primarily direct their attention to the business plans and scaling strategies of different projects. The second category comprises *community driven* initiatives, those that focus primarily on creating community among social enterprises and social entrepreneurs and, in general, use participatory governance models. The support organizations lie somewhere in the middle.

SOCIAL ENTERPRISE DEVELOPMENT ECOSYSTEM

For an ecosystem to foster the formation and consolidation of new and improved organizations there must be collaboration throughout its entire structure. Ecosystems involved in social enterprise development have been depicted as closely interconnected structures comprising government, university, and industry. Government includes the federal, regional, and local levels of government, as well as other public institutions. University refers to both public and private institutions. Industry involves companies, sector networks, and associations, as well as other platforms that support the social enterprise sector (see also Freeman, 1995; Hwang and Horowitt, 2012).

Drawing on the outstanding work of Etzkowitz and Leydesdorff, the Triple Helix model is used to graphically illustrate the social enterprise development ecosystem. This model depicts the mutually beneficial interactions that can exist among universities, governments, and industry, which ultimately encourage innovation while maintaining the autonomy of each sector (2000).[1] Moreover, this model reveals the potential of these entities to adopt the capacities of their counterparts, including their particular role and identities—their ability to interact and coevolve. In turn, this process triggers interesting forms of innovation that have the potential to lead to the development of new networks and hybrid (social, environmental, and financial) organizations able to function as support structures for social enterprises.

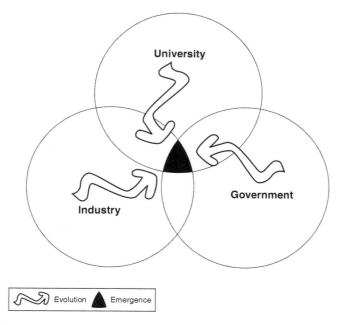

Figure 4.1   Triple helix: Evolution and emergence of support structures.
Source: Adapted from Etzkowitz, H, & Leydesdorff, L, 2000.

Within the area of convergence among sectors, "entrepreneurial" universities are dedicated to transferring value to society and to supporting social innovators and entrepreneurs. At the same time, they develop a theoretical framework that addresses these new paradigms. The government becomes increasingly involved in the process of redefining a regulatory framework that embraces these tendencies and actively promotes this nascent ecosystem. Finally, industry organizations facilitate new spaces for self-organization and develop new financing tools—all the while validating relatively unconventional business models.

As can be observed in figure 4.1, on the one hand there are *evolutionary dynamics* that are to some extent exogenous to the world of social enterprise. These dynamics reside within traditional sectors. On the other hand, there are *emergent dynamics*, many of which are, by nature, self-organizing, peer-to-peer, or chaordic.[2] This space of emergent dynamics is where the fourth sector is able to achieve new models of property and governance to engender companies that are socially oriented and environmentally friendly.

The Role of Government as a Support Structure for Social Enterprises

On an international level, there are concrete experiences demonstrating the government's important role in fostering diverse entrepreneurial models associated with social enterprise. The role of government is not only related to the consolidation of social enterprises but also incorporates dimensions such as encouraging a culture of collaboration among citizens who become more responsible and aware when it is time to make decisions.

There are four roles that governments can take to create support structures for social enterprises (see also chap. 2).[3] First, it can intervene in regulatory frameworks to develop a legal-fiscal framework designed specifically to recognize and regulate this type of company. Second, it can provide or promote the necessary financial support, both through direct support and incentives offered to the financial industry as a means of encouraging impact investing. Third, it can promote the development of networks and connections among the social enterprises that emerge in the sector, as well as between these enterprises and the various stakeholders within the impact-investing ecosystem. Finally, government can be the driving force that ensures social enterprises have access to incentive programs, the market, and government procurement processes, such that they are recognized on the same level as small- and medium-sized enterprises (SMEs) and traditional companies.

Evolution of the State and Support Initiatives for Social Enterprises in Latin America

The state has played an active role in creating links and building alliances with key social actors. Progress has also been made in areas that directly affect these new trends, such as deepening democracy and open government, or the cobuilding of public policies and development incentives aligned with this new economy. Furthermore, this progress has enabled government to identify new opportunities and to move closer to the emergence of social enterprises.[4]

This evolution of the state as it moves closer to these new enterprises and their support structures can be seen at several levels. On one level, there are the various programs or instruments to develop the sector and build networks, such as intermediary organizations and platforms. An example is the Social Innovation and Enterprise Program (Programa de Innovación y Emprendimiento Social, PIES) launched by the Chilean Economic Development Agency (CORFO),[5] one of the pioneer donors discussed in chapter 7.

On another level, we find governmental efforts specifically to develop social innovation initiatives. In the case of Colombia, the recently created Social Innovation Center (Centro de Innovación Social, CIS[6]), which is part of the National Agency for the Eradication of Extreme Poverty (Agencia Nacional para la Superación de la Pobreza Extrema, ANSPE), has been tasked with the challenge of strengthening the sector. In the words of its director, Luisa Fernanda Acevedo, "we asked ourselves what the government's role should be and we came to the conclusion that we needed to be the hub that would bring together all of these actors."[7]

Finally, there have been initiatives such as the intersectorial commission, specifically requested by the Economy Ministry, which was created in mid-2012 to study and present a draft bill for Fourth Sector Businesses in Chile. Further, both Sebrae (the Brazilian Service of Support for Micro and Small Enterprises) and BNDES (the Brazilian Development Bank) are sponsoring social enterprise initiatives in Brazil, including an assessment of how the agencies can become more involved in social enterprise development.

Challenges and Opportunities

The role of the state in areas related to social enterprise is a relatively recent development in the region that dates back only a few decades. On a national level, in addition to the basic support that the state can and should provide in designing public policy, the state can also contribute to creating and consolidating support structures for social enterprises. Structures for financing enterprises, generating networks within the ecosystem, and ensuring fair access to development instruments and public procurements provide transparency and alternatives for this new ecosystem.[8]

Given the hybrid nature of social enterprises, support structures specifically tailored to these types of organizations need to be developed, primarily to support the financing and development of the sector. Similarly, there is a need for intermediary organizations from traditional sectors that understand these dynamics and can act as a bridge between these emerging organizations and the market. There is also a demand for initiatives supporting collaboration among key actors to successfully promote the emerging ecosystem.

The recent Social Enterprise World Forum in Rio de Janeiro (2012), in which the majority of organizational leaders in the Latin American ecosystem participated, concluded that the public sector has a crucial role in advancing legislation that encourages and protects these new models of hybrid organizations. Chile, for example, is following the successful approach adopted by the United Kingdom with its Community Interest Companies,[9] Italy with its Social Enterprises law,[10] and the United States with its Benefit Corporations[11] legislation (introduced in more than 15 states).

At the same time, the state needs a thorough review of its various development instruments to analyze how these currently support or could support this emerging sector, such as through access to public procurement. Furthermore, current processes, communication, and bureaucracy must be evaluated to ensure that these organizations can really take advantage of the existing instruments.

Another area to consider is the state's role at a regional or local level in promoting the development of social enterprises; successful initiatives exist in Quebec, Germany, and the United Kingdom. One interesting example from Latin America is decree N. 5,940 of Brazil, firmly implemented by the State of Bahía, which required public institutions to recycle solid waste and give these materials to local recycling cooperatives.[12] In many cases, these cooperatives are supported by enterprise incubators that were specifically created in federal universities through public incentives to support this type of social enterprise.

UNIVERSITIES

Role of Universities in Supporting Social Enterprises

Universities are a key part of the ecosystem of innovation and social enterprise. O'Shea, Allen, and Morse[13] state that the role of universities has evolved over time, and according to the Etzkowitz and Leydesdorff Triple Helix model (1997, 1998, and 2000), universities are embarking on a third mission (in addition to their two historical missions of teaching and research) of contributing to the economic development and social well-being of their local environments.

According to these authors, the inclusion of this third mission represents the 'second academic revolution'[14] that is shaking universities from their ivory towers. Where previously their main goal was to educate individuals and provide them with a high degree of knowledge, universities today have become agents that contribute to the local economy and to society overall.[15]

Universities in Latin America have been supporting this "third mission" for many years through their traditional areas of work. An example of this is the university incubator system where spin-offs emerge, leveraged by applied research and backed by entrepreneurs. Another example is the growing interest by local universities to encourage interaction with industry and the wider public through initiatives such as technology business parks. All of these processes have been developed to a large extent following the models and approaches of the world's leading higher education institutions, particularly those in the United States and Europe.

Evolution of Universities and Support Initiatives for Social Enterprises in Latin America

Although there are few links with the emerging world of social enterprises among universities in Latin America, some efforts are already bearing fruit. An example is the Social Enterprise Knowledge Network (SEKN), composed of ten higher education institutions. It aims to broaden knowledge beyond traditional university practices by creating a socioeconomic impact network to generate and share information on practices in social enterprise, corporate social responsibility, and other associated areas. As a result of the SEKN, issues that affect hybrid organizations have become embedded within the majority of these universities and many are including the experience of these social enterprises in their curriculum and promoting their development through extracurricular activities.

One such example is the Universidad del Pacífico in Peru, which has various initiatives to foster innovation, enterprise, and particularly the new hybrid models. In addition to supporting applied research and a joint initiative with national and international institutions, the university is developing local community links through projects such as Campaña Recicla tu Ciclo (Recycle your School Year Campaign) and Para Crecer (To Grow). Through Recicla tu Ciclo, waste paper from the university is collected by Fundación Fundades,[16] with the support of Acción Sostenible. They sell the paper to Kimberly Clark and use the proceeds to buy school materials for children living in extreme poverty. Para Crecer is a university-wide initiative to encourage students to participate in developing sustainability solutions for specific communities.

Another interesting example is the Anacleto Angelini INNOVA Center at Chile's Universidad Católica. This initiative emulates the global model for technology parks and offers the university as a center of innovation for business and public policies. Social enterprise and innovation are key issues, and the university has sponsored events such as the Social Enterprise IDEA competition organized by the Chilean Solidarity and Social Investment Fund (FOSIS). Furthermore, the Center is working closely with the university's embryonic Social Innovation Laboratory, which has been actively involved in developing the Chilean social enterprise ecosystem. Among other initiatives, it is supporting the creation of the sector's first association, Asociación Gremial de Empresas Sociales de Chile (Social Enterprise Association of Chile, or ASOGES), advising on the regulatory framework for a Fourth Sector Enterprises statute, and developing a report for the Economy Ministry on "Social Innovation in Chile and the Role of the State in Its Development."[17] In summary, this is a new space for interaction and collaboration among sectors that support the development of the social enterprise industry, and the university is leading the way.

Challenges and Opportunities

The role of universities has gradually evolved in ways that support the development of hybrid organizations, as illustrated by the examples just given. However, multiple challenges will need to be addressed as the process consolidates and the practices expand to other universities in Latin America.

As new spaces emerge for universities to create links with traditional and emerging support structures, some interesting lessons can be learned from the European experience. More than a decade was spent researching social enterprises, particularly through the EMES[18] network (founded by European research centers to build a body of knowledge relating to social enterprises). However, the research agenda has not focused on practices that allow us to learn more about support or intermediary organizations and their important role in building the sector.

In addition, the restrictions and limitations of traditional universities worldwide have stymied many initiatives and leaders in the field of social innovation and social enterprise. These leaders have had to look elsewhere and set up their own teaching and training initiatives that embody the vision and spirit of this interconnection with other sectors, particularly with industry. This was the case in Europe with the Kaos Pilots in Denmark, Team Academy in Finland, and the School of Social Entrepreneurs in England, to name just a few.

Collaboration among stakeholders in the system needs to be greatly strengthened by designing new opportunities for transferring and creating knowledge related to innovation and the new hybrid models. With collaboration, universities in Latin America will be better positioned to become catalysts in developing the social enterprise and impact ecosystem.

INDUSTRY

Role of the Industry in Supporting Social Enterprise

The private sector obviously plays a key role in the evolution of local entrepreneurship and impact-innovation ecosystems in Latin America. These efforts have traditionally taken diverse forms, including providing technical assistance services, helping promote linkages in the sector, providing financing, and developing sector validation and negotiation agendas, and are often led by industry associations and chambers of commerce.[19] Another key role concerns promoting business-to-business relationships that include these types of organizations. In recent years, these various roles have gained importance and there is growing activity in three areas: linkages (intermediaries), financing, and value chains.

International experience provides important examples of how linking social enterprises appears to play a major role in their development. One example is the Social Enterprise Coalition[20] in the United Kingdom, which has been in existence for ten years and now counts almost 70,000 social enterprises contributing more than 2.4 billion pounds to the local economy. The Coalition played a key role in building a public agenda and a special regulatory framework for social enterprises in the United Kingdom. Another example is the Social Enterprise Alliance[21] in the United States. This organization, which defines itself as "the champion for social enterprise in the United States," has forged links and developed a strong agenda to provide tools and resources that contribute to the success of social enterprises (see chap. 1).

Beyond this kind of intrasector organization, there are also a series of initiatives that have enabled certain regions to make progress in terms of intersector innovation. Some notable examples of this are the Social Innovation Europe[22] platform created by the European Community and the Social Innovation Exchange,[23] both of which are quite active. These initiatives are known for providing platforms for exchange and connections among the ecosystem actors in Europe and elsewhere (see chap. 3).

With respect to financing, the industry is developing and provides support for different types of hybrid models (and at difference stages of development). An entire industry has been created around networks of angel investors and venture capital. Today, around the world, the impact-investment sector is growing rapidly, with more than 64 funds, 50 countries, and USD 2.5 billion placed.[24] However, its presence is still quite incipient in Latin America (B Lab, 2012) and there are very few early-stage impact-investing funds or philanthropic funds for start-up and incubation (see chap. 8 for additional information).

Finally, there is another role for industry in the development of the impact ecosystem: forging industry connections through business-to-business relationships. As confirmed by the different panels at the Social Enterprise World Forum in Rio, social enterprises must increase their competitiveness through training, technology, and addressing other challenges in order to directly link with the private sector (see chap. 5 on scaling best practices and chap. 7 on pioneer donors).

Industry Evolution and Intersector Partnerships to Promote Social Enterprise

The social innovation and social enterprise industry is also evolving in Latin America. While hybrid models are often not considered by the more traditional sectors of the business world, interest in sustainability is gradually increasing among corporations with philanthropic and shared value practices.[25] In addition, public institutions and civil society organizations are also developing the industry. Several studies are underway to explore and quantify the efforts of new entrepreneurs in Latin America; one is a study of B Corps in Latin America, which is being financed by the Inter-American Development Bank and involves researchers in Brazil, Colombia, and Chile. The Avina Foundation, the Rockefeller Foundation, and Omidyar Network have also recently begun to fund efforts to develop policies and best practices in social enterprise development (see chap. 7).

Incubators can also play a fundamental role in developing and supporting social enterprises. However, a thorough scan of incubators in Latin America demonstrates that while there are a few hundred business incubators (particularly in Mexico and Brazil), those that are directly linked to social enterprise are few and far between (less than 20).[26] Brazil has one of the higher numbers of business incubators, yet few focus on social enterprise or social impact overall. However, early-stage impact-investment fund research indicates strong interest in incubator and accelerator programs that help prepare social enterprise for investment (see chap. 9). Box 4.1 outlines several examples of these incubators, and the challenges confronted by these support structures.

The impact ecosystem in São Paulo, Brazil, illustrates how an industry can help develop more actors by taking on the three roles described earlier. The HUB (http://saopaulo.the-hub.net/) has played a key role in linking social entrepreneurs in São Paulo, which has facilitated linkages with different agents in the impact ecosystem. In addition, various organizations are working in the financing dimension, including Vox Capital (http://www.voxcapital.com.br/), a venture capital fund that invests in innovative, high-potential businesses that serve low-income customers. Finally, in terms of the value chain, several leaders who also participate in the HUB networks have raised the possibility of a "game changer" by using their purchasing power in the supplier market. An iconic example of this is *Natura* (http://www.natura.net), the Brazilian multinational cosmetics company with a commitment to social and environmental issues. In 2001, *Natura* decided to purchase its packaging exclusively from recycling cooperatives in Brazil. This has directly contributed to the development of a sector that includes more than 1 million collectors of recycled material who live in precarious conditions.

Pending Challenges for the Industry

There are many diverse challenges that remain for the social enterprise and social innovation industry. Because this is an emerging and still somewhat limited phenomenon within the business world, the first major challenge for the social enterprise industry is linking and validating the sector in terms of its value proposition and new business models. These models are clearly disruptive to the prevailing business approach in Latin America. The challenge of connecting social entrepreneurs is being addressed (e.g., in Chile with the recently created ASOGES for social entrepreneurs, as well as the efforts of Sistema B, TECHO, and other organizations), but there is still much work to be done.

Possibly one of the greatest challenges for the industry and the growing number of social enterprises is the development and consolidation of structures that facilitate financing for these types of initiatives. Beyond the exponential increase in collective financing platforms, such as Idea.me, Nobleza Obliga, and La fondeadora,[27] which are certainly important, the larger challenge is related to the development and consolidation of impact investment in the region. As mentioned, this industry is of considerable size on a global scale and is beginning to make a strong entrance into Latin America. However, as evidenced by the conclusions at the 2012 Social Enterprise World Forum in Rio de Janeiro, the problem is not related to the availability of resources. Rather, the problem is the lack of investor awareness about this emerging impact ecosystem and new hybrid organizations that serve as support platforms or intermediary entities, as well as the lack of early-stage patient capital, which is critical to building a pipeline of investment-ready enterprises.

Box 4.1   Social Enterprise Incubators

Incubators are a vital part of the industry. Typically, incubators provide support through a mix of services, such as capacity building, access to financing and specialists in marketing, business planning, law, accounting, and, in some cases, performance measurement. Many support organizations of social enterprise only employ these services at certain stages of the enterprise's development, primarily for enterprises that already have a proven concept and are ready for high growth.

The few social enterprise incubators that do exist in the region usually provide high-quality programs that last 6–12 months, and usually focus on more developed enterprises. Agora Partnerships is a nonprofit organization working principally in Mexico and Central America with a mission to nurture early-stage companies. It focuses on entrepreneurs and companies with a proven product and an average of USD 250,000 in sales. Agora works to accelerate the growth and social impact on communities.[28] In Brazil, Artemisia was founded in 2003 by Potencia Ventures to provide incubator and accelerator services to enable social entrepreneurs to become investable. Artemisia's initial model focused on an intense period of incubation and acceleration of about 6–9 months, but realized its resources would be more effective supporting only those enterprises that demonstrate a serious capacity for scaling their product or service. Njambre in Argentina was founded in 2011 to catalyze the creation of a community of impact enterprises. It assists early-stage entrepreneurs via business development coaching and related services, with the goal of establishing a consortium of social enterprises. (See chapter cases for more information).

A study conducted by NESsT on incubators in Latin America suggests the following:

- The vast majority of incubation models come from the private sector.
- In Chile, Peru, and Ecuador, incubators are generally associated with universities and fail to transcend their academic origins. The incubator functions more as a teaching model, meaning the projects often do not launch into civil society, and momentum ceases once the students involved with the projects graduate.
- Brazil has the most developed incubation sector: According to a 2006 study by the National Association of Entities Promoting Innovative Enterprises there were over 377 incubators and over 40 technology parks. Many are connected to universities but receive funding from the government and other sources.
- More incubators should focus on supporting social enterprises at the early stage and with a long-term view.
- A balance is needed between effective state-sponsored incubation initiatives and experimentation and flexibility within the regulatory environment.

- More incubators that are created by universities need to transcend the institution and become more market driven.
- More support needs to be provided for incubators to identify and cultivate investors.
- Long-term support of incubators is vital for them to scale, replicate, and become self-sustainable.

SUPPORT STRUCTURES: PATHWAYS TOWARD IMPACT

It is evident that the support structures have gradually begun to build a pathway toward impact. The structures created by governments, universities, and industry are moving toward a central overlapping focal point, which is often referred to as the triple helix model of innovation. In this central place, innovation is stimulated more effectively and the impact is multiplied due to synergies generated by collaborative work.[29] Also, it is precisely in this intersection where the new dynamic of support structures emerges, based on interaction and collaboration among entrepreneurs and innovators. These emerging dynamics can be considered an endogenous creation to a certain extent, and in many instances they have a strong self-organizational component.

Using the analytical framework for the emergence and evolution of social enterprise support networks, this section will describe some new dimensions that are part of this phenomenon. We will examine five Latin American organizations—Simón de Cirene, SociaLab, The Hub, Njambre, and NESsT—to clearly illustrate each dimension. This information was gathered from the literature, from each organization, and from a questionnaire completed by the leaders of each organization. The new dimensions are the following:

a. Mission and theory of change
b. Governance
c. Approach, tools, and methodology
d. Support target/impact instrument
e. Entrepreneur support stage

Mission and Theory of Change

Organizational mission plays an important role in social enterprises. Kim Alter has created a typology of social enterprises that classifies them according to their mission orientation.[30] One type is mission-centric companies founded to serve a social purpose—rather than an economic purpose—differentiating them from traditional companies. The mission guides their strategy and objectives, the structures they adopt, their internal culture and decision-making process, and their programs. Economic issues are important, of course, but not primary.

Nevertheless, it can be quite challenging for these hybrid organizations to adhere to their mission at all times. In fact, as described in the Echoing Green study of more than 3,500 applicants to its fellowship programs, "Hybrids also must strike a delicate balance between social and economic objectives, to avoid 'mission drift'—in this case, a focus on profits to the detriment of the social good."[31] Likewise, a variety of efforts and strategies are required to keep the organization connected to its mission and operating in line with it.

The expression of how the organization addresses these challenges is the organization's theory of change. Each organization seeks to establish the actions and results necessary to achieve the change expressed in its mission, while providing a roadmap based on its evaluation of the environment. At the same time, the relevance of the social enterprise's theory of change is that it offers logical consistency to the different elements within the organization and guides those elements toward the mission, helping the organization achieve its social purpose more successfully.

Among the mission-centric hybrid organizations that are explicitly utilizing a theory of change are the HUBs. These initiatives have integrated the theory of change concept and contributed to a reinterpretation of Margaret Wheatley and Deborah Frieze's article, "Using Emergence to Take Social Innovation to Scale" (2006). This study examines the important stages required to scale social innovation and socioeconomic initiatives. According to the authors, this process begins with networks, where the focus is on finding and sharing common goals. They then move to creating communities of practice where new practices are shared and developed. Finally, they progress toward a system of influence in which the new practices become the norm.[32] Thus, from the perspective of the HUBs movement in the region, and in each city where these inspiring spaces have been implemented (São Paulo, Curitiba, Oaxaca, Bogotá, and many others now under development) their vision is clear: "People taking collaborative action for a better world."

Governance

The governance dimension refers to the mechanisms created to guide each support system, including the predominant leadership styles and shared criteria for decision making. As described in the Schwab Foundation study, governance is key for social enterprises since it enables them to oversee the fulfillment of their mission and policies, strengthening leadership and helping to ensure the success of the social enterprise. The Schwab Foundation study notes, among other issues, that impact investors in these organizations often require the creation of an external advisory committee to ensure adherence to the mission.[33]

There is a great deal of diversity in this dimension among the organizations that serve as support structures for social enterprise. At one extreme are leadership-oriented approaches that conserve certain elements of the stewardship model of traditional companies, with centralized and hierarchical decision-making processes, while at the other extreme are more collaborative approaches, presented as stakeholder models, which are inherently democratic and hence open to cocreation.[34] Between both extremes is a continuum with different degrees of depth of participation: from consultative and inclusive participation to reliance on decision making by interest groups.

The HUBs, for example, have a global governance model that is broken down into HUB Companies and HUB Associations. Each local HUB has a vote in these and they follow a democratic logic. At the local level, there is diversity in HUB governance. In Latin America, the São Paulo HUB is driven by a core of directors led by Pablo Handl of Argentina, whereas the Bogotá HUB was founded by a collective that arose out of a leadership workshop organized by La Arenera, Somos Más, and Fábrica-Industria Creativa y Cultural. This particular initiative is a model of collaborative action in Latin America.

Approach, Tools, and Methodology

The approach used by each of the support structures depends to a great extent on mental models, which are defined as the set of shared beliefs that each organization has regarding how it functions and the role it plays in its specific environment.[35]

When considering the mental models that underlay the tools and methodologies of support organizations, we find some initiatives use tools traditionally associated with business management, which is based on linear and sequential logics within a mechanical paradigm.

The "Social Enterprise Management Manual"[36] published on Simón de Cirene's website is a good example of how tools traditionally associated with for-profit business management are being applied to social enterprises. These tools include strategic planning, marketing, human resources management, and others that involve linear, systematic processes that follow the classic management cycle: plan–organize–direct–control.

NESsT takes a portfolio approach, preparing social enterprises at different stages of development with capacity support and mixed financing. It uses the language of the financial world, such as portfolio performance, but also displays a more tailored approach to its consulting services. These services incorporate recent methodologies such as coaching and learning by doing, as well as cutting-edge concepts such as engaged philanthropy.

Other initiatives apply tools and methodologies based on approaches that are inspired by collaborative models with organic paradigms. At this extreme is Socialab, which bases one of its main social innovation programs on large-scale collaboration (using crowd sourcing) to generate innovative proposals.

The HUB network's operating system DNA is found in the so-called Art of Hosting,[37] a name that is associated internationally with collaborative facilitation and participatory leadership practices, such as Open Space, World Café, and Appreciative Inquiry.

Support Target/Impact Instrument

Support target or impact instrument is the mechanism used by the support structures to impact the ecosystem. Beyond the mission, governance model, and tools that can be developed, there are alternatives regarding the pathway toward impact. In articulating their visions, missions, and theories of change, organizations determine whether they will work with entrepreneurs, the community, or projects. These constitute the target of their support or their impact instrument.

The experience of traditional entrepreneurship and the world of start-ups provide a different perspective that can help describe this dimension of impact instrument. In this case, the focus is on the entrepreneur and the type of assistance needed, differentiating, for example, between the support provided by an incubator, an accelerator, or a coworkspace. Likewise, by understanding the differences between a well-articulated ecosystem, such as entrepreneurship, and an incipient ecosystem, such as social enterprise, we find some interesting lessons for our cases and their support target.

In fact, a central characteristic in the literature on social enterprise has to do with the change agent. As Bill Drayton, founder of the prestigious social enterprise network Ashoka,[38] has said, "Social entrepreneurs are not content just to give a fish or teach how to fish. They will not rest until they have revolutionized the fishing industry." To a certain extent, all of these organizations have a common support target—the entrepreneur—in their efforts to accelerate talent.

Nevertheless, a deeper examination of these cases reveals two complementary approaches to the entrepreneur. On the one hand is a group of support organizations *focused on collective or community actions*. The main example of this group is the HUB, with its explicit value proposition related to generating "critical connections," as well as SociaLab, whose mission is to facilitate a cocreation process that is both virtual and in person. There are also groups *focused on projects, plans, or business models*, which adhere more closely to business and management methodologies. This group includes traditional incubators linked to universities, social enterprise accelerators, as well as organizations such as Simón de Cirene and NESsT.

Enterprise Support Stage

For the purposes of this analysis, we have divided the social enterprise formation cycle into four phases. In the first phase, the concept is created and the problem is identified. During this "seed" phase, the enterprise passes through a "death valley" moment where the difficulties faced are such that the effort required from the entrepreneurs often exceeds their capacity and the enterprise is very likely to fail. In the second phase, the enterprise begins to generate income by testing its business model, which must be continually revised until a scalable business model is identified. During the third "plateau" phase, certain aspects of client understanding are improved and fine tuned, finance is leveraged, and strategic alliances are established. In the final phase of our cycle, the enterprise is either scaled to other economies, or new ways of generating income based on the original model are found and the enterprise creates an impact on the ecosystem.

Social enterprises, in general, are affected by *chaordic* processes, or processes that are both chaotic and ordered. For a social enterprise, knowing exactly what stage it is at and what the next steps should be is even more uncertain than it is for traditional enterprises. This is because enterprises that are aiming to achieve social value often focus on far-reaching objectives and as a result, the finance models or short-term profit objectives during the early stages are not always compatible with the social value aim. For example, among the cases studied, organizations such as Njambre and the HUB work with enterprises during the early stages of maturity. Similarly, there are initiatives like NESsT that focus on giving social enterprises the tools and support they need to mature, either by expanding their business model or by reaching new niches and economies. To map the processes experienced by social enterprises and determine at what stage of the process the support organizations are situated, we propose the following phases of maturity, based on the work of the SESAME program in the United Kingdom:

i.   *Seed*: During this phase the team is developing the idea and generating working models, often without any planning. Beneficiaries are reached but there is a lack of methodology and little conclusive knowledge of the problem.

ii. *Start-up*: The start-up phase of most projects, businesses, and social enterprises is energy driven; this is the time when social entrepreneurs are called upon to show their determination, commitment, and focus in order to get things done. It is also the time when a sustainable economic and leadership model begins to emerge.

iii. *Scaling*: The enterprise becomes more established and consolidated. It is then replicated in some way or it focuses on expanding its social impact, attempting to resolve some other social "pressure point."

iv. *Maturity*: During this phase, a sustainable business model that is highly likely to succeed takes root. At the same time, there will be a consolidated work team generating internal working protocols, which, depending on the degree of rigidity that the organization acquires, could pose a risk. Nevertheless, this is typical in the majority of consolidated social enterprises.[39]

Illustration of Key Points

In the previous section, we saw how the organizations studied constitute a group of emerging support structures that provide various products and services to help social enterprises achieve their aims.

Figure 4.2 depicts four of the five dimensions discussed previously (governance, approach, instrument of impact, and support phases). The fifth dimension, relating to the mission and change theory, was not included because of its abstract nature. The figure provides a comprehensive overview of the differences among the five cases studied.

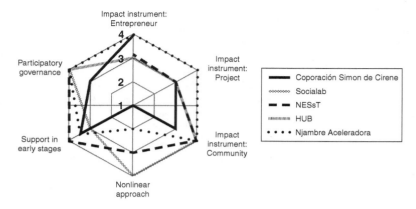

Figure 4.2   Case comparison by dimensions.

As mentioned earlier, each support structure may offer several choices regarding which aspect will become the instrument for impact on the ecosystem. Of these, three were identified: the entrepreneur, the project, and the community.

Focusing on the entrepreneur is commonly associated with traditional notions of entrepreneurship and the world of start-ups, and it poses the question: what type of help would be needed to intervene from this angle? Our findings show that in each of the selected cases, the entrepreneur was considered key. Similarly, in terms of projects, we can see that both Njambre and SociaLab differ from the other initiatives by focusing mainly on plans or business models as the key elements for achieving an impact. Finally, in terms of the community as the instrument of impact, most cases studied claimed that they focus strongly on the community as a support object. This reflects the extent to which they encourage the building of communities of social entrepreneurs and intervene in fostering networks and links. Corporación Simón de Cirene has begun to move gradually toward the incorporation of diverse stakeholders, developing new practices that involve them in more participative ways.

The approach chosen by the support structures reflects how the organization views itself and its role, and determines the methodologies and instruments it utilizes. It can range from a more traditional focus that follows managerial, linear, and systematic processes, as in the cases of Corporación Simón de Sirene and Njambre, to a more collaborative and organic focus as in the cases of SociaLab and HUB. NESsT is in the middle—more flexible than the first two but with certain predefined linear processes for working with social entrepreneurs. It is worth highlighting that this dimension of focus is where the greatest comparative differences can be seen among the five organizations.

Social enterprises go through different stages of development, during which they require different types of support. Based on the data we have gathered from various sources, it is evident that despite their differences, the selected support structures are concentrated primarily in the seed and start-up phases. However,

SociaLab and especially NESsT also assist in the scaling process. This enables these support structures to plot the potential pipeline and timeframe for the long-term maturity of social enterprises, as well as bring other relevant stakeholders into the ecosystem (e.g., impact investors).

Finally, regarding the governance model, all of the organizations reported that feedback, ideas, and the active participation of beneficiaries and other stakeholders in the decision-making process are part of their short-term objectives. This style of governance, while adding complexity to traditional management processes, appears to stem from the new hybrid characteristics of these models. The Corporación Simón de Cirene, which uses a support structure driven by the efficiency and effectiveness associated with business, is being gradually challenged by these new ways of governance and stakeholder involvement.

CONCLUSIONS AND LESSONS LEARNED

This analysis was driven by the growing need to identify and explain the ecosystem of emerging support structures for social enterprise and the dynamics that characterize it. The analysis has shed light on the areas that deserve further exploration to enrich the discussion of support structures for the fourth sector and social enterprise.

The triple helix model shows how the private sector, universities and the social enterprise industry converge and lead to the emergence of hybrid organizations such as social enterprise support structures or social enterprises themselves. In this context, the model is quite useful in organizing the discussion and reflecting on the dimension of support structures (both traditional and emerging ones). The model provides value in terms of its capacity to recognize the dynamism of the system in which these structures exist. However, there remains the need to create new models that can help us interpret and explore both the micro and macro aspects of these structures, including new methodologies that will deepen our understanding of them.

With respect to the evolutionary dynamics of traditional support structures, there is a latent need and opportunity in Latin American countries to provide a regulatory and policy framework that addresses the requirements of social enterprises. There is also work to be done with government to simplify bureaucratic procedures and stimulate the ecosystem with new incentives. Intermediary organizations appear to play a key role in stimulating and making connections among different actors in the ecosystem, particularly in bringing together traditional and emerging actors. Simplified procedures and incentives should be designed with this role in mind.

Universities are implementing new courses, applied research, immersion programs, and even creating special units focused on social enterprise, but they do not have a clear mandate to generate real involvement with well-articulated, long-term work plans with the different actors. One pathway that has recently arisen is the INNOVA Center of the Universidad Católica de Chile, where the Social Innovation Laboratory is working on disruptive innovations to develop the impact ecosystem, and particularly new hybrid organizations. Scaling up such efforts in the region may in part require a review of existing indicators, incentives, and expectations regarding the role of the university in society, and in particular its position in relation to local challenges for these social enterprises.

In addition, it is clear that the industry needs to further provide capacity and investment support and increase impact. This requires improving metrics and developing competencies among entrepreneurs and their organizations. Furthermore, investors need to be made more aware of emerging opportunities, which require more and better intermediary organizations. Social enterprises will have to more fully integrate into the dynamics of government and industry to seek financing. This will enable them to become more competitive, increasing the possibility of scaling up their social and environmental impact. In light of international experience, the sector would benefit from the development of membership associations to promote it from within.

Across the three traditional spheres of support, it is imperative to develop clearer and more efficient channels for transmitting information among government, universities, and industry, as well as emerging intermediaries. This could be key to progressing toward better support structures to develop social enterprises. It is important to understand the challenges faced by support structures, and that there is no model or type of structure that is superior to another. The use of any approach will depend on the ecosystem and the gaps and resources to build upon it.

Emerging support structures, as well as social enterprises, must reinforce their missions to prevent mission drift. The challenging task is to pursue their social and environmental objectives while at the same time ensuring their financial autonomy. In response to this challenge, initiatives are now instilling in the organizational culture a mission and an explicit theory of change that is central to the social enterprise's work.

It is also important to mention the valuable contribution made by emerging support organizations. These organizations bring new methodologies and approaches, including processes that are not necessarily linear, as well as open governance, which facilitates endogenic and self-organized processes. Similarly, there are organizations in a support structure role that foster skills, encourage the use of new tools, and ensure efficient management to enable social enterprises to scale their impact. One of the outcomes of this work is that it brings together the impact investors and other agencies that are attempting to understand and progressively support this emerging sector.

Table 4.1 summarizes possible incentives to encourage more and better support structures (based on responses from the questionnaire).

Support Structure Case Studies

SociaLab

SociaLab, founded in 2012, was the first spin-off initiative from the Un Techo para Chile ("A Roof [House] for Chile"; now TECHO-Chile) Innovation

Table 4.1 Incentives to promote social enterprise support structures

Organization	Proposals
Corporación Simón de Cirene	Generate a culture that incentivizes civil society to take responsibility for the country's social challenges
	Raise awareness of the social challenges facing these organizations
	Develop a legal regulatory framework that facilitates and incentivizes donations, while demanding greater administrative accountability from the donor organizations
SociaLab	Provide more incentives for project implementation, as opposed to only project proposals
	Encourage uptake of the projects by the target segment
NESsT	Make available different types of financial resources, including philanthropic patient capital, according to the different development stages of a social enterprise
	Subsidize certain "social costs" when the social objective, once proven, prevents the enterprise from competing under equal market conditions (e.g., the cost of drug rehabilitation for employees of a social enterprise)
	Create a special tax regime for profits that are reinvested to increase the social impact of the social enterprise. Support an environment that encourages transparency and provides recognition through procurement requirements and other purchasing, hiring, and financial incentives
	Provide free or low-cost access to advisory services and capacity support during the early planning and launch stages.
HUB São Paulo	Establish closer links with public policy development to create more programs that nurture social innovation
Njambre	Recognize that these are economically sustainable models (for investors, universities, employees, governments, etc.)
	Create impact-investment funds for first and second rounds

Center. As a platform for disruptive social enterprises, it identifies solutions to major social problems by involving the various stakeholders in cocreation and networking. The organization's aim is to help identify, create, and accelerate transformative technologies and businesses that can create sustainable well-being for the poorest members of society.

There are many subsistent families at the base of the economic pyramid and a lack of suitable products and services for their needs. The starting point is to work with the most vulnerable communities to identify a problem and then cocreate solutions based on input from each of the stakeholders. For example, methods and techniques may be proposed by universities; core business ideas from the private sector; or observations from vulnerable families based on their experiences. Because these solutions create value, they can be the basis for generating sustainable, scalable enterprises that do not require donations.

Change Theory and Mission

SociaLab's mission is to cocreate innovative and transformative enterprises in a way that ensures everyone benefits from the eradication of poverty.

SociaLab's work is based on three action lines.

1. *Competitions:* SociaLab, together with a private company or the government, identifies social problems or challenges and provides a web platform for open innovation, which allows businesses, educational establishments, entrepreneurs, and local residents to interact and cocreate solutions. The best ideas are developed, financed, and accelerated before being converted into social enterprises.
2. *Start-ups:* SociaLab has created an entrepreneur support program that focuses on strengthening the social enterprise ecosystem. The program creates networks and communication strategies to increase the visibility of social enterprises. It supports enterprises during the application process with prizes, grants, and competitions, and during funding rounds with investor meet-ups and networking. SociaLab also facilitates direct cocreation with users, validating the project from the outset and training entrepreneurs in different methodologies. SociaLab provides a collaborative working space that favors learning, feedback, and networking through weekly meet-ups and mentoring sessions with experts from various fields.
3. *Consultancy:* SociaLab offers a consultancy service to develop business models for low-income markets using a qualitative methodology that increases the competitive capacity of enterprises. This consultancy service is delivered over the course of eight days and includes the company's senior management. SociaLab also hosts Social Innovation Workshops for businesses.

Governance

SociaLab has 15 employees, 8 volunteers, and 1 partner (TECHO). It receives permanent support from cofinancing institutions such as the Inter-American Development Bank's Multilateral Investment Fund and the telecommunications company Movistar-Chile.

Wherever possible, decisions are made collaboratively. Similarly, needs identified by the target audience are included in SociaLab's medium-term objectives. The Accelerator Council, composed of a multidisciplinary team including social leaders and representatives from organizations, is responsible for accelerating the implementation of projects, proposing networks with possible users, and contributing to the resolution of any subsequent problems.

Approach, Tools and Methodology

SociaLab takes a holistic approach that requires commitment and contribution from all those involved—entrepreneurs, companies, and communities—to ensure that its activities are carried out effectively. The actions undertaken by SociaLab are always based on cocreation and collaborative work.

The methodology and tools used by SociaLab are designed to generate sustainable business models via a platform of open collaboration. During the second phase, SociaLab seeks to scale these projects through coaching and market inter-mediation, and by supporting product placement, the production and com-mercialization stages, and the sales of social services to clients. It also provides support with cross-subsidization, which allows social activities to be financed by the sale of products and services, which in turn means that the commercial and social activities are aligned.

Area of Support/Instrument of Impact

This organization focuses on the entrepreneur, the project, and the community on the premise that solutions opening up space for enterprise need to be cobuilt and continuously tested by the users. SociaLab uses an innovation process that ensures unviable projects will fail quickly and without significant resource invest-ment. It provides ongoing support for entrepreneurs through methodologies that build their capacity to create projects.

Support Phases

SociaLab tackles social challenges by encouraging new ideas that are poten-tial solutions; therefore, it primarily supports enterprises during the seed and start-up phases. However, SociaLab has also created a support mechanism for scaling projects to increase their impact and benefit to communities. By 2014, SociaLab hopes to generate more than 5,000 ideas and implement the best 127 projects, of which at least three will be scaled to impact more than one million people.

The HUB

The HUB movement was founded in London in 2005 to facilitate sustainable development through collaboration. It provides a space that allows entrepre-neurs to generate global networks and connect with people from every profes-sion, background, and culture to imagine and develop enterprising ideas for the world.

The HUBs offer a comprehensive service that combines a community char-acterized by trust and participation with an innovation laboratory, a business incubator, and the comforts of home to help innovative projects grow and develop around the world. Above all, HUBs are spaces for meaningful encoun-ters, exchange, and inspiration.

The HUB was created to address the lack of collaboration and support struc-tures that are essential to the development of ideas. According to the HUB founders, ideas are the fundamental social technologies that facilitate the process of building value in society. There are currently more than 30 HUBs around the world, with 50 more in the process of being developed, and close to 5,000 members across all five continents.

We will focus on two HUBs in Latin America: the São Paulo HUB, the first in Latin America, founded in 2008 by Pablo Handl; and *La Arenera* HUB in Bogotá, Colombia, created in 2011 by La Arenera, Somos Más, and Fábricca as an Enterprise and Innovation Center.

Change Theory and Mission

The HUB aims to build a unique ecosystem by creating spaces that inspire and connect people, thereby enabling them to develop ideas for enterprises that will have a sustainable impact. The HUB's mission is to create a transformative force that creates and promotes sustainable social and economic systems based on values of trust, courage, and collaboration. In order to achieve this objective, HUB's work is focused on three specific aims:

1. *Creating inspiring spaces.* In a world dominated by social networks and online interactions, the HUBs aim to become spaces that reinforce existing relationships and promote encounters and collaborative work. To do so, they provide coworking office space, meeting rooms, event halls, a lounge, a cafeteria, and a public meeting space that connects entrepreneurs with the wider public.
2. *Facilitating and nurturing the development of a vibrant and creative community of entrepreneurs, innovators, and social organizations.* It encourages social innovation among its members and offers opportunities for personal development, mutual support, networking and the development of collaborative projects.
3. *Generating significant events that help develop the network and support members.* The HUBs aim to become spaces that channel support services for the development of social entrepreneurs.

There are also specific aims that steer the work of local HUBs. For example, the goals of the São Paulo HUB include becoming a key actor in Education for Social Innovation in the next three years, incubating social enterprises with a focus on low-income regions, and facilitating the development of a collaborative environment for social entrepreneurs by hosting spaces for social innovation.

Each HUB is unique; however, the core principles and values are the same. By developing different activities that are aligned with these core values, HUB aims to become a movement that transforms society. Among its global activities are the development of clusters to bring together people working on similar projects; a practical academy to share knowledge and talent across the HUB network; and the European Union (EU) cluster, which groups initiatives from various European HUBs that want to become part of the EU's social innovation agenda.

The HUBs also develop activities at a local level. The La Arenera Hub provides information and training on topical issues, executive coaching, management consultancy, and technical assistance. It also seeks to increase contact among entrepreneurs, projects, and potential partners. There are also activities aimed at strengthening the social innovation community such as the Social Innovation Weekend.

Governance

The HUB has a global governance model that is divided into a HUB Company and a HUB Association. At a local level, the governance models vary greatly.

The São Paulo HUB has a nucleus of three directors. Meanwhile, the Bogotá HUB originated from a Leadership Workshop initiative that was driven collectively by Arenera, Somos Más, and Fabricca-Industria Creativa y Cultural. The HUB's ownership structure adheres to the logic of a distributed network—it belongs to everyone. It has a global principle for decision making across the worldwide network of "1 vote per HUB." In return for membership in the network and access to the benefits of being part of a global network, each HUB contributes financially to maintain global operations and invest in the network's future projects. Each new HUB must be approved before joining the network to ensure that it meets certain quality standards.

Approach, Tools, and Methodology
The HUB uses a holistic approach to create networks to achieve its core objectives. The methodology and tools used by the HUBs create inspiring spaces, vibrant communities, and meaningful events.

Area of Support/Instrument of Impact
The HUB support model is primarily bottom up, emerging from the social entrepreneurs themselves who begin to self-organize in supporting, connecting, and sharing spaces. Thus, the primary focus is on creating a community as opposed to the success of any specific project.

Support Phases
The HUBs are focused on creating ideas, and they support projects during the seed and start-up phases.

NESsT

NESsT was created in 1997 with the purpose of catalyzing social enterprises in emerging markets and around the world. It provides training, mentoring, and both financial and social capital, as well as facilitates market access for high-impact social enterprises. NESsT combines the tools and strategies of leadership, entrepreneurship, innovation, and investment with the mission and values of the social sector to improve the administrative capacity and growth of enterprises, thereby increasing their social impact.

NESsT is an international, nonprofit organization that develops and invests in sustainable social enterprises that solve critical social problems in emerging market economies. NESsT has launched and invested in more than 130 social enterprises in 10 emerging market countries, improving the lives of over 320,000 marginalized people. NESsT works with three categories of organizations with social missions: nonprofit organizations, small and medium businesses, and start-ups by individual entrepreneurs. NESsT has helped these groups create innovative and sustainable solutions to economic and environmental problems that affect marginalized communities.

Change Theory and Mission

NESsT's theory of change is based on the unique potential of social enterprises to address the social barriers faced by marginalized communities. Emerging markets are growing, but there is growing inequity and marginalized communities face social barriers—discrimination, lack of skills, isolation—and are being left behind. NESsT believes that social enterprises offer enterprising solutions to address and confront these barriers.

NESsT develops social enterprises in three impact areas:

- Inclusion in the labor market for people with disabilities, at-risk youth, ethnic minorities, and other individuals who are excluded from the labor market.
- Sustainable income for artisans, small-scale farmers, and other producers that require access to markets.
- Accessible technologies for low-income communities that enable them to improve their quality of life.

NESsT believes that social enterprises generate markets that are open, fair, and productive. They increase access to dignified work, sustainable incomes, and quality basic services. Furthermore, they improve living conditions and create products and services that are socially and environmentally responsible.

Governance

NESsT has six country offices, representative offices in San Francisco and London, and works throughout Central Europe and Latin America. The majority of the 35 person staff is composed of emerging market professionals and the organization counts on the support of over 300 volunteer business advisors to help mentor its enterprise portfolio. The International Board of Directors, elected for six-year terms, is composed of professionals from the private and philanthropic sectors with a strong commitment to NESsT's mission. All of the board members are donors.

NESsT's consulting services have taken its work to 48 countries and over 100 clients to advance social enterprise around the world. Self-generated income covers about 15–20 percent of the organization's budget.

Approach, Tools, and Methodology

NESsT uses a long-term portfolio approach to develop social enterprises. The organization provides business-planning support to identify and select the best ideas. Annual social enterprise competitions generate the pipeline for business ideas and business planning. NESsT then selects and launches the most promising enterprises and incubates them with capacity support and tailored financing for 2–3 years. NESsT then scales those enterprises for 3–4 years with patient investments to multiply their impact.

NESsT offers workshops on business planning, leadership development, sales and marketing, performance management, human resource and governance, financial management, and communications. Each workshop is followed by a period of individual mentoring in these areas, governed by a Memorandum of Cooperation that it signs with each social enterprise. On average, each enterprise receives 34 days of support per year, provided by NESsT staff and complemented by the support of external advisors. Using a range of financial instruments, NESsT invests approximately USD 220,000 per enterprise during the entire process.

Area of Support/Instrument of Impact

NESsT works with the social entrepreneur and his or her team to develop their capacity to launch, consolidate, and scale their business. The organization works with the social enterprise to develop a hybrid team that is best suited to lead and manage the business.

NESsT plans to reach 250,000 marginalized people in the next four years through social enterprises that will provide dignified permanent employment, sustainable income, and/or access to affordable technology—ultimately improving their quality of life and that of their families.

As a thought leader, NESsT has been at the forefront of social enterprise development, conducting extensive research and disseminating many publications on best practices. The organization has led numerous forums on this topic, and is the founder of Social Enterprise Day, an annual event that focuses on fostering an enabling environment for the sector. NESsT leverages its thought leadership to promote policies that further increase the impact of social enterprise.

Support Phases

NESsT offers support during three stages: planning, incubating, and scaling. Each stage is informed by the previous one and has specific aims and indicators to measure its success during the following stage. Entrepreneurs may receive up to four years of support during the initial stages of their projects, followed by another four years during which NESsT supports the scaling of the projects and provides financial and technical resources to ensure their success.

Simón de Cirene

Corporación Simón de Cirene was founded in 1995 with the aim of converting nonprofit organizations into actual social enterprises. Its objective is to strengthen these organizations and accompany them throughout the process of change that this transformation requires. Simón de Cirene recognizes that the only way to ensure the success of a social enterprise is by providing it with the necessary tools to tackle the problems it may face.

Simón de Cirene works with microbusinesses, individual entrepreneurs associated with the third sector, and community organizations by providing them with management tools and supporting the development of their businesses. Simón de Cirene's ultimate goal is to create a society that builds itself, in which social enterprises are the leading figures in the fight for a more developed, integrated, and humane society.

Change Theory and Mission

The aim of Corporación Simón de Cirene is to strengthen and support small entrepreneurs in the management and administration of their businesses. The end goal is clear: increase the quality of life and employment opportunities in Chile.

Simón de Cirene's programs help nonprofit organizations manage their operations, and, to this end, it provides manuals for social enterprises. It also works with microbusinesses, which are major employers among the vulnerable sectors of society and an important vehicle for inclusion. The development of good management practices in these businesses creates additional employment, income, and social mobility for vulnerable families. Simón de Cirene also works with community organizations, as these are the first organizations to emerge spontaneously in communities and, if well managed, they help communities develop and function effectively.

Its specific near-term objectives are as follows:

- Train 1,600 microentrepreneurs.
- Train 250 directors of foundations and corporations.
- Create indicators to measure the impact of programs on beneficiaries.
- Coaching, personal business services, and consultancy services are used to achieve these objectives.

Governance

The corporation has 33 employees, 8 volunteers, and 7 partners, and is governed by a board of directors. It is legally constituted as a foundation and operates through donations. Its structure is typical of the third sector.

Approach, Tools and Methodology

The processes are linear, with manuals to help the management of organizations and a schedule to guide the stages. These manuals can be downloaded for free, making the information readily available to a wide audience.

Simón de Cirene has a Social School to transform nonprofit organizations into social enterprises. It provides management manuals for social organizations that enable them to diagnose how they function. The School offers specific courses on finance and legal frameworks, in addition to coaching and advisory support on specific topics relating to business models.

There is also a Small and Medium Business School for microbusinesses, which gives participants the opportunity to deepen their understanding and implementation of management tools. All of the courses offered are designed to generate financially sustainable microbusinesses that create employment.

Area of Support/Instrument of Impact

Simón de Cirene focuses on the entrepreneur rather than projects or building communities. This is evident in the range of courses and activities it offers. These are designed to provide individual entrepreneurs with specific knowledge and tools, and none of the activities is aimed at building communities or generating shared ideas among entrepreneurs.

Simón de Cirene equips entrepreneurs with the tools they need to develop their existing projects successfully and realize their potential. In its 2012 annual report, it states that 910 entrepreneurs were supported. Interestingly, 84 percent of these clients belonged to the second quintile (of income), which demonstrates the important role Corporación Simón de Cirene plays in eradicating poverty.

Support Phases

Simón de Cirene supports entrepreneurs during the initial stages, concentrating on projects at the seed or start-up phase. The projects that are developed usually satisfy a local need and seldom seek to be scaled. Primarily, the projects are based within local communities and operate on a small scale.

Njambre

Njambre is an Argentine social enterprise founded in 2011 with the goal to identify, catalyze, accelerate, cocreate, disseminate, and create a community of impact innovation enterprises.

It works with social and environmental impact enterprises that are designed to improve the quality of life in disadvantaged communities. It has also contributed to the development of a social enterprise and innovation ecosystem in Argentina. Njambre's seeks to increase the number of social enterprises, and to achieve this it believes that it must identify and support social enterprises during their embryonic phases. It wants to contribute to the ecosystem by helping to generate financing and an appropriate legal framework for these organizations.

Change Theory and Mission

Njambre's objective is to create a consortium of impact innovation enterprises and entrepreneurs with the potential to influence the impact economy. The lines of action followed by Njambre are based on three mutually reinforcing strategies:

i.   Stewardship, shared management, training, coworking, building communities, and finance for social entrepreneurs
ii. Contribution to the ecosystem of social enterprises and impact investments in Argentina
iii. Generation and dissemination of knowledge

Njambre seeks to strengthen enterprises that will always prioritize the distribution of their products or services to vulnerable communities and that attempt to include more vulnerable people in their value chain.

Governance

There are certain characteristic elements that help Njambre carry out its mission. Impact entrepreneurs who are members of the community are able to exchange stock options with Njambre, which in turn invests in individuals who are committed to the impact economy. Njambre has a pioneering legal structure: it is a nonprofit civil association that is legally organized as a public limited company. Njambre supports organizations with participatory and transparent decision-making and governance processes. It conveys these values through its own example and strives to be collaborative, participatory, and transparent in all its processes.

Approach, Tools and Methodologies

Njambre uses a holistic approach, aimed at cobuilding social enterprise projects with all the relevant stakeholders. Njambre provides support for entrepreneurs through coaching, personal business services, and consultancy services. It assists projects through market intermediation; supports product placement, production, and commercialization; and provides organizational support in aligning the enterprises' social and financial objectives. In 2012, Njambre created a seed capital fund for impact enterprises, designed and implemented a management system for cardboard recycling cooperatives with Clase X and Avina, and supported and strengthened 50 entrepreneurs in the Mugica neighborhood in Retiro, Buenos Aires. Njambre has also helped disseminate the new paradigm of the impact economy through a series of lectures and via Internet.

Area of Support/Instrument of Impact

Njambre's goal is to create a community in which each enterprise is seen as part of a system of change agents seeking to transform the world through social innovation. However, Njambre also desires to strike a balance between providing tools for specific projects and equipping individuals with knowledge that goes beyond the particular project they are developing.

Support Phases

Njambre helps entrepreneurs during the seed or start-up phases. In its first year, it supported the emergence and development of four initiatives. Mamagrande develops biorefineries for ethanol and bioplastics, thereby contributing to efforts to decontaminate water. Lyara provides hydraulic energy for fishermen. Energe provides thermal energy solutions. Finally, Amagi makes clothing for people with reduced mobility. All of these businesses are examples of impact innovations that have three aims: delivering social value, delivering economic value, and protecting the environment.

5

First-Stage Scaling: Moving Early-Stage Enterprises to Expansion

Introduction

This chapter focuses on the appropriate approach to move early-stage social enterprises from incubation/proof of concept to their first-scaling process. This process, referred to as "first-stage scaling" because it is the first true attempt of the enterprise to grow or replicate, has many implications for social enterprises in terms of their business model, leadership team, governance, and financing. This chapter will highlight some of the common issues that arise when growing socially driven enterprises, and ways to overcome these challenges.

As in the case with the term "social enterprise," scaling has a wide array of meanings that are often the topic of heated debate. This becomes particularly challenging when referring to scaling social enterprises, since there is no baseline or common meaning for either term or no consensus on how to measure the "social" aspects of scaling. For some, scaling may mean adoption of the model in public policy; for others, it may mean large societal impact through behavior or cultural change; and for still others it may mean reaching a specific number of beneficiaries or enterprise revenue level.

While there is a lack of consensus around the definition, most donors, investors, incubators, and social enterprise managers increasingly agree that scaling is important. Scaling can be summarized as one way to maximize resources. Given the dearth of resources for early-stage social enterprise development, it could be inefficient to support a large number of small enterprises that, while sustainable, do not reach large impact—with some exceptions for donors/investors interested in specific causes where scale is a secondary priority. By focusing on scaling impact, effort can be concentrated on enterprises that demonstrate potential. This is an effective use of financial and human resources, and also a way to attract new forms of capital to this early-stage sector.

This chapter addresses one aspect of scaling, first-stage scaling, and specifically how to prepare enterprises to approach first-stage scaling and succeed. The emphasis on first-stage scaling is significant: an enterprise that has incubated its

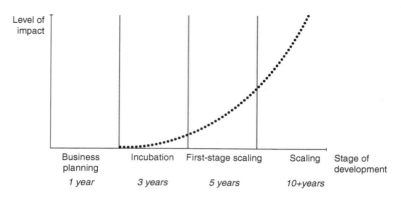

Diagram 5.1   First-stage scaling.

operations for two or three years and has a demonstrated proof of concept will not be able to scale with its current governance, team capacity, and financing. Scaling requires the careful design of an appropriate first-stage scaling strategy that leads to the right model and puts the enterprise on course for large impact.

Diagram 5.1 depicts the positioning of first-stage scaling in the enterprise development process. During this phase, social enterprises evolve their model to grow within their communities and/or replicate from one community to a select number of additional ones. This process leads to significant increases in the level of impact and activities compared to incubation, typically in the order of magnitude of four or five times. While this growth is impressive, it does not meet the exponential growth definition of typical scaling initiatives reaching hundreds of thousands or even millions of people. Nevertheless, first-stage scaling is a precondition to reaching these higher numbers.

The path to scaling requires approaching the process in stages, as social enterprise offerings are adapted to new users, and/or new products are developed to reach the same users. Moving too quickly to reach very high beneficiary numbers can be detrimental in cases where the beneficiary group requires training to use the product.

Scaling also includes trying out different approaches until the right model is selected as the enterprise embarks on its first growth strategy. For example, the governance model may require adaptation to comply with the business model and legal environment. Marketing and distribution may evolve as different strategies are tested until the most efficient model leads to the first significant increase in revenue and impact. These adaptations may take place over the course of a few years, and first-stage scaling provides the necessary time frame to tweak the model to facilitate large-scale impact later.

Social enterprises in first-stage scaling tend to have USD 100,000–150,000 average level of sales. This is consistent with the stage of their development at incubation. Enterprises should be breaking even or generating a small profit to be confident that the model can be replicated sustainably. Those directly employing persons from marginalized communities and that have high social costs—operating costs related to training and lower levels of productivity by their employees—may still be at 80–90 percent cost recovery rates. In these cases, one of the objectives of first-stage scaling could be to significantly grow the number of beneficiaries and sales, while reducing the total cost per item or service and reaching 100 percent self-sustainability to position the enterprise for large-scale impact later on.[1]

PREPARING FOR FIRST-STAGE SCALING

Social enterprises need to have a number of elements in place to become ready for first-stage scaling. There is a set of first-stage scaling readiness factors and best practices that are fundamental, and the greater the degree to which these are in place, the greater the capacity and readiness of the enterprise to move toward their first growth strategy. These best practices include the following:

- *Leadership and vision*: The need for a strong, capable leader committed to scaling is probably the fundamental driver of first-stage scaling success.
- *Performance oriented*: Exceeding on both the social and financial side of performance is a basic premise for first-stage scaling since it reflects that the model is proven and has the potential for high impact.
- *Scaling opportunity and interest*: There is a model in place that has both the business and social drivers[2] present that would allow for first-stage scaling. Both internal and external indicators demonstrate that this opportunity should be explored.

Social enterprises ready to move to first-stage scaling should have all three of the readiness factors in place. In some cases, one-off issues of concern can be addressed during the first-stage scaling design process (e.g., in the form of a business plan), as long as these issues are identified up front. For example, enterprises may have the right leadership and vision, but they need to strengthen the management capacity of the team with additional resources. Furthermore, a scaling opportunity may have been identified, but the exact scaling strategy is not clear yet and needs to be assessed through the business plan.

Social enterprises not meeting the above readiness factors should continue to consolidate their operations before moving to first-stage scaling. It is common for the leadership factor to be missing, and/or for the management or board to not agree on the opportunity to scale. Given the importance of this factor to the first-stage scaling process, enterprises need to prioritize building the right leadership and management team, and reaching consensus at all levels.

For donors and investors supporting social enterprises, the due diligence and selection process is a central ingredient to identifying the right first-scaling candidates. Obviously, relying on a large pipeline of social enterprises that have successfully incubated and can move to first-stage scaling is a benefit. Ensuring that all of the factors and drivers are lined up requires not only time, but also a strong understanding of social enterprises. Having an existing relationship with the enterprise, preferably developed during the incubation phase, reduces uncertainty for donors and investors. Local intermediaries very familiar with the enterprises' strengths and weaknesses, and a realistic plan for reducing the weaknesses, can also enhance the prospects for investment. This relationship must be balanced with an objective decision-making process, otherwise the risk of "falling in love" with the scaling idea is always a possibility.

Finally, to facilitate the first-scaling process, there need to be tools, training, and models available to social enterprises and the intermediaries that support them. Donors can play an important role in ensuring that these are supported and that models are documented and systematized, in order to foster a pipeline of healthy first-stage scaling enterprises.

Getting the Right First-Stage Scaling Strategy

As mentioned in the introduction, social enterprises with successful proof of concepts considering their first expansion need to carefully evaluate their current model. First-stage scaling incurs significant operational changes that require planning. Developing the right first-stage scaling strategy and business model is critical.

Three types of first-stage scaling strategies are available for social enterprises (see table 5.1). The first, grow enterprise, is implemented directly by the enterprise and includes taking the existing product to a significant number of end users (multiplication) or diversifying into new products (diversification), or a combination of both. The second and third strategies, replication and adoption,

Table 5.1   First-stage scaling strategy and business model framework

	Grow enterprise		Replicate with partners	Adopt through behavior change or public policy
	Multiplication	Diversification		
Strategy[a]	Scale by expanding existing product to a significant new number of end users	Scale by diversifying into new products	Scale by replicating the model	Change behavior, attitudes of a large number of people; adoption of practice through policy
Business models	Single entity		Franchising	Legal and regulatory change
	Branches		Licensing	Significant social marketing (can apply to all business models)
	Distributors		Partnership Joint ventures	

Note: [a]In all cases, expansion to new geographies could be a component of scaling.

are implemented in partnership with or through other organizations to reach the intended impact. Replication strategies take the model to new sites through an entity that is responsible for operating the model, while adoption focuses on changing policy, behaviors, and attitudes in order to ensure the broader impact of the social issue(s) that are being addressed. In all cases, the expansion can also happen geographically to new cities, regions, and countries.

During first-stage scaling, an enterprise may choose more than one strategy. It is common for enterprises to opt to first grow their businesses in their current community (i.e., during the first two or three years of first-stage scaling) before replication to new communities. The enterprise team needs to weigh the various costs and benefits of the scaling strategy to ensure that scaling is done effectively, and without compromising either the impact side or the enterprise side. As will be seen below in the cases on selecting the appropriate strategy, scaling is not an exact science, and the same scaling strategy applied to one enterprise is not necessarily appropriate for a similar enterprise. However, scaling does require careful analysis of drivers and goals and only when these are clear, can the most effective strategy be selected.

Once the strategy is clear, the business model needs to be selected. The business model varies depending on the scaling strategy, including the following:

- Growth strategies are executed directly by the enterprise and the business models typically include expanding the existing enterprise structure and/or opening up new branches (or offices) in different locations. Another option is to expand the reach of the enterprise through distributors that can cost effectively reach vulnerable communities.
- Replication business model strategies include the classical models of franchising and licensing, as well as partnerships and joint ventures. For example, "social franchising" is a tool that is increasingly considered and applies concepts of commercial franchising to achieve socially beneficial ends.
- Adoption of the enterprise model in policy can come from legal and regulatory changes, though that is more likely to happen once first-stage scaling has demonstrated the potential large-scale impact of the approach. Furthermore, adoption could come from any of the business models as long as there is a strong social marketing approach to achieve specific behavioral goals for social good.

SOCIAL PROGRAM COSTS

Social enterprises are in some instances associated with costly up-front social programs. It is important to decide how much of the program should be included in the scaling strategy and what should be separated out or perhaps streamlined. Reciduca is an Argentine enterprise located in Buenos Aires that trains and places at-risk youth in companies while they continue to go to school. Argentina has a very low secondary education completion rate and the high school dropout rate approaches 40 percent;[3] the problem of high school abandonment in Argentina is acute and has numerous repercussions for the country's development. Reciduca's training lasts two years and costs approximately USD 2,360 per youth. The program begins by engaging youth through an environmental education volunteer opportunity that is key to building their self-esteem. During the second year of the program, youth are trained in basic employment skills such as preparing for a job interview, meeting employer expectations, and conducting day-to-day tasks. This training is accompanied by internships that provide opportunities for the youth to acquire work experience and apply their skills. It is only in year three that they are ready to be placed in a permanent position and that Reciduca is able to charge a placement fee to the client companies. Reciduca's "soft skills" training program is no doubt an integral part of scaling the job placement enterprise. The program builds a steady flow of employment-ready youth. However, the cost of the internship placement increases significantly if the enterprise needs to cover the two-year training costs of the program as well.

During first-stage scaling, Reciduca's challenge is designing the appropriate strategy to increase its presence from 6 high schools to 35 in a period of 5 years in a way that is cost effective and does not jeopardize the quality of the youth training. To reach this goal, Reciduca is developing various training modules that more closely match the needs of the youth and lower costs at the same time. The enterprise is also redesigning its environmental education volunteer program to handle growth more cost effectively.

A similar situation relates to Asociacion Grupo de Trabajo Redes (AGTR), a Lima-based Peruvian social enterprise that provides high-quality training to domestic workers and places them with employers who are interested in and willing to respect legal contracts and requirements. Over 3 percent of working women in Peru are domestic workers (approximately half a million women),[4] most from poor rural communities who migrate to the city and who often work 12–14 hour shifts; and there is a high incidence of child domestic labor in the country.[5] AGTR's employment agency receives a fee from the employer after the training and after a contract is signed. However, AGTR must build a pipeline of trained workers who are not always placed right away. This pipeline is required to supply domestic workers who match the specific desires and expectations of prospective employers—expectations related to the type of service (cleaning, sewing, ironing, childcare, or elderly care), working hours (part time, full time, six days a week, or live-in), as well as the costs of service. AGTR must invest in training a wide range of domestic workers, and bear this cost until the worker is placed.

For enterprises like AGTR and Reciduca that provide employment opportunities to vulnerable groups, identifying who covers the costs of the training programs is critical. Although the costs can be evaluated and potentially reduced, significant reduction could compromise the social side of the business. If either of these two enterprises were to reduce the training component for their beneficiaries, it would likely not only reduce their "employability" but also the "social inclusion" of these marginalized groups. As part of its first-stage scaling process, AGTR reduced the length of its core training from one week to two days, which has allowed facilitation of placements without losing the quality of training, and gave flexibility to many women who prefer to participate in a core curriculum and continue with additional training in the future. Rather than eliminate the training program, another option is to have the program initially subsidized by grants until the enterprise breaks even (in the cases of Reciduca and AGTR, the possibility of the beneficiaries paying for the full cost of the training is not an option). This would require careful management of the grant, until the cost of training the youth or domestic worker could be covered by the enterprise income, and ensuring that these enterprises do not become dependent on subsidies in the long run.

High program costs are not always tied to high-quality training. In the case of Andar, an Argentina social enterprise that manages a bakery and Kék Madár, a Hungarian enterprise that runs a restaurant—both staffed by people with disabilities—first-stage scaling also entails the high costs and complications associated with replicating a capital-intensive business. In Argentina[6] and Hungary,[7] where 70–90 percent of people with disabilities are unemployed, one important goal of these enterprises is the training and support that prepare people with disabilities for work in the food service industry.[8] However, another goal is running a well-equipped, well-functioning, and well-located food service establishment. The high rate of failure in food start-ups is well known, and this becomes especially complicated when the restaurant employs people with disabilities. The selection of the first-stage scaling strategy will depend on whether these two enterprises decide to replicate the full business on their own or through a franchising or licensing model. On the one hand, remaining loyal to the social side will need to be weighed against giving control to someone else who might have a great deal of experience in the food business, but knows very little about employment of marginalized individuals. On the other hand, replicating through an entity that works with marginalized communities but knows very little about running a restaurant or bakery will also require overcoming significant obstacles.

ECONOMIES OF SCALE AND BUSINESS EFFICIENCY

Another important factor to consider when selecting the right strategy is the question of economies of scale and business efficiency. This issue is relevant for enterprises whose key business driver is high-volume potential (this is not the case for restaurant social enterprises, for example).

In the case of Magrini, a social enterprise located in Puno, Peru, the scaling potential is based on diversification and the ability to offer different agricultural machine products to the same users in that region. In Peru, there are over 65,000 families engaged in the production and conservation of Andean cereals.[9] Of these, about 60 percent use manual labor rather than machines to harvest the land. This is not only a slower, more laborious process, but can also cause premature aging and physical ailments for agricultural producers. Based on its market research, Magrini realized that there was a large market demand in the region for a number of different agricultural machines that it could manufacture. Rather than doing a first-stage scaling process by taking the same single product to new locations, both social and business considerations point to the need to deepen impact in the same region through product diversification. A second phase of scaling could potentially adapt the products to other locations in order to reach new users. This could potentially also be done through multiplication and the use of distributors or branches. However, depending on the level of complexity related to adaptation and distribution, replication through franchising or licensing might be more appropriate.

Ingenimed, a Peruvian social enterprise, can reach more end users of its Neoled phototherapy technology for the treatment of jaundice by multiplying to all rural clinics in Peru. Unlike the case of Magrini, the product does not require adaptation and fills the huge demand for low-cost and efficient care of jaundiced newborns in rural communities. This demand currently is not being met by expensive imported machines that are only found in urban hospitals, or by ineffective locally handmade machines. The potential for doing first-stage scaling through multiplication is excellent given that neonatal jaundice is highly prevalent in the rural regions of Peru. Ingenimed needs to decide whether to grow through distributors or branches. The need to replicate is less important in this case given the low degree of adaptation needed.

Some social enterprises find that balancing efficiency and mission considerations is extremely challenging. In the case of Viitor Plus, a Romanian enterprise that produces ecofriendly organic-cotton shopping bags, the enterprise employs at-risk mothers and youth to produce the bags. This has caused incessant production challenges that would not exist if the bags were being produced en masse. There is a very high potential to scale, and an early scaling issue Viitor Plus must consider is the advantage of achieving greater environmental impact by getting more cotton bags into the hands of shoppers—in a country where five million plastic bags[10] are used annually—versus employing people who would otherwise have a very difficult time getting employment. In this case, potential for impact seems to indicate that the enterprise should not apply an employment model to its enterprise, but rather to scale through a very intense growth multiplication strategy.

Finally, the case of Upasol also has a first-stage scaling efficiency dilemma. This social enterprise, located in a medium-sized city in the north of Chile, is a recycling business that collects solid waste (plastic, cardboard, and glass) from community residents and public entities. The collected waste is sold to large companies that use them in their recycling and production processes, generating revenue for the organization and environmental benefits overall. The business is quite successful, engaging more than 1,500 community residents and generating a 10 percent annual increase in sales. The interesting dimension about this enterprise is that all of the profit generated is used to fund the parent organization's rehabilitation center for children with disabilities. The only direct link between the recycling business and the rehabilitation center is that the families, who benefit from the free or reduced fees of the center, collect and provide the solid waste to the enterprise as an indirect form of payment. So unlike the employment models mentioned in this chapter, there is no direct social link between the enterprise and the center, but rather, there is an indirect link that also leads to social impact. In terms of scaling, Upasol is considering replicating the recycling business to other cities in the north of Chile and delinking the business from any specific impact other than the environmental one. This will make replication efficient, since the model can be adopted by a wide variety of organizations, which can decide whether to link the business to a social cause or not.

Leveraging Procurement Opportunities

In some cases, government policies and incentives, including those related to procurement, will provide the scaling opportunity. In the case of INCORES, a Brazilian enterprise that trains and places at-risk youth in the job market in Bahia, the training side of the program is paid for through placement fees charged to companies. In Brazil, where there is over 17 percent youth unemployment and underemployment,[11] the law requires that between 5 and 15 percent of staff at private companies with more than 7 employees must be apprentices in training. Companies must pay for the training and mentoring of these apprentices by a certified training agency. Unlike the case of Reciduca in Argentina where there is no legislation requiring that companies must pay for training services, the policies in Brazil allow INCORES to pass the training costs to the employer and also guarantee a healthy supply of clients interested in contracting its services. This opportunity facilitates INCORES's scaling potential and indicates that replicating the model to other urban centers in Brazil will allow the enterprise to reach thousands of at-risk and low-income youth. INCORES has the training know-how, and the variable costs of growth are paid by clients, which makes the model highly efficient. It points to a replication strategy that is managed by INCORES through the use of branches rather than the need to sell the license or franchise to a third party.

Another interesting example is Fundatia Cartea Calatoare (FCC), a Romanian social enterprise that produces audio books and educational materials for the blind and sight impaired. Of Romania's 5,300 libraries and bookstores,[12] only a few offer disability-friendly technologies to meet the needs of approximately 90,000 visually impaired citizens.[13] At the same time, there is very low availability of audio books, which the visually impaired need to gain access to literature and professional material. After a successful incubation of three years, FCC is embarking on its first-stage scaling process by significantly expanding its current selection of feature-rich, navigable recordings targeting public libraries and individuals. The enterprise also plans to sell the devices and software necessary to play the recordings to public libraries, which are required by law to accommodate visually impaired readers. Key to its first-stage scaling success will be if the government decides to recognize the FCC devices as equipment needed by people with sight disabilities, and subsidizes its purchase price (as is the case with wheelchairs, for example). FCC is working hard with other partners to lobby the government to adopt this legislation. If it does not succeed, the enterprise will consider working with alternative lenders to offer low-interest loans to blind and sight-impaired individuals to purchase this hardware. Building alliances is essential for implementing either one of these options.

IMPLICATIONS OF FIRST-STAGE SCALING ON SOCIAL ENTERPRISES

As demonstrated above, first-stage scaling requires complex decisions to ensure that the right strategy and business model are selected to move an early-stage enterprise from incubation to its first attempt to grow significantly. Once the strategy is in place, execution will have important implications for the social enterprise. This section analyzes how first-stage scaling affects the enterprise leadership and the team, the governance structure and relationship with the enabling environment, and financing.

Leadership and Team Practices

The need for the right leadership is fundamental to the success of the enterprise. Leadership is necessary at all stages of development, including at business plan, incubation, first-stage scaling, and beyond. Leadership traits evolve from one stage to the next. At business planning and incubation stages, strong leadership entails bootstrapping and having very good knowledge of the product side. At first-stage scaling, it entails flexibility to redesign the enterprise strategy and business model and not only having the commitment to scale, but also the vision of what it takes to do it right.

First-stage scaling leaders need to know how to obtain and assess the relevant information for taking calculated risks. Openness to learning and learning from mistakes is crucial. The old adage that failure is the key to success should become the mantra of all leaders at scaling stage. Fear of failure will surely lead to unwillingness to take calculated risks, risks that oftentimes are important to meeting scaling goals. Leaders at scaling stage also need to be opportunistic and leverage opportunities that will contribute to the success of the business. A central component of this is having the ability to assess the costs and benefits of the opportunities that come their way. For early-stage social enterprises, having support mechanisms that buffer some of the costs of risks and opportunities becomes critical to growth and scaling.

Across the board, leaders need to be transparent and accountable. This becomes particularly acute at first-stage scaling when the levels of investment and sales begin to grow significantly. One small mistake tied to the way money is managed or spent can be detrimental and lead to the loss of buyers, suppliers, clients, and/or investors. This relates to the need to invest in external experts who have the know-how and are able to ensure that the business is meeting its legal and accounting obligations.

Perhaps the single most important leadership asset of first-stage scaling is to develop a multidisciplinary team that can meet the demands of the scaling process. This not only means getting the right leader, as mentioned above, but also making sure that he or she has the team needed for the job. In the case of Kollyor, a social enterprise that sells highly efficient and environmentally friendly cookstoves and other technologies in Peru, complementing the invention and engineering skills of the founders with someone who has strong business acumen and can run the day-to-day enterprise management is critical. In addition, bringing on board an experienced salesperson can ensure that the stoves will get to the hands of end users, which in this case include families, tourist agencies, and non-profit organizations (NPOs). The same can be said of Ingenimed (see above), the social enterprise launched by four engineering students who have added a business entrepreneur to the team. This combination will allow the enterprise to continue improving its line of products, while ensuring that the business is structured and managed in a way that allows it to scale to rural clinics throughout the region and eventually the country.

For Kék Madár, the key to success is having an extremely visionary and apt leader who knows how to build a multidisciplinary skilled team. She has staff who train and provide therapy and other forms of support to people with disabilities; staff with disabilities who are the servers and cooks in the restaurant; and finally, a very high-caliber chef, who knows how to create meals that can be cooked by people with disabilities and are extremely popular with the customers (mostly families) who frequent the restaurant. Achieving this combination is not easy, but is vital to Kék Madár's replication strategy.

A central element of first-stage scaling is for enterprise leaders to know when to delegate tasks to the team, and knowing when to make the complex decisions on their own. In the case of nonprofit social enterprises, often led by people used to taking some risks but who often are reluctant to share the risks with their staff, this requires learning to transfer responsibilities and decision making to middle managers. In some cases, the enterprise leaders lack the necessary management capacity to make some of the difficult scaling decisions. This capacity is essential and needs to be built before first-stage scaling begins (see box 5.1).

Box 5.1   Andar: Learning to build a leadership team

As is the case with many NPO leaders throughout the world, Raul Lucero, founder and director of Andar, is a visionary who has built his organization from the ground up. A strong advocate of the right to work for people with disabilities, Raul launched a bakery soon after founding Andar. It was not until years later that with NESsT's support Andar developed the more profitable accompanying catering business, which is currently at incubation. A key success driver of the new business and its readiness for scaling was the need to better organize the team, requiring them to adopt new responsibilities and the capacity to make certain day-to-day decisions on their own.

There was, however, some resistance to this training and, above all, to the implementation of the new production and administrative processes. The middle managers were not used to taking responsibility and following formal processes beyond the technical training they had received. This resistance to the implementation raised a very critical and sensitive issue.

Raul, a national leader known for his entrepreneurial vision and strong service, was no doubt the main driver behind Andar's strong reach and performance. However, this same leadership style was also becoming a limitation for the organization and enterprise. The high concentration of functions, roles, and decision making in one director acculturated the team to not take responsibility for complex decisions. There was a high reliance on the director's decisions and little space for group analysis of situations that should be resolved day-to-day. Consequently, the director handled most solutions and was overwhelmed with daily tasks, which prevented him from focusing on and advancing strategic decisions of the association.

Given this diagnosis, shared by the director, NESsT began working with him and his team to change this way of operating. To assist in this task, NESsT returned to a member of its Business Advisory Network, a human resources specialist who had previously worked with Andar. The aim was to change this paradigm of dependency, to delegate operational decisions to each coordinator, and at the same time to empower middle managers to assume responsibility for decisions and their outcomes.

Work began by interviewing the entire team to understand their expectations and capabilities to carry out their tasks. At these meetings, it became clear that the organization relied too heavily on its leader to make decisions. It was determined that during the year middle managers would be trained on the importance of their roles and of assuming responsibility for their work. For the human resources specialist, this work was critical in order to overcome feelings of uncertainty among staff and reestablish confidence and bonds of trust among the team.

The process was designed to be gradual, with the director delegating, on the one hand, and middle managers assuming decisions tied to their duties, on the other. Nevertheless, an unforeseen situation arose that accelerated the process: the leader of the organization accepted a public office, with the intention of using it to bring about policy changes related to disability and social integration. This changed the timing of the process, but fortunately they had acted early and middle management had already started to gradually assume leadership and responsibility in their work areas. Given the situation of the director, the new human resources plan for Andar also included a new high-level position defined as "operations manager," which would replace the director in production management. Thus, the new HR structure organized the positions, defined roles and responsibilities, empowered middle managers for decision making, and replaced the director with a new manager who received strategic guidance to help the transition at Andar.

Once this new structure is consolidated, Andar should be well positioned to begin the scaling process.

Governance and Enabling Environment Practices

First-stage scaling sometimes requires changes in the social enterprise governance structure. This stems from having to adapt the governance model to the first-stage scaling strategy of the enterprise to facilitate growth. The reasons to adapt the governance model may be to comply with the legal environment, to strengthen the overall management of the enterprise, or to attract financing.

With regard to the legal environment, as seen in this book, there is a lack of an enabling legal framework for social enterprises in emerging market countries. A good case in point is RODA, a pioneering organization in Croatia commercializing organic-cotton products to promote natural childbirth and breastfeeding. The enterprise was incubated as a nonprofit entity, and quickly showed the potential of the model by reaching close to USD 500,000 in sales during proof of concept. As the enterprise began to plan its first-stage scaling process, it quickly realized that it would not be able to grow significantly under current Croatian law, which restricts the type of distribution channels through which nonprofit enterprises can sell. Importantly for RODA, the law severely limits nonprofit enterprise exports, which is a key market for the enterprise's first-stage scaling. To circumvent this issue, RODA is currently incorporating its enterprise as a for-profit entity to reach a wider set of distribution channels, including exports.

The governance structure may also be modified during first-stage scaling to strengthen overall management. The enterprise leadership may decide to bring in additional skills to the enterprise, allowing outside experts to join the board or become partners in the business. In Argentina, Reciduca expanded its board to integrate professionals with experience in entrepreneurship and private equity in order to assist with the growth of the employment agency. In addition, the organization (a nonprofit) created a committee of the board tasked with oversight of the employment agency, and external experts were invited to join the committee to advise on the growth and first-scaling strategy.

A similar idea includes creating an expert advisory group for the enterprise to access know-how and contacts. The benefit of an advisory group is that it is consultative and is relatively easy to manage, compared to expanding the board. An advisory group can be extremely useful during first-stage scaling since the enterprise often needs to expand its access to clients, suppliers, and distributors.

A final reason for modifying the governance structure is to attract financing. For nonprofit social enterprises, attracting any type of equity investment requires incorporating as a for-profit business. For example, the social enterprise Fruit of Care, a Hungarian enterprise that sells attractive home decor and gift products made by people with disabilities, was spun off from a foundation and set up as a business, which attracted the necessary capital from management and three other business partners to set the entity on its first-stage scaling process (the enterprise now employs two hundred people with disabilities—see box 5.2). Furthermore, accepting debt or equity may require policy changes in nonprofit enterprises. Upasol, the recycling enterprise in Chile, successfully incubated its business with grants. In first-stage scaling, the enterprise was offered a patient investment in the form of a loan to expand its facilities. Until that time, the organization had an

Box 5.2   Fruit of Care: Spin-off to enable financing and growth

Fruit of Care sells decor and gift items made by people with physical and intellectual disabilities. The concept was developed as a program of a foundation that advocates for the rights of people with disabilities in Hungary. As the program grew, the foundation realized that it did not have the capacity to run the business, which it spun off as a separate limited liability nonprofit company.

Under Hungarian law, the limited liability nonprofit company was created for social enterprises to attract capital, similar to a limited liability partnership. The difference is that the limited liability nonprofit company restricts any dividend distribution to investors, and all profits need to be reinvested in the business.

By incorporating under this business form, Fruit of Care was able to attract three investors (in addition to the founder) to provide the initial capital to relaunch the enterprise and embark immediately on a first-stage scaling process.

explicit policy to fund itself only through grants, and it had to revise this policy to secure the necessary loan to facilitate growth.

For-profit social enterprises may also need to modify their governance structure to attract financing. As will be seen below, first-stage scaling is oftentimes the first moment when a social enterprise attracts investment. Working with one or several equity investors requires significant governance changes. The most obvious one is to share equity with an outside investor, which comes with a host of implications. There are many benefits to bringing investors into the social enterprise governance structure, including the injection of capital necessary for first-stage scaling, the expertise and skills the investor brings to the enterprise, and the large network of contacts that can help the enterprise access new resources. At the same time, it also means sharing decision making with the investor(s), and in some cases sharing board seats. It is important for the social enterprise to carefully screen investors to ensure that they have the same vision for the first-stage scaling process. The added complexity of a social enterprise is the social side—how to grow it, and how to balance this growth with the financial side. Entrepreneur and investor must be in agreement with what comes first, and how decisions will be made to prioritize the social side.

Social enterprises entering their first significant growth phase often face these challenges on their own. A driver of success is building strategic alliances and ensuring that with these allies, the enterprise is able to push on all fronts related to first-stage scaling. As already mentioned above, in emerging market countries there is a lack of incentives, tax benefits, and long-term growth funding and support mechanisms for early-stage social enterprises. In many instances, the products and services that are offered by the social enterprises are so innovative that there are no regulations and processes in place to recognize and mainstream them.

This makes creating strategic alliances even more important, since it is a way to affect the environment through the contacts, networks, expertise, and resources of a larger group. The capacity to identify these allies and set up the right partnerships is not always intuitive and needs thoughtful assessment and time. In some cases, a loose partnership is all that is needed, whereas in others, it is important to formalize the process, ensuring that roles and responsibilities are binding and that intellectual property or confidential information is being respected and adhered to.

FCC and INCORES mentioned earlier are cases of how an enabling environment can positively affect the scaling potential of social enterprise. Another good case in point is the experience of Ingenimed, the social enterprise that sells Neoled phototherapy equipment to address the needs of jaundiced newborns. The enterprise is the first ever biomedical company incorporated in Peru. Prior to its creation, there were no other Peruvian companies addressing the needs of jaundiced newborns in the country. The enterprise is now in the process of obtaining its certificate to legally manufacture and sell the technology. It had to wait until the first law for biomedical certification was enacted, which took over a year. Now that the law has been enacted, it can begin the process of complying with the certification procedures, including manufacturing the technology and preparing to fully enter the market after a successful proof of concept has been conducted.

In addition to improving the regulatory environment, enterprises in first-stage scaling need to engage in changing behaviors in order to maximize impact. In the case of RODA, the sale of organic-cotton products is only one side of the enterprise's current impact. Building awareness of breast-feeding and less intrusive birth practices is the other, and in many ways just as—if not more—important. The same can be said in the case of Viitor Plus where the use of cotton bags as a tool to change overall behaviors that are harmful to the environment could have far-reaching societal impact. For Kék Madár and Andar, showcasing that people with disabilities are able to work in skilled jobs on a regular basis sends a clear message to both the private and public sectors on the need to provide labor inclusion opportunities to this community. The same applies to the case of AGTR, in Peru, which provides legal, fair-wage employment to domestic workers. Alongside its enterprise activity, the organization advocates for the rights of domestic workers and to prevent child domestic work, building awareness on the need for dignified employment among this sector in Peru and throughout Latin America.

First-Stage Scaling Investments

The evolution of social enterprises from incubation to first-stage scaling opens up the need to attract different types of investments to finance growth (see chap. 8

for more details). At incubation, the use of grants is critical to support innova-tive ideas, particularly since there is little cash flow. Grants can cover the social costs that enterprises incur, such as beneficiary training to gain access to formal employment or to sell in higher-value markets. Also, during incubation, other types of financial support such as bank loans or impact investments are generally not available, given the perceived risk of the enterprises operating at this stage; grants tend to be the only means to fund a proof of concept. In some cases, social enterprises can access loans during incubation for specific uses, such as working capital or secured loans (e.g., to purchase property or equipment).

Grants continue to be relevant during first-stage scaling, but they have a dif-ferent purpose—to prepare for or ramp up in year one of first-stage scaling. The case of Reciduca is a good example. As noted earlier, the enterprise invests heavily in a two-year training program to prepare each group of at-risk youth for place-ment (at which time it gets paid). As the enterprise moves to expand its services to new schools as part of its first-stage scaling, a grant that helps to ramp up its staffing and cover other operational costs until it breaks even makes a great deal of sense.

Grants can also be important in those cases where the model is being rep-licated and there is heavy up-front investment in a new entity. As noted earlier regarding Andar and Kék Madár, replication of the bakery and restaurant would be quite costly, and it would be very difficult for the replicating entity (e.g., licensee or franchisee) to take on a loan for all start-up expenses. These models usually take at least three years to break even, and profit margins are low.

First-stage scaling also offers the opportunity to provide the first nongrant investments to social enterprises. It is important to find the right funding mix between grants and investments: first-stage scaling is not about only philan-thropy anymore, but not about impact investing yet either. The typical size of investments for financing first-stage scaling ranges from USD 75,000 to USD 300,000, which is several times larger than typically provided at incubation/ proof of concept (see table 5.2).

Managing a loan or equity investment, as opposed to a grant, requires a new set of skills. At first-stage scaling, the introduction of investments is important for the enterprise to build a track record and to prepare for additional rounds of financing in later phases of the scaling process. It is also a way for social enter-prises to begin to understand the cost of capital, and to build those costs into the first-stage scaling plans. For an enterprise to know that it needs to meet projections in order to comply with a repayment schedule is a healthy exercise. Having a more diverse capital structure may also allow the enterprise to attract new and larger forms of financing: some donors and investors view favorably an enterprise that successfully has raised donations and patient investments for its first-stage scaling. This is certainly the case of Kék Madár restaurant (as explained in chap. 8), whose loan to purchase its building unlocked European Union (EU) funding for refurbishing the restaurant.

Preparing social enterprises to take on their first investments requires time. Investment-readiness programs exist for social enterprises to become acquainted with different investment types, and to understand the benefits and drawbacks

Table 5.2 Financial support for social enterprise development

Social enterprise stage	Planning and incubation stages	First-stage scaling	Investment-ready[a] social enterprises
Type of financial support	Grants, working capital loans, and infrastructure loans	Debt or equity, includes soft loans and quasi equity;[b] grants complement investments	Debt and/or equity, often convertible loans[c]
Amount	Up to USD 75,000	USD 75,000–300,000	USD 300,000+
Expected returns	No return expectations on grants; social return first on investments and more flexible expectation of financial return	Social return first and expectation of financial return on the investments	Social return or financial return first

Notes:
[a] "Investment-ready" means that the social enterprise has the financial performance, leadership, and systems in place to receive commercial loans or equity investments based on investor expectations of market returns.
[b] A special form of financing for social enterprises that fills the gap that exists between a grant/loan and equity. It "has equity-like qualities without conferring ownership rights to the investor. Forms of quasi-equity include use of underwriting, royalty share finance, and repayable grants. It should be noted that some current definitions of quasi-equity also embrace use of subordinated, unsecured debt." The Social Investment Bank, The Commission on Unclaimed Assess, UK, March 2007, http://socialfinance.ca/knowledge-centre/glossary/term/quasi-equity.
[c] Convertible debt is repaid as one lump-sum payment when it reaches maturity. At that point, the investor has the option of asking for repayment in full of the loan, or taking a percent in the form of equity in the company.

of each. Often a precondition to attracting investments includes developing appropriate accounting and financial systems that give investors the assurance that the investments will be allocated properly. Many social enterprises fail to attract investments because their accounts are not investment ready. In some cases, such as Upasol described above, social enterprises need to warm up to the concept of using investments to finance first-stage scaling. It may require modifying internal policies to allow nongrant financial instruments. In other cases, it entails working with the enterprise management and board to explain the benefits of taking an investment. This process of investment readiness can take six months to a year.

For investors and social enterprises alike, scaling-financing decisions should be made based on capacity to help enterprises achieve their impact. Although the ability to repay or offer a return is important in selecting the right financial instrument, the main driver should be whether this is the right financial instrument for what is being sought. An important factor is where the social enterprise is in its development. As mentioned above, an enterprise that is just getting off the ground and needs to cover social costs and significant start-up costs requires a very soft form of capital, most likely a grant. However, once there is cash flow and capacity to repay, the use of low-interest loans, loans with long grace periods, or loan guarantees should be considered. Human resources and other soft assets should be paid through grants or equity, until the enterprise is able to finance these costs.

Hard assets such as the purchase of a building for a restaurant or bakery, or equipping a workshop for the manufacture of technology, should probably be funded with infrastructure loan capital and paid back through future sales or through equity and returned upon final sale (see box 5.3).

Box 5.3   Motivation, UK, and loan for first-stage scaling

Motivation is a UK-headquartered, global social enterprise that provides training and mobility products for the physically disabled in the developing world. It was founded in 1991 after students David Constantine and Simon Gue designed an award-winning wheelchair for developing countries. This affordable wheelchair worked well on rough paths and was sturdily constructed with easily accessible materials. Today, Motivation manufactures a range of quality, affordable mobility products designed specifically for developing countries.

Providing mobility is one of Motivation's four areas of work. It also focuses on survival, empowerment, and inclusion of individuals with physical disabilities. Motivation trains the parents of children with cerebral palsy to prevent children from dying of malnutrition, pressure sores, and respiratory problems. Its peer group training empowers disabled people to learn wheelchair skills, prevent health problems, and discuss their rights. Its products and training programs have reached over 135,000 people in 90 countries around the world.

Motivation knew that wheelchair manufacturing had great impact— each product changed lives, opened opportunities for training, and provided income for the organization. However, it did not have the reserves and could not obtain large enough grants to scale its impact. Traditional banks would not finance this project.

In 2009, Motivation approached Venturesome—a UK social investment fund that provides affordable repayable finance to charities, social enterprises, and community groups (see chap. 8 for more details)—with an ambitious plan to increase production sixfold in five years. After discussions with the Motivation leadership team and extensive review of its finances and business plan, Venturesome determined that it could loan GBP 200,000. Venturesome made this loan conditional on Motivation strengthening its financial capacity and systems, including hiring a new finance manager. The loan was divided into two different types of instruments. It provided a GBP 125,000 five-year loan with interest-only payments for the first three years. Short-term loans are standard instruments for Venturesome, with an interest rate between 5 and 8 percent.

The second part of the funding, GBP 75,000, was secured by a right to a small proportion of Motivation's revenue. Venturesome had confidence in the leadership team and the high social returns of the product. It targeted about a 10 percent internal rate of return (reflecting the higher risk), and the total repayment was capped. For Motivation, it received a timely investment and repayment would come from future revenue.

Equity investments are the more complex form of investment, particularly at first-stage scaling, when the business model evolves and financial projections are difficult to develop with certainty. In the case of Ingenimed, the enterprise needs approximately USD 200,000 to build a laboratory to increase its manufacturing capacity of Neoled phototherapy machines. Were the enterprise to take a loan, based on cost and revenue projections, it would take at least five years before the enterprise could begin considering repayment. The possibility of taking equity is very attractive to the enterprise, particularly if the investor is able to provide strong capacity support to assist the team of young inventors to meet the enterprise goals.

For investors and social enterprises, the question of control over decision making is also important and not always equated with ownership. For an investor taking an equity stake, control might be advantageous under certain circumstances, but it is not always the way to influence decisions. Ideally, the relationship between investor and enterprise should be constructed so that key decisions are made jointly and are based on the respect and value that the investor gains and adds to the enterprise and the scaling process. Goals and expectations should be outlined up front, as well as what is nonnegotiable. In those instances where having influence means gaining some level of control, a spectrum of options should be considered—this could range from holding a seat on the board of directors, to limiting the voting rights of management, to taking partial or majority control of the enterprise. With each level of control comes a certain level of additional responsibility and exposure that needs to be taken into consideration. The degree to which any one of these measures is adopted should be assessed carefully.

There are four key considerations that should be taken into account when selecting which financial instrument, or combination of instruments, should be used. These are the purpose for which the financing is sought; the type of risk that is tied to the instrument; performance indicators, including the historical and expected social impact and income growth of the enterprise; and external considerations such as the supply of capital that is available.

Table 5.3 classifies all three instruments along these criteria, and shows that there is a wide range of possibilities for using these financial instruments. It is important to understand these various uses to apply the right financing package.

Table 5.3   Financial instrument criteria

Purpose	Grant	Loan/loan guarantee	Equity and equity-like investments
Consolidation	x		
Working capital	x	x	
Infrastructure	x (early stage only)	x	x
Bridge cash crunch		x	
Start-up capital	x		x
Social enterprise operations	x	x	x
Growth/expansion	x	x	x
Preparation for exit	x	x	
Risk			
Length of financing need	Short/long	Short/long	Long
Good credit history exists		x	
Service other loan	x		x
Performance			
Years of operation	Any	Minimum one	Minimum two
Cash flow exists to ensure repayment		x	
Investment horizon	Any	Minimum one	Three to five years
External Considerations			
Alternative financing options not available	x	x	
Coinvestor exists	Not necessary	Preferable	Preferable
Financial return minimum 0%		x	x
Investible entity (not a nonprofit)			x

A high-level assessment of the first-stage financing requirements of social enterprises incubated by NESsT reveals the need for all three types of financing instruments. All the enterprises received grants during incubation, and all will receive some form of investments (either debt or equity or a combination) at first-stage scaling. The need for investments demonstrates the necessity for social enterprises to open up their capital structure to investors during their first-stage scaling process.

For donors and investors providing financial support to early-stage social enterprises, first-stage scaling also has implications on the relative financial influence of these organizations/investors on the capital structure of the enterprise. As enterprises move into first-stage scaling, their financing needs increase, which leads to a search for new sources of funding and diversification of the donor and investor base. This can be considered a benefit, because as the enterprise works

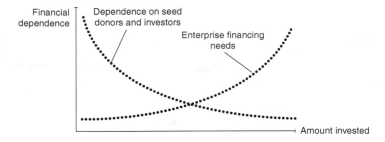

Diagram 5.2 Financial dependence and financing needs.

with a large pool of donors and investors it becomes less dependent on any one source and the financial risk decreases (see diagram 5.2).

CONCLUSIONS AND RECOMMENDATIONS

Scaling early-stage social enterprises is increasingly viewed as necessary and at the same time very challenging. Focusing on the social side first and ensuring that social ends are not compromised is fundamental. However, the timely and strategic use of scaling best practices is no less important for success.

For social enterprises embarking on their first-stage scaling, a number of factors need to be in place. Getting the leadership right is the first step in the process. Having a leader who is committed to building a team and growing the enterprise beyond him or her, and who has the vision needed to grow and scale, is crucial. With this comes the need to consolidate the social enterprise, which might take several years before first scaling. Having resources and capacity support during this phase is extremely important.

Selecting the right first-stage scaling strategy and business model is also important. The costs of the social program and the need for economies of scale and business efficiency should be clearly assessed when making this decision. Although commitment to social impact should be the ultimate aim, identifying the right business and social drivers and determining whether to adopt a growth or replication strategy (to multiply or diversify or both) can make a great deal of difference in terms of reaching that impact.

With this comes the need to decide what components of the social enterprise are being scaled. In the case of the social enterprises highlighted in this chapter, social impact is the key scaling indicator. Whether moving from 100 to 1,000 job placements, or 1,000 to 30,000 end users, there must be a clear understanding of the end goal and how the enterprise will get there.

Systems to establish and clearly track financial and social performance data are also critical. This must start at incubation, so that there are clear indicators for measuring success, an understanding of the obstacles to overcome, and realistic expectations on what the scaling business will achieve. In addition to concrete outcomes, quality of life indicators should be set, including those that take into account changes in policy, behaviors, and attitudes.

For those supporting first-stage scaling social enterprises, such as incubators, donors, and investors, their level of involvement in the process is also important. They should offer strategic advice and provide access to information, experts, and networks. Enterprises often need external support to become investment ready and to modify their governance structures for scaling. Knowing how to build strategic alliances, multidisciplinary teams, and to invest in visibility and positioning are proven practices that need to be implemented at first-stage scaling.

For these support organizations, understanding the local context is fundamental, both for identifying the scaling potential of the enterprise and for informing the investor. Growing an at-risk youth labor inclusion model in a country with a population of 36 million such as Argentina versus 203 million such as Brazil is quite different and so the assessment needs to be quite different. If there is a procurement policy that facilitates the hiring of this group, the scaling potential will be quite different.

Donors and investors should align their expectations with those of early-stage social enterprises and understand the resources needed to prepare these enterprises to grow and maximize their impact. Just as social enterprises need to prepare for first-stage scaling, so do investors and donors need to prepare for that phase by analyzing the time and resources required to make this process successful.

Donors and investors should consider supporting development of the methodology and tools that are specifically appropriate for scaling social enterprises is fundamental. This can be done through intermediaries, as mentioned in other chapters of this book, or directly with social enterprises. There are very few tools available, and those that do exist, mostly standard industry tools for scaling, are not appropriate for early-stage entrants. Tools should range from selection to implementation, and should include frameworks for assessing and making decisions that can be adapted on a case-by-case basis, manuals on best practices with checklists to ensure that all areas are being considered, and business-plan templates, as well as performance management and measurement tools. Workshops would be extremely helpful for first-stage scaling enterprises to have access to this know-how and resources. Exposing them to peers who have successfully scaled, providing them with opportunities to learn from others with similar models, building their own strategic and management capacities, and helping them balance the social and financial goals and challenges of scaling are all important learning areas.

Support also needs to be provided for experimentation and cross-learning. Scaling early-stage social enterprises is a risky business, and resources need to be allocated that allow for some of these to be piloted so the industry can learn from failures and successes. Documenting these experiences and disseminating lessons learned will help to reduce risks and to identify the fundamental ingredients that need to be in place for more scaling success.

Part III

CAPITAL FOR GROWING SOCIAL ENTERPRISES

6

DONOR GIVING AND SOCIAL ENTERPRISE IN LATIN AMERICA— A FRAGMENTED LANDSCAPE

INTRODUCTION

The current funding environment for social enterprises in Latin America reveals a major obstacle to their development and a cost that must be borne by stakeholders if the sector is to grow and flourish. To appreciate the funding situation of social enterprises in the region, it is important to understand how civil society organizations (CSO) are funded overall, since most of the social enterprises remain CSO operated. CSOs in the region are still very grant dependent and require donations to support them in delivering their services to society and to survive as organizations. Although some CSOs do practice some form of self-financing, as a proportion of their financing it is for the most part too low to sustain the organizations in the long term.

The funding landscape is not encouraging, as a large percentage of donations fail to address the long-term and planning needs of many CSOs that operate in Latin America, or often the structure of giving encourages inefficient use of funds. The investment of time and energy on fund-raising is disproportionate to the amount of funding obtained, resulting in very high transaction costs and a diversion of time away from project outcomes and impact.

Most donations (in monetary terms) to Latin American CSOs still come from international cooperation agencies with origins in Europe and North America, followed by Brazilian companies and foundations, and then by North American foundations. Although the number of Latin American private institutions, individuals, and foundations has been increasing, there is not yet a "culture of giving" in Latin America capable of serving the needs of the region. A possible exception to this rule is Brazil, a country noted for its plethora of donors among foundations and businesses.

Another important trend to point out is that donor priorities are changing. There has been a transition from contributions to charitable activities aimed at health, education, and extreme poverty reduction programs to a current focus on issues such as democracy, corruption, and human rights. Another area with increasing interest is the promotion of economic development via support for micro-, small-, and medium-sized enterprises. This movement away from charity and toward more systemic solutions provides an important opportunity for social enterprise.

Donors putting social enterprise on the radar have emerged. These donors are still very much a minority, but a larger minority than a decade ago. Some of the new and interesting opportunities are not only with international foundations and agencies, but also with national governments and corporations. These pioneers will be featured in chapter 7, but some of these opportunities and trends will be highlighted here.

This chapter is based on 10 years of collecting donor information related to NESsT efforts to develop and support social enterprises in the region; an experience that includes working with a total of 73 current and past donor organizations in Latin America. Additionally, an investigation of donors with an identified potential interest in social enterprise development in Latin America was conducted, increasing the number of donor organizations to 230.[1]

Using this information, a database was constructed that includes the average duration of grants; the levels of funding; areas of donor giving in the Latin American context (e.g., education, health, etc.); the donors and trends in giving by donor type as they relate to social enterprise (e.g., foundation, corporations, government, individuals, etc.); and the terms and conditions that define most donor funding in the region.

Additionally, this chapter relies on information derived from NESsT's own country analyses completed prior to its entry into each country in the region where it has operated. This extensive analysis includes interviews with over 40 institutional donors and summarizes their views on the challenges regarding sustainability and social enterprise, both within specific countries and the region overall. A summary of these interviews reveals consensus on the part of donors for CSOs to diversify their funding base and reduce dependency on one or two key donors. There is also a strong call for CSOs to consider social enterprise as an alternative way to fund their important work and to develop market-driven business plans. Donor comments in various interviews indicate their interest and intention to help empower social enterprises, while admitting that they themselves have done very little in this area, given their own funding constraints.

These findings are very much corroborated in this chapter, which reveals a low level of funding committed to social enterprise development on the part of donors. Additionally, donors often create barriers and even hinder the options that many enterprises have to grow and become self-sustaining organizations. Based on this data, the research offers an overview of the fragile environment in which social enterprises, CSOs, and donors coexist in Latin America. However, the chapter also points to some new and interesting opportunities that, if recognized, supported, and built upon, could change the overall landscape and begin to channel real resources toward the sector and the growth of social enterprises in the region.

Grant Duration

From the start of NESsT's work in Latin America in 1999—when it began operations in Chile—until 2012, it has collaborated with 73 different donors in the region, 74 percent institutional and 26 percent individual. Understanding how these donors operate and the type of giving that they provide is critical to understanding the overall funding landscape and potential funding opportunities for social enterprises in the region.

Graph 6.1 shows the status of donations to NESsT in Latin America in terms of the duration of each grant. *The vast majority of donors only commit for one year.* Although some are willing to renew these annual grants for several additional years, as demonstrated in graph 6.2, the fact that the donation is only provided for one year has implications for the work of CSOs and social enterprises in the region.

First, it requires the institutions to work on short-term projects and diverts them from the longer-term projects that are needed to overcome poverty and exclusion, as well as other systemic problems that social enterprises and CSOs overall are trying to resolve. Although CSOs would prefer to design longer-term initiatives, they tend to move away from, delay, or take longer to develop these efforts since they cannot be certain if there will be funding to carry them out. In the case of social enterprises, this issue is particularly acute since it usually takes most businesses at least five years to develop a business plan, launch, and consolidate. One year funding can be a large deterrent to making these longer-term commitments.

Second, it creates social enterprises or CSOs that are permanently dependent on external financing. The lack of longer-term funding prevents organizations

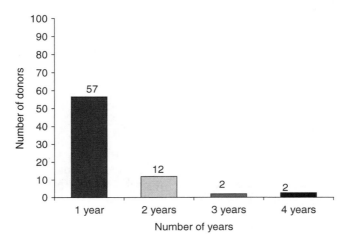

Graph 6.1 Duration of donations.
Source: Compiled from NESsT database, 2012.

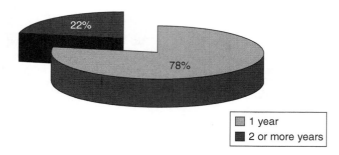

Graph 6.2   Donors by years of support.
Source: Compiled from NESsT database, 2012.

from having the capacity and time needed to diversify their funding base and dedicate time to self-financing and social enterprise activities. This results in organizations that are unable to sustain themselves therefore remain under the wing of the donors for long periods of time.

Third, it leads to unrealistic expectations on the part of donors who want to see immediate results from their short-term contributions and corresponding unrealistic promises on the part of CSOs on what they can deliver in such a short period of time. This need for short-term results creates a baseline from which all grantees are expected to perform, and which in turn leads to unrealistic measurements for the social sector overall.

There is a subset of these "one year only" donors that are willing to repeat their funding for more than one year. Eighteen percent of donors that start out with a one-year commitment repeat their donations, usually in the same amount for a second and third year. This is important to point out since by providing repeat grants, the donors show an interest in supporting social enterprise development. However, the majority of these short-term donors are not willing to consider repeat donations, either because they are constrained by institutional policies, or in the case of individuals, because the donations are perceived by the donors as one-off donations.

Although there are some institutions that support longer-term projects, these are a minority. From its experience in Latin America, NESsT was only able to identify 16 of its donors who committed to donations longer than one year.[2] Of these, 12 have given financial support to NESsT for 2 years, 2 institutions have contributed financially to NESsT for 3 years, and only 2 institutions have committed for 4 years. In sum, as shown in graph 6.2, only 22 percent of donors have provided this type of longer-term funding to NESsT. These cases include mostly international and family foundations such as The Ardeola Trust, The Ashmore Foundation, The Ausherman Family Foundation, Avina Foundation, The Lemelson Foundation, and the Tinker Foundation—all organizations that have worked with NESsT and committed economic resources for longer periods of time. It also includes cooperation agencies such as the Inter-American Development Bank Multilateral Investment Fund (FOMIN) and the US Agency for International Development.[3]

Further, it is important to point out that donors overall are very reluctant to support the same project for another cycle. Those that provide funding for one year will in some cases repeat funding for two additional years if they are happy with the results. And those that provide funding for three to five years will seldom support the same project twice. Although it is quite understandable that donors like to support innovative projects and do not want grantees to become dependent on them for a longer time, this does have implications for the development of social enterprises that usually require much longer periods to reach maturation.

Exit Strategies

In Latin America, there are a small number of institutional donors—particularly, bilateral development assistance agencies—which do provide longer-term funding to a select number of grantees. However, the majority of these donors do not enter the relationship with a view toward preparing their grantees with an exit strategy that will allow them to sustain their activities once the donor is no longer providing funds. As a result, many CSOs in Latin America have become totally dependent on one or two donors, and have become accustomed to a culture of dependency that often prevents them from adopting more entrepreneurial or market-driven practices—even though in many cases CSOs understand the need for developing these entrepreneurial activities.

The withdrawal of many of these agencies from the region in the past ten years—which is still ongoing[4]—has had devastating effects for many organizations that came to rely on them for their survival. NESsT has seen cases of donors who announce to their grantees one year before departing that the grantee will no longer receive their support. To compensate, these donor agencies try to implement short-term activities as stopgap measures, hoping that the grantees that they invested in for 10 or sometimes 20 years, will quickly develop sustainable strategies. Needless to say, these efforts are usually not helpful and do not achieve their intended objectives. Box 6.1 describes the experience of a social enterprise that was created when its parent organization lost its international funding.

The lack of exit strategies is prevalent among all donors, not only bilateral development assistance agencies. Although many ask grantees to describe how they will continue to sustain themselves after termination of the project, few neither really know how to help their grantees do this, nor are they really willing to expend the funds needed to build the capacity of their grantees to do this. Program officers within foundations are very well intentioned but do not always have the final say. They are not always able to convince the higher echelons to invest in fewer grantees, but for longer periods of time and with an exit strategy.

Box 6.1   Templanza: Developing a culture of independence while transitioning to become a social enterprise

In Chile, international cooperation organizations left the country after the transition to democracy in the late nineties. Many CSOs that were very good at developing and implementing projects lacked the skills and attitudes needed to become more market driven. This same dependency was fostered among their beneficiaries, who became accustomed to receiving free services. This entrenched culture of dependency made it very difficult for CSOs to make the transition, which led many entities to close at a time when the need to consolidate democracy was most important.

Templanza, a social enterprise that sells psychological counseling to low-income women who are victims of domestic violence, is a case in point. Originally, Templanza was part of La Morada, a highly reputable organization located in Santiago whose mission is the development of women's rights and their position in Chile. With the transition to democracy in the late nineties, a large amount of La Morada's funding from international cooperation agencies was cut.

To solve its financial problems, La Morada decided to transform the mental health clinic into a self-sustaining social enterprise. Beginning in 2002, La Morada and NESsT collaborated to develop and implement a business plan that would meet the needs of the clinic. As a result, the social enterprise was launched in January 2004. For years, it experienced sustained growth, and in 2008 the clinic spun off from La Morada and established itself as Templanza, a self-sustaining social enterprise.

This transition came with some very high internal costs. When the decision was made to begin charging for its services through a differentiated fee scale, several members of the team were opposed to it. They felt that the organization should continue to offer its services free of charge, and felt that they would drift from their social mission if they charged for their services. The leader of the organization had a different perspective and realized that the organization had to become market driven if it was to survive. With the support of several team members, she worked diligently to develop and grow the enterprise while staying true to its social mission of empowering victims of domestic violence to lead normal healthy lives.

In 2011, the social enterprise exited the NESsT portfolio, having achieved 90 percent self-sufficiency, and serving 300 patients a month with an 85 percent success rate. With its revenue, Templanza not only supports its highly professional team of psychologists, but also dedicates part of its time to raising awareness and influencing public policy on the issue of domestic violence in Chile, a country with a high domestic violence rate.

Templanza's experience illustrates the importance of donors planning an exit strategy before they decide to stop funding an organization. Had Templanza not had the vision to restructure its model and reach out to NESsT for assistance, they would probably not be a highly successful social enterprise today and model for others to follow.

Levels of Funding for Social Enterprise Development

It is important to also consider the levels of funding available in the region for social enterprise development. To investigate the funding amounts, NESsT used its database of past, present, and potential donors—a total of two-hundred-plus donors supporting the social enterprise sector in the region. These donors, which will be described in greater detail later in the chapter, include corporate foundations, family foundations, high-net-worth individuals (HNWIs), banks, and government agencies.

Graph 6.3 highlights that 44 percent of donors have provided funding at USD 25,000 or less, with many giving amounts of USD 10,000. Only 34 percent of donors are in the USD 25,000–100,000 category, demonstrating that the higher the commitment, the lower the number of donors. These higher-range donors are for the most part donors who give for more than one year, although there are a few who have given for only one year. Finally, only 22 percent of donors have given donations above USD 100,000. It is very important to note that the majority of donations exceeding USD 100,000 are commitments for periods longer than one year.

These figures reflect the scarcity of donors willing to provide significant funding to support social enterprise development in the region. No doubt, they view the problem with a more traditional project-based funding lens. However, the fact that 18 percent of donors are willing to repeat their donations, as discussed above, means that over the course of time, total funding levels do increase. The amounts given to NESsT are often to support the planning stage of social enterprise development, often organized as national business plan competitions. And in some cases, this is followed by one or two years of additional support toward incubation. There are very few donors willing to provide a single social enterprise with significant support; rather, they opt to provide many with very

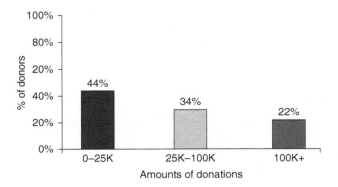

Graph 6.3 Amounts of donations.
Source: Compiled from NESsT database, 2012.

little support. The notion that the social enterprise chosen might not succeed in achieving its goals represents a risk that donors are not willing to take in most cases. Furthermore, donors often prefer to communicate and report to their stakeholders that they are helping many social enterprises.

It has been previously discussed that the development and growth of the social enterprise sector in Latin America requires donors with the capacity and commitment to provide long-term financial support in amounts that will achieve the goals of self-sustainability of these organizations. As will be discussed in chapter 7, there are a handful of donors—both public and private—that are investing these higher levels of grant funding in the region, and are role models for others.

DONOR INTEREST IN SOCIAL ENTERPRISE

The first thing that should be emphasized is the small number of donors in the region who openly affirm interest in social enterprises (i.e., they use this or similar terms), and support social enterprise development directly. The donors that fall into this category are few considering the total number of donors with which NESsT has worked. This analysis considered the donors who support or have supported NESsT, as well as other donors on the continent.

As illustrated in graph 6.4, of the 230 donors investigated by NESsT, only 3 percent affirm to directly provide financial support to social enterprises at this time. Twenty-two percent are donors from the private equity sector. They do not necessarily focus on social enterprise but NESsT has cultivated them over the years and they have provided support to NESsT's portfolio of social enterprises.

The remaining 75 percent represent donors in Latin America who support social enterprises indirectly—that is, they support a social enterprise through another sector focus that falls under one or more of their program activities. Within these various sectors, education, community development, and social development are among those that most closely touch social enterprise. This seems to be consistent with the fact that many social enterprises are solving

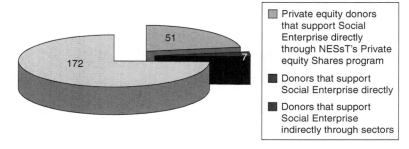

Graph 6.4   Donors that support social enterprise.

problems in these three sectors but are doing so using an enterprise approach. The entry point for the donor is the social problem that they are solving. So, whether a donor is addressing lack of access to education, employment, or health, they see the value addition of doing so through a social enterprise and by taking a more sustainable approach.

The paradox in this situation should not go unnoticed. On the one hand, donors are very interested to support entrepreneurial solutions to the problems that they are trying to address. However, few actually approached this from the social enterprise point of view. This offers an opportunity to work with these "thematic" donors to more formally integrate social enterprise in their giving, in terms of strategy and higher amounts. This would unlock resources for social enterprise development. This change would allow donors to view CSO social enterprise as a way to deliver sustainable long-term social impact linked to education, health, community, and social development, as well as other sectors.

SOCIAL ENTERPRISE SUPPORT BY TYPE OF DONORS

The analysis of NESsT's donor database and experience reveals some important differences in social enterprise development support by type of donor. Understanding these different types of donors and differences in social enterprise development increases opportunities to leverage donor support and to attract donors that are willing to fund different stages of the social enterprise development process.

International Donors

1. *International foundations*: This type of institution is characterized by support to a particular project for longer periods of time (two to three years on an average). They provide high levels of funding, at times exceeding USD 100,000. Additionally, foundations tend to support research and innovation in the field of social enterprise development. In many cases, they also have the objective of creating sustainable organizations, meaning that they support capacity building.

   Their funding is often tied to social enterprise applied research, social enterprise capacity building, and the development and dissemination of tools and best practices. Their support is extremely important for showcasing innovation to other stakeholders in the field and identifying needs for further field building. The models and cases that are developed through their initial giving can catalyze support and interest from others. They should not be viewed as funders that support social enterprises for the entire duration of their development, but as funders that demonstrate, through research and case studies, the benefits of doing so to other donors.

2. *International banks*: These institutions commit for short periods of time, usually no more than one year. The amounts vary according to each bank, and sometimes are as much as USD 100,000, but at other times do not

exceed USD 25,000. The contributions are directly related to projects within their areas of work, and therefore, many of the projects they finance involve job creation and promotion. Social enterprise tends to be a good fit for their giving. They are usually involved with project marketing and promotion, as well as employee volunteering.

Their funding is often tied to social enterprise business competitions, including award ceremonies and other events. This support is important for early-stage enterprise business planning and pipeline building. International banks are often willing to provide repeat funding as long as they continue to see the benefits for their institutions. There is a great opportunity to work with these banks to make the connection between their social giving and their direct business services.

3. *International corporations*: In this category, there is considerable variation, with some corporations contributing substantial amounts (as much as USD 50,000) to the social enterprise sector, but others that give less than USD 10,000. Similar to banks, corporations like to give to communities tied to their business or to the locations where they are working.

Significant social enterprise support by these funders is often tied to developing alternative economic activities for surrounding low-income communities, such as helping to build supply chains for their own business. The opportunity lies in helping corporations develop enterprises early on when first entering countries, and to structure parts of their business around these activities. Often called "inclusive businesses," these social enterprises can become suppliers or providers of the corporation. Some of the support can be offered by the companies themselves and other needs can be outsourced to incubators and other experts. There is a need to assist corporations conduct early assessments of the social enterprise potential of the regions and sectors where they operate. A good example of how corporations can include local communities as part of their business is Masisa, a major forestry group operating in Latin America. From 2007 to 2009, the company supported 68 training courses that were delivered to 1,267 low-income carpenters. This contributed to securing its future customer base, while building the capacity and livelihoods of a neglected group.[5]

4. *International cooperative agencies*: In many cases, international aid agencies hold open calls or requests for proposals in which they commit resources for longer than one year and for amounts exceeding USD 100,000. The challenge is that these calls are extremely competitive without any guarantee that resources will be awarded. In 2012, Japan Poverty Fund, administered by the Inter-American Development Bank, received more than 1,885 applications for one grant award program.[6] Given this level of competition in the region, the probability of not receiving the grant is very high (in the case of the Japan Poverty Fund, fewer than 10 projects were selected). This becomes challenging when trying to create, incubate, and grow social enterprises. Some donor agencies do accept unsolicited proposals, but the funding probability of these is very low given that there is often very little discretionary funding available for activities other than those already planned.

International cooperative agencies do not for the most part fund social enterprise development since they usually prefer direct social provision. They are less interested in capacity and financial support. A great but challenging opportunity exists to work with these donors to include a social enterprise dimension into their calls for applications and to convince them of the power of these enterprises to solve the social problems that they are trying to address. This would also require convincing their governments that are often more interested in seeing short-term improvements as opposed to long-term systemic changes.

5. *Embassies*: Embassies from developed countries in Latin America commit funds for very specific activities, such as bringing experts from their countries to speak at events or providing industry expertise. They often also offer access to tangible assets provided by their national companies. Contributions are generally for a period of one year. The amounts range from USD 10,000 to USD 25,000. Social enterprise development is usually not provided unless it is tied to one of their existing grantees or to a specific training or asset opportunity.

National Donors

1. *National banks*: Unlike international banks, domestic banks only engage in small contributions, and generally focus on more charitable or visible socially focused activities.

   Social enterprise development support is usually tied to a specific enterprise in their community. The key opportunity here is to make sure that the banks provide the ongoing capacity support, from their own staff, that is often needed for these enterprises to maximize impact. National banks that have a strong rural or community presence can help develop social enterprises whose business models can leverage the expansive reach of bank branches. There is a lot of room for innovation here and for banks to increase their impact significantly.

2. *National foundations*: These institutions typically donate for a one- or two-year period, and the amounts vary depending on the size of the foundation. There are very few national foundations and most are interested in funding more visible activities related to education and health.

   Social enterprise is funded as a related activity but not as the main entry point. As mentioned earlier, there is an opportunity for national foundations to bring an enterprise impact strategy to their more thematic approach, so that they can ensure the sustainability of the endeavors they are supporting. There is also a need for them to fund the development of tools and methodologies and the dissemination of best practices based on these experiences so that others will follow.

3. *Corporate foundations*: These are mostly tied to larger companies in industries such as mining, oil, and gas. The donation levels can be quite high, over USD 100,000, but similar to international corporations they give in their own backyard and to the communities they serve.

In terms of social enterprise, they are interested in short trainings or capacity building, although an increasing number are also interested in supporting social enterprise development. Similar to international corporations, there is an opportunity to develop social enterprises that can offer products and services needed by the parent company as well as by the communities they serve. Support for these enterprises can be provided by the companies themselves—if it can be continuous—or outsourced to incubators or other entities that can offer this expertise.

International and National

1. *Family foundations, family offices, and HNWIs*: This is a growing class in Latin America and globally, as more families accumulate higher levels of capital and are interested in philanthropy. The grant amounts can range from USD 1,000 to more than USD 100,000. The use of donations can be quite flexible in terms of the organization's focus and the type of activities. However, this donor group usually prefers to be close to their donations and requires very specific impacts and results.

   Giving for social enterprise development is a potential growth area. However, family foundations, family offices, and HNWIs in the region are leery of giving to third parties and prefer to support their own initiatives. One entry point might be to assist them to convert some of their existing grantees into social enterprises. Another door could be to start with impact investing and then move into philanthropic capital to support early-stage social enterprise.

2. *Private equity*: With a few exceptions, private equity firms do not have foundations or philanthropic funds. Most donations come directly from the partners of the firm. This industry has committed to donation amounts from USD 1,000 to USD 100,000 for a one-year period of time (some firms have committed for up to three years).

   Given its investment and portfolio approach, NESsT has a special affinity with this sector, which is why it has been able to leverage their support. The strategy used is described in greater depth in a section below.

Private Equity Shares

The private equity sector has become a significant source of financial support for NESsT in recent years. It is a sector that has been cultivated and introduced to the concept of social enterprises by NESsT through its work on 2 continents during the last 15 years.

NESsT created the Private Equity Shares program as a way to make philanthropic involvement and giving easier and more effective for the private equity industry. In many respects, NESsT works in a manner similar to private equity firms. It conducts rigorous due diligence to identify and invite scalable social enterprises into its portfolio; it provides philanthropic capital "investment" to this portfolio of social enterprises; and it supports the portfolio with ongoing mentoring and tailored funding until the enterprise is sustainable. NESsT then "exits" the enterprise from the portfolio, creating a high social return for the donors that have provided philanthropic support.

The affinity of the approaches has made private equity investors interested in becoming engaged and identified with the Private Equity Shares program. There are currently more than 50 firms participating in the program. It has become a mainstay of committed and recurring funding for NESsT. In the past two years, Private Equity Shares represented 41 percent of the total NESsT budget in Central Europe and 15 percent of NESsT's overall budget. The funds are usually quite flexible and have supported the NESsT portfolio and operations wherever needed. NESsT reports the allocation of this funding and its impact through "Making the Grade," an annual report that it disseminates to all supporting firms.

Another aspect of the Private Equity Shares program that should be highlighted is the pro bono technical support and advice provided to NESsT from partners and other professionals of the firms. Hundreds of hours have been provided to review and score business plans, and to provide strategic advice and training to the enterprises in the portfolio. More than 149 private equity professionals from the private equity sector are part of the NESsT Business Advisory Network (BAN) in Central Europe and Latin America.

Support from the industry tends to be very flexible, since most private equity professionals understand the strategic use of capital. They also understand the importance of capacity support in building and growing enterprises. Although some might question the 50 percent capacity/50 percent capital division of NESsT support, they tend to come around once they learn of the very close mentoring and training needed by these early-stage social enterprises. The same is true of the early use of grants versus loans or equity in terms of financial support. Given the high social costs of many of the enterprises in the portfolio, supporters quickly understand the reasoning behind grants.

Despite the many positive aspects that have been mentioned about the private equity industry, it is important to note that the sector requires an extended period of time for "cultivation" of each professional. Private equity firms are not the actual funders or donors; rather, professionals working in this sector are the donors. They are also reluctant to commit for more than one year, or provide very large amounts of funding. Interestingly, in the case of some of the firms, the decision is made to select NESsT as their only philanthropic partner, whereas in others, the firms leave it up to the discretion of each partner to decide. This extends the cultivation period.

The private equity industry has been one of the cornerstones in building NESsT in the regions it operates in, and it should be considered for future advisory services and financial support. It has demonstrated a specific interest in social enterprises, which has been demonstrated by the support and confidence in the daily work of NESsT.

Donors and Knowledge Creation

There is another donor category that has focused on the development of social enterprises in Latin America; this type of donor has worked mainly in the development of research and knowledge in the field to affect policy and practice. It has directed significant resources toward the generation of research that has been applied by organizations throughout Latin America. There is not a clearly defined type of donor in this category (they do not come only from a specific sector). Rather, these are institutions that recognize the value of generating, systematizing, and disseminating knowledge. They are interested in case studying and assessing experience in the social enterprise sector and in disseminating best practices and recommendations for others to adopt.

During its years in Latin America, NESsT has worked closely with three organizations that support such research: the International Development Research Center (IDRC), the Tinker Foundation, and FOMIN. Each of these institutions has funded extensive investigations on social enterprises in Latin America.

IDRC

IDRC is a Canadian entity focused on resolving fundamental issues for the progress of society, such as finding new ways to stimulate employment or to protect public health. IDRC is a key component of Canada's aid program, with the objective of providing the answers to social problems and improving the quality of life in developing countries.

IDRC has worked with NESsT on analyzing and understanding how local innovation can be brought to a larger scale and on creating and strengthening avenues of support to boost innovation in rural Latin America. This objective was translated into an investigation, conducted by NESsT and funded by IDRC, that analyzed different practices for scaling successful technology-based social enterprises that bring accessible technology to low-income communities and improve their quality of life.

The investigation consisted of four parts:

- *Research*: Investigation on innovators who develop technology social enterprises and their needs for scaling.
- *Proposal*: Documentation of 20 case studies of scaling technology innovations and the development of an approach to scaling local technology-innovation social enterprises.
- *Implementation*: Testing the scaling approach with local innovations in Peru.
- *Dissemination*: Disseminating information about the approach throughout Peru and the region.

A second objective of the research was to assess the scaling of technology-innovation incubators and to develop a methodology for replicating these incubators.

The outcomes of the research supported by IDRC have extensive implications for the field. First, at an immediate level, the research allowed NESsT to develop a scaling methodology for its own portfolio of technology-innovation social enterprises. The best practices and lessons learned proved critical to this effort. Second, the research was and is being disseminated widely to other incubators and innovators in the region as well as institutions that support them. In 2012, IDRC organized a major international conference in Peru to share the results of the research and the implications for field building. As the research is adopted by universities, think tanks, and government entities, it will no doubt impact future research and policy initiatives in the region and at a global level.

Tinker Foundation

The research activities of the Tinker Foundation are directly related to its mission "to promote the development of an equitable, sustainable and productive society in Latin America and to enhance understanding in the U.S. of Latin America and how U.S. policies may impact the region." NESsT established a relationship with the foundation that recognized the importance of developing an enabling environment to foster social enterprise as a way to strengthen civil society, democracy, and the ties between the private and public sectors in the region.

As a result, NESsT and the Tinker Foundation collaborated for six years to conduct research to understand the legal, regulatory, and policy environment as well as the overall state of the social enterprise sector. The objective was to understand the series of changes that have occurred in the social enterprise field in terms of new opportunities, barriers, restrictions, and/or possible legal "loopholes." The research produced the following:

- *Legal guides*: Documents that have provided a basic understanding of the legal landscape for social enterprises in countries such as Argentina, Brazil, Chile, Colombia, Ecuador, and Peru. Such research is critical because an analysis of the legal situation in these countries reveals the current allowances, as well as legal barriers that may exist in the areas of taxation, state support, and so on.
- *Case study series*: NESsT has also created a series of case studies of particular organizations in Latin America to depict their situations, including the challenges and barriers they have faced, best practices within the organizations, and work methodologies. These experiences serve other organizations that are initiating self-sustaining business activities.
- *Country assessments*: Nationwide assessments of the state of the social enterprise sector, including the overall support provided by both the private and public sectors as well as the experiences of donors, social enterprises, social enterprise support centers, the government, academic, and private sectors have been done.

FOMIN

As will be shown in chapter 7 on pioneers, FOMIN plays a fundamental role in fostering the development of social enterprises (also referred by FOMIN as inclusive businesses) in the region. Part of this role is to support research, systemization, and development of best practices and knowledge management for the field. In the case of NESsT, FOMIN supported research related to the expansion and replication of the NESsT model in Chile to Argentina, Ecuador, and Peru.

Similar to the Tinker Foundation, the focus was on understanding the legal, regulatory, and policy environments for social enterprise specifically in those three countries. It also consisted of a legal guide, case studies, and country assessments. For FOMIN, it was important to disseminate and support regionwide communication efforts as well as events held to launch the final publications and outcomes. In addition, FOMIN also funded several external evaluations of NESsT's work, which highlighted key lessons learned and changes needed to foster the development of social enterprises in the region. Specifically, the objectives of the evaluation were to

- review the relevance of the program;
- conduct a comprehensive assessment of program success; and
- generate recommendations and observations about the program.

Recommendations validated the methodology used to develop social enterprises and the need for longer term financing to help the social enterprises that were launched through the program reach full sustainability. It also recognized the important role of the private sector in leveraging its financial, intellectual, and social capital toward these ends, and the importance of increasing this type of support. The study also called for a loan fund that would provide new financing to early-stage social enterprises. The dissemination of this study reflects FOMIN's demonstrated interest in supporting the ecosystem of social enterprises in the region.

The research funded by these three institutions plays a unique role in the identification and assessment of opportunities and barriers to social enterprise in the region and is fundamental to the sector's emergence. Undoubtedly, more such research is needed to really push the field to the next level so that new initiatives and efforts are based on existing lessons, cases, models, and failures.

Grants giving practitioners the resources to assess and systemize their work can play a pivotal role in not only improving what they do, but also demonstrating the importance of this work to the overall sector, including in academia and policy circles. Rather than be studied by others, this allows practitioners to study themselves and to make needed changes in their practices. This can be very empowering for them, for their peers, and for the field as a whole.

CULTURE OF GIVING

A great deal has been written on the culture of giving, and how it often runs counter to results that are being sought. Rather than dwell on this, this section will mention a few donor practices that have a direct bearing on social enterprise development. Some donors resist funding operational costs of their grantees, believing that this will cause dependency and/or divert funding from their ultimate beneficiaries. Although in some respects this is true, it seems to run counter to the idea that successful businesses and institutions are the product of the people that run them. Once a grantee has already been vetted by a donor, and has demonstrated its ability to effectively manage donor funding, the need to have resources to run operations should be supported. Leaders and managers need to be supported particularly at the early stages of organizational development or when launching a new initiative. This is especially true in the case of social enterprises, which by their very nature are developed and designed to become sustainable and lessen their dependency on grant funding.

The unwillingness of donors to support operational costs makes building and growing organizations and social enterprises extremely challenging; no doubt, this partly explains the reluctance of many people to launch them and the failure of others to grow them. The overreliance on consultants (paid by grants when paying in-house staff is forbidden) builds a healthy consulting industry, but does little to produce sustainable impact.

Another important point is in relation to transaction costs for fundraising and grant management. Fundraising requires an inordinate amount of time—from prospecting and cultivation to concept and proposal presentation, to reviewing and rewriting, to complying with legal and grant reporting requirements. Although donors have every right to feel confident that they are selecting the right grantees and that their funds are being spent as effectively as possible, the resource demand for donor cultivation, grant management, and reporting can often be excessive.

There seems to be no relation between the size of a donation and the amount of reporting and monitoring required by donors. Often donors who give reduced amounts of funding have extensive reporting requirements. This is the case of "open calls" or "requests for proposals," which have numerous criteria for participation, creating a high transaction cost for organizations that compete for them.

One unfortunate consequence of high transaction costs is that grantees are very cautious about highlighting them to their donors, preferring to invest the time and energy to comply with requirements rather than to threaten relationships with funders. The need for open dialogue between donors and recipients is essential to change this paradigm and find a healthy balance of transaction costs and reporting requirements that satisfies both parties, allowing them to get on with the business of impact.

Conclusions and Recommendations

This chapter has presented different perspectives on the work and contributions made by donors in the social enterprise sector. An analysis of types of donors and what they are willing to support, the amounts of their contributions, the time periods for which they customarily pledge, the lack of exit strategies, and the use of overbearing donor management and reporting demonstrate some of the barriers and challenges to the development of social enterprises in the region.

Perhaps what is most disheartening is the fact that of the 230 donors assessed in this chapter, only a handful are directly and specifically supporting the social enterprise sector. Though there is general agreement on the need to support enterprising solutions to poverty and exclusion, there is really a very low appetite for undertaking perceived and real risks associated with these efforts. No doubt, the malpractice of certain CSOs and social enterprises has led to this resistance. However, malpractice has been more the exception than the rule, and should not be generalized.

Yet, in spite of these barriers, it is important to recognize the vital role that donors play in the development of social enterprises. They are part of the solution to grow the sector. Donors channel critical funding for early-stage social enterprise development. Currently, donors are really the only funding available to launch and grow these businesses in the region. The fact that they are willing to do so is important and provides a platform for communication on how to go about expanding this pool.

Highlighting the obstacles is in no way meant to discourage the sector as a whole. The purpose is to recognize that these donors are certainly a mainstay in facilitating the emergence of social enterprises in the region, and to identify the challenges that need to be addressed to ensure that social enterprises can develop and ultimately solve the region's most pressing problems. A new culture of philanthropy, or at the very least, a new culture of understanding the limits of the current culture of philanthropy, is needed.

The most obvious recommendations are for more donors to recognize the vital role of social enterprise in solving critical social issues, and to give more constant and greater amounts of funding toward these efforts. The approach of developing sustainable entities must be embedded from the beginning, and not toward the end of the funding cycle. Donors should enter relationships with a view to exiting, and making sure that there is a sustainable model in place once they withdraw their funding. Fewer grantees—but stronger ones—should really be the dogma.

Different donors have different roles to play in creating an infrastructure to support and foster these social enterprises. Foundations should be called on to help ignite new thinking, demonstrate models, and disseminate tools, methodologies, and best practices. Corporations and banks need to build this into their core businesses. They should not see social enterprises as a side activity of their charitable activities, but rather part and parcel of their overall business impact. They should continue to support early-stage pipeline building through competitions and other efforts. This is a way to help many CSOs strengthen their sustainability by developing social enterprises that expand their social impact and generate funding.

Bilateral and multilateral agencies should include social enterprises in the projects they support and not shy away from supporting intermediaries that can play an important and cost-effective role in developing these enterprises. Family foundations, family offices, and HNWIs should continue to provide the flexible funding that is often needed at incubation and later stages of the social enterprise development process. Those from the United States and Western Europe are role models, and should contribute to fostering local philanthropy among their peers in the region. Finally, foundations and other research entities can play an extremely important role in developing the knowledge to assess what works and to influence policy and awareness building on behalf of the social enterprise sector.

Donors should work together to leverage resources and maximize impact. More dialogue and joint planning is needed so donors learn from one another and their grantees. They should reach consensus on definitions and what is needed to build the appropriate infrastructure and policy to build and improve the sector overall.

7

BETTING ON HIGHER SOCIAL RETURNS—PIONEER DONORS SHOW THE WAY

INTRODUCTION

As interest in market-based solutions to problems of poverty and inequality grows, philanthropists question what role they will play in engaging these solutions. Monitor Group's research publication, "From Blueprint to Scale" concludes, "Impact capital alone will not unlock the potential of impact investing for the global poor. Because of the extreme challenges facing those who are pioneering new models for inclusive business, truly realizing the impact in impact investing will require more, not less, philanthropy, and will need that philanthropic support to be delivered in new ways."[1]

In this chapter, NESsT surveys 14 philanthropy providers committed to long-term social enterprise support, and explores how they use patient capital (longer period of support), mixed financial instruments (use of grants, debt, and/or equity), and creative uses of grants to support capacity building and scaling. In effect, these 14 organizations are "pioneer" philanthropists, social investors who are well positioned in the current environment to play a leading role in bridging the gap between the enterprise and the investment that it needs.

Pioneer philanthropists practice the principles of "engaged philanthropy,"[2] a hybrid approach to giving that integrates the philosophy and practices of long-term investment and venture capital models of the for-profit sector with the grant-making principles of the nonprofit sector (it is sometimes called venture philanthropy). Engaged philanthropists in this sector combine financial grants and social investments[3] in socially minded nonprofit and for-profit organizations with additional capacity building, mentoring, or management assistance to help nonprofits and social enterprises succeed in meeting their goals. Social enterprise development pioneers practice engaged philanthropy by focusing on long-term support, and are often willing to give grants at a very early stage.[4] They are willing to take an entrepreneurial approach despite the risks involved. They recognize the value of capacity building, the use of mixed financial instruments, and the commitment to patient investing. These enlightened donors can be found in government agencies, multilateral institutions, corporate foundations, family foundations, and private equity firms; they can also be high-net-worth individuals (HNWIs).

While some organizations fitting this pioneer profile have already been profiled publicly, the case studies in this chapter are programs that have had a relationship with NESsT and have worked in Latin America and/or Central Europe,[5] or have demonstrated a replicable capability that could provide guidance for emerging or maturing regional donors/investors. NESsT views these actors not only as pioneers in their own sector, but also in the broader field of social enterprise development.

The case studies include an understanding of the pioneers' primary objectives and mission. Additionally, broad strategy in the social enterprise field was considered, as well as areas of operation and sectors of impact, use of financial instruments, capacity-building initiatives, important partnerships or networks, and evidence of field building. NESsT based these case studies on a combination of desk research, NESsT documentation, and primary interviews. The organizations listed in table 7.1 have been included in this chapter.

The pioneer quality is defined by four main elements, described in figure 7.1: early-stage support, patient capital, mixed financial instruments, and capacity support.

Table 7.1   Pioneer donors assessed

Pioneer	NESsT donor	Description
Actis	Yes	A private equity firm that supports philanthropic initiatives that deliver sustainable social impact across emerging markets by leveraging its network, global footprint, and financial and human capital.
Avina Foundation	Yes	Avina Foundation contributes to sustainable development in Latin America by forging alliances between civil society and business in pursuit of the common good in communities, countries, and Latin America as a whole.
The Ausherman Family Foundation	Yes	The Ausherman Family Foundation supports community and nonprofit organizations (NPOs) in Frederick County, Maryland, but has expanded its giving to similar organizations outside the United States.
Banco Bilbao Vizcaya Argentaria (BBVA)	No	BBVA develops social entrepreneurship in Spain through a support program for the most promising social enterprises, so they can consolidate, grow, and scale. BBVA has expanded its reach with efforts in Peru and Mexico.
Charities Aid Foundation (CAF) Venturesome	Yes	A social investment fund set up in the United Kingdom over a decade ago that holds 70 charities and social enterprises in its portfolio. Its birth from CAF was meant to make giving more efficient and far reaching.

Pioneer	NESsT donor	Description
KL Felicitas Foundation	No	A family foundation that enables social enterprises worldwide, focusing on rural communities and families. It is founded on the premise that an impact-investment strategy can cause real social change to occur.
Citi Foundation	Yes	Citigroup's foundation fosters job creation and development of programs connected with the work of social enterprises.
Corporación de Fomento de la Producción (CORFO)	No	A government organization that was created in 1939 to develop and improve industrial capacity in Chile. It has been a pioneer among Latin American government agencies in terms of promoting social enterprise.
Inter-American Development Bank/ Multilateral Investment Fund (IDB/FOMIN)	Yes	Part of the Inter-American Development Bank (IDB), FOMIN aims to create economic opportunities and reduce poverty in Latin America through innovative models that benefit lower-income communities and entrepreneurs.
Halloran Philanthropies	No	Halloran Philanthropies invests in entrepreneurs who implement catalytic initiatives that address inequality, structural poverty, and foster the well being of communities.
The Lemelson Foundation	Yes	The Lemelson Foundation uses the power of invention to improve lives, by inspiring and enabling the next generation of inventors and invention-based enterprises to promote economic growth in the United States and social and economic progress for the poor in developing countries. Established by prolific US inventor Jerome Lemelson and his wife Dorothy in 1992, to date the foundation has donated or committed more than USD 175 million in grants and Program Related Investments (PRIs)[a] in support of its mission.
Omidyar Network	No	Omidyar Network is a philanthropic investment firm dedicated to investing and scaling social enterprises.
Romanian-American Foundation (RAF)	Yes	RAF is a philanthropic foundation focused on making social investments in entrepreneurship, strengthening education, developing community-centric solutions to marginalization, and technological innovation.
Shell Foundation	No	Shell Foundation is a UK charity that aims to develop, scale, and promote enterprise-based solutions for development issues.

Notes: [a]PRIs are mission investments made by foundations to generate specific program outcomes. Like grants, PRIs make inexpensive capital available to nonprofit or for-profit enterprises that are addressing social and environmental challenges. Unlike grants, PRIs are expected to be repaid, often with a modest, risk-adjusted, rate of return. Once repaid, the money used for a PRI is recycled into new charitable investments. https://www.missioninvestors.org/mission-investing/program-related-investments-pris.

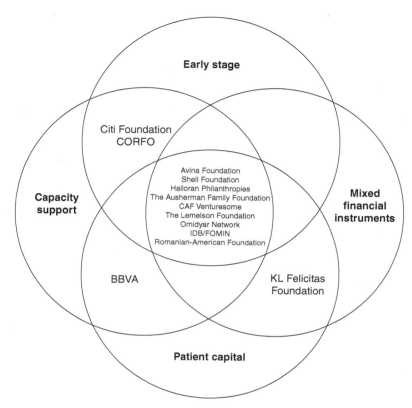

Figure 7.1   The pioneer space.

TRENDS AND ANALYSIS

Patient Capital Is Necessary

The use of patient capital is a defining characteristic of the pioneers profiled in this chapter. The Ausherman Family Foundation, which has supported social enterprise development in the United States, in Central Europe, and in Latin America (the latter two in partnership with NESsT), has a focused approach and a long-term outlook. As Lisa Ausherman, cofounder of the foundation, said, "Our trustees want to focus our giving more on major projects and funding fewer organizations for longer periods of time, for greater impact."

The BBVA Momentum Project focuses on supporting social enterprises that are at two to three years of development with capacity support and financing. Enterprises in the yearlong program are then eligible for soft loans with an eight-year repayment period. The bank set up a separate EUR 3 million fund to provide this financing, realizing that these enterprises would not be eligible for commercial support given their riskier profile.

The Shell Foundation also recognizes that, given the high risk in the field, patience is key and failures will occur. In fact, Chris West, director of the Shell Foundation, credits some failures for helping shape the evolution of the foundation's strategy, which is now focused on finding catalytic and disruptive opportunities, smart subsidies, and market-linkage support. West says that their original assumption was that reaching people through proof of market would lead to a growing pool of interested impact investors. Yet, over time, this has not proven to be the case. The foundation has stayed with their portfolio partners longer than anticipated—ten years. There is still a need for enterprise philanthropy (which Shell calls "angel philanthropy") to create a pipeline for impact investors. Their focus on supporting a select number of programs and concentrating their efforts on making these programs successful has been instrumental in filling some of this gap.

Omidyar Network, which supports, invests in, and helps to scale social enterprises, also takes a very long-term outlook with its portfolio. It sees exits happening in a period of 10–12 years and emphasizes that the scaling cannot detract from social impact or quality of service to customers at the base of the pyramid.

The Lemelson Foundation, which focuses on invention, innovation, and entrepreneurship, has found that technological invention has the potential for profound impact, but inventors need support to turn their ideas into products and businesses that reach the people who need them most. The foundation believes that the path to scaling inventions that address the needs of the poor—and building the invention and entrepreneurship ecosystem in developing countries where technical capacity support is often lacking—can take 10, 20, or even 30 years of development and sustained efforts.

Tailoring Financial Instruments Provides Flexibility for Sustainability

As will be highlighted in chapter 8, finding an appropriate fit between an enterprise and the range of financial tools available is, arguably, one of the most important aptitudes of incubators and the philanthropic investors who fund the sector. Creative use of grants and tailoring instruments to fit specific contexts and needs are hallmarks of the pioneering donor or social investor.

Early-stage grant making is not a new concept, but in a nascent and growing field it is important to remember its merits. Grants are an integral part of KL Felicitas's impact-investing strategy, for example. Grants are typically made alongside investment support to early-stage enterprises that require some subsidy or capacity-building assistance in preparation for scaling social impact.

For years, Omidyar Network has experimented with making grants to both for-profit organizations and NPOs. Their investments take a long-term view, ranging from grants, venture capital, debt, and program-related investments. However, there is a strict division between for-profit investments and grant making: the foundation does not provide grants to the same entities that receive investments from Omidyar Network's for-profit arm.

Avina Foundation, after years of commitment to building awareness and refining its robust program of incubation and investment support, has decided to focus on investing in early-stage ventures as well, realizing that a secure start-up phase can ensure long-term financial stability. Avina observed that further developing financial instruments in the region is key, so it partnered with Equitas (Argentina) to provide seed investment capital (USD 50,000–300,000) to early-stage social enterprises, developed microcredit fund for rural co-ops, and provided loans in Brazil for NPOs that had revenue streams (e.g., hospitals). Avina has moved toward sophisticated investment vehicles, including "microprivate equity" funneled to companies that have proven models and require growth capital. In some cases, Avina invests directly. In fact, Avina recently created a for-profit entity, which has been used to make for-profit investments in some of the impact-investment funds Avina supports. One of the objectives of the for-profit entity is to demonstrate to the most conservative investors that there are true business opportunities, with social impact, at the base of the pyramid.

CORFO, the preeminent government entity in the Chilean entrepreneurship sector, has taken an enlightened approach to grant support. Programa Capital Semilla, for example, provides seed capital to small- and medium-sized businesses, which could be made available to social businesses, is a manifestation of their vision for improving the productivity of Chile and leading the way for competition in the entrepreneurial market.

FOMIN, or Multilateral Investment Fund, prioritizes access to finance in their diverse programming. Early-stage equity, "angel investment," seed capital, and grants are financing instruments they believe foster an ecosystem that is more conducive for scalable enterprises to develop and flourish.

Halloran Philanthropies takes a case-by-case approach to financial instruments. Typically, the type of capital deployed is decided in partnership with the investee after the opportunity has been analyzed, and often includes a grant component. Halloran's investment size ranges from USD 50,000–500,000. Halloran sees value in using grants for scaling social enterprises. Even when core operations no longer need to be subsidized, social enterprises still need philanthropic capital in order to continue innovating and scaling their impact.

The Lemelson Foundation views mixed financial instruments as vital for early-stage support, recognizing that donors and impact investors should be more creative in deploying capital. The foundation uses various types of financial instruments to allow greater flexibility in working capital. It sees an evolution taking place in the sector, and it knows that a point of inflection, where a large number of donors and social investors use tailored financial instruments, has not yet been reached. The foundation hopes that its tolerance for risk and willingness to explore new types of financial instruments will help to inform the path forward for the sector.

Shell Foundation views the impact-investor market as still risk averse, and the foundation provides loan guarantees to offset risk and make social enterprises more attractive for investment. Currently, the predominant instrument—85 to

95 percent—is still grant making, though the organization is expanding beyond grants and including loans and guarantees.

Innovation in financial tools is exactly the theme that the CAF Venturesome Fund adheres to in practice. Venturesome recently announced the start of the CAF Social Fund, which it manages. Donors invest money into a revolving loan fund, and Venturesome supports NPOs ("charities") and social enterprises with working capital, underwriting facilities, and bridge loans. Working capital, Venturesome says, helps a charity to grow, and finally to transition to generating income. Bridge loans are critical in helping organizations avoid going into arrears while waiting for payments. Standby facilities allow charities that potentially need support but do not want to take out a loan until necessary to have access to cash if willing to pay an up-front fee and interest only if and when funds are drawn.

CAF's Innovation Fund tests new and financially innovative ways of supporting charities and social enterprises. The fund provides riskier loans for social enterprises that are consolidating or scaling, such as loans whose repayments are tied to performance. Over time, Venturesome's write-off of its mixed financial instruments has been fairly low, though not all experiments have gone exactly as planned. The reality of being a pioneer is that mixed results are part of the learning process.

Capacity Support Is Part of the Critical Path

Bringing early-stage enterprises to financial self-sustainability or scalability is dependent on many factors (see chap. 5), but success is almost always related to capacity support. Performance management, systems design, organizational development, strategy, and business planning are all key areas entrepreneurs must endeavor to excel in. The question is, how? And who will provide the know-how and funding, or at the very least, the connections to capacity-support providers?

In the corporate foundation sector, BBVA has pioneered the Momentum Project, which targets social entrepreneurs who have projects underway and need to consolidate and guarantee the feasibility of these businesses. Momentum assists with training, advice, and plan development. The program fosters collaboration and exchange of knowledge among entrepreneurs, students, and managers. As the program works with universities, it also channels fresh ideas/businesses into the line of sight of impact investors. BBVA has expanded Momentum's reach globally, including a pilot program in Peru through training programs with Universidad del Pacifico, and in Mexico, through the Technological Institute of Monterrey.

Citi Foundation, another corporate foundation pioneer, supports very early-stage social enterprises (often start-ups) and sees a great need for training, mentoring, and business planning. The foundation focuses on employment models and supports capacity building as well as provides access to capital. Results focus on increases in the number of micro or small enterprises and social enterprises that provide new income generation and employment opportunities for low-income individuals.

Actis, the private equity fund, is a pioneer in private equity for its support of social enterprise in emerging markets. Actis understands the need for management support to grow early-stage businesses and takes them to scale, and it has developed a program to tap the expertise and know-how of its investment professionals and portfolio companies to provide pro bono capacity support to social enterprises. They offer feasibility study and business plan review, training for early-stage social enterprises, and individual coaching.

Omidyar Network, through its focus on "high-quality" entrepreneurship, has demonstrated a model of capacity support. Omidyar provides its portfolio members in-depth expertise in its investment areas, bringing knowledge and direct experience to bear on investees' operations. Additionally, it connects enterprises with investees' insight and guidance in areas such as strategy, management, operations, human resources, legal matters, and marketing. In fact, management development is a key feature of the Omidyar approach to capacity support. Omidyar believes deeply in the strategic importance of human capital. It has internal recruiters that recruit on behalf of portfolio entities, help to manage and motivate employees (particularly in high-risk businesses), and develop compensation strategies, all because Omidyar sees this support as an integral responsibility to investing at an early stage. Omidyar uses a highly engaged approach to ensure that the early-stage investment must provide and add value.

KL Felicitas has observed that many promising social enterprises have viable business models and proof of concept, but often are unable to access critical technical assistance, mentoring, and funding to enable the enterprise to go to scale. The foundation uses targeted interventions, either internally or through capacity-support providers, such as peer-to-peer learning, mentoring, and networking to access critical investment capital, and business planning.

FOMIN recognizes the need for capacity support, as illustrated through its Social Entrepreneurship Program (SEP), which provides financing to later-stage social enterprises (see chap. 8 for more details). Social enterprises receiving SEP financing can access nonreimbursable (i.e., grant) funds for strengthening their technical, operational, or administrative capacity. In most cases, the maximum amount of funds for technical assistance is USD 250,000 (social enterprises receive USD 700,000 on average in financing).

The Lemelson Foundation sees capacity support as a critical part of getting organizations to reach self-sustainability. With capacity support, organizations and social enterprises can exist permanently as "agents of change" in the ecosystem in which they operate, becoming role models for both public and private sectors. Therefore, capacity support is linked to developing local competencies and the ecosystem for promoting entrepreneurial endeavors that serve the poor.

The Shell Foundation provides business advice, market access, and governance support to complement its financial investments. Social enterprises should be guided by market principles, and the foundation's staff drives business models, business thinking, and business discipline in the portfolio.

Robust Networks for Partnership and Investment Are Necessary for "Pipeline" Flow

A common observation in the field is that "deal flow" (the number of investment-ready enterprises) and partnerships are not streamlined, not visible enough, or present gaps where tailored financing or patient capital are necessary to weather the risk of early-stage impact investing. Field interviews revealed ways in which to grow the pipeline, including the development and expansion of incubators and accelerators.

Omidyar ascribes some of the challenges with deal flow to a disconnect between capital sources and needs in Latin America. Much of the impact capital that has been raised has been later-stage private equity and debt finance where many of the high-growth ventures are in need of earlier-stage venture capital. In addition, there is a human-capital challenge—many of the investment funds dedicated to impact ventures in the region are likewise not accustomed to working with earlier-stage ventures in a high-growth mode where operational expertise and skill sets are critical in addition to experience in investing. Omidyar overcomes these challenges by providing an investment product geared toward fast-growing, early-stage businesses and pairs it with investment staff with the operational and investment expertise to effectively support these businesses. Omidyar also builds critical relationships with local coinvestors to couple their domain expertise with deep experience in the local market.

Halloran Philanthropies, a family foundation, believes its network is its biggest asset, according to cofounder Adriana Fernandes-Halloran. Though the foundation has not established formal alliances with other institutions, it takes a very collaborative approach to its work. On the investment side, it has developed a close relationship with a small core group of fund managers, coinvestors, and entrepreneurs who have been crucial for Halloran as it refines and identifies its role in the impact-investment field.

For Avina, relationships are key. With the support of IDB, Avina has started the Latin America Donor Index initiative, an online database organizing information concerning donations to Latin America and the Caribbean, which continues to grow as a reference for philanthropy in the region. The goal of this index is to promote and advance the field of philanthropy in Latin America. It follows that such an endeavor helps NPOs find partners and assist philanthropic organizations to better coordinate with their peers, who are working on similar issues or in the same geographical area. This index, focusing exclusively on Latin America, is the first of its kind.

Avina's coordination efforts in the investment sector include linking mostly foundations and HNWIs with NPOs. Avina observes that traditional investors, such as banks, are emerging in the sector, but the Latin American investor sector is ripe for leadership by family offices. Avina plans to improve partnerships with HNWIs and encourage them to enter in the early stage. Avina believes in catalyzing change for a robust pipeline development across the continent, and it focuses on articulating partnerships with Latin American partners and institutions around the world to scale and enhance their actions.

HNWIs are on the radar of many field participants, whether they are incubators and accelerators, or other philanthropic pioneers. And rightfully so, as enlightened HNWIs can build networks to increase deal flow. Charly Kleissner, a pioneer HNWI impact investor, cofounded Toniic, an international impact-investor network. Members in the network benefit from access to prevetted deal flow, due diligence, educational opportunities, Global Impact Investing Rating System (GIIRS) ratings for investments, impact measurement, connections to impact-investment service providers, and access to the broader impact-investment community.

Field Development Is a Nascent but Necessary Area for Pioneers

There can be a nexus at which policy, entrepreneurs, incubators, and investors meet and produce enterprises with high social impact and great potential to scale. Consequently, pioneers, similar to the donors in chapter 6 that emphasized knowledge creation, know that part of their responsibility is to foster advancement in the field. Research, results dissemination, policy-level alliances, and general advocacy and awareness raising of social enterprise development are among the various ways in which these individuals and entities are trying to fulfill their responsibility. In the words of the Shell Foundation, enterprise scale is not enough, and systemic change and sustainable ecosystems are necessary to drive impact.

Partnerships come not only in the form of investment and capacity support, but also in the form of knowledge building. Avina partnered with Harvard Business School (HBS) to create the Social Enterprise Knowledge Network (SEKN).[6] This initiative helped Avina research inclusive businesses, with the help of local partners, and was able to build knowledge and awareness. Additionally, Avina notes that pioneers need to be more engaged at the policy level and try to positively influence public policy. In the context of investment, Avina has been active in providing advice to the government of Colombia. This has led to collaboration on designing policies to promote inclusive businesses and social enterprises. In Ecuador, Avina has helped to create programs for co-ops and associations, as well as support for microfinance institutions. Avina sees an increasing opportunity to further the social enterprise sector by including provisions for social enterprises in existing legal frameworks, rather than creating new government programs. For Avina, field development is not static: its early efforts on social enterprise development were focused on raising awareness of the concept to encourage new players to enter the sector. As this happened, Avina shifted its field-building strategy to strengthening linkages between incubators and accelerators, which it saw as critical to providing the needed capacity support to social enterprises.

Halloran Philanthropies has a history of making high-impact grants in very early-stage enterprises and initiatives such as Benefit Corporations (B Corps)[7] and Social Capital Markets (SOCAP),[8] to help establish key infrastructure for the overall development of social enterprise. Halloran has supported other important initiatives in Latin America, such as events on impact investing and the expansion of incubators and accelerators, which it sees as playing critical roles in efficiently supporting social enterprises to validate and strengthen their business models to scale. Halloran has convened social enterprise accelerators and incubators at both

SOCAP11 and SOCAP12 to share best practices and common challenges, and to strategize on how to overcome them together. Halloran believes it can leverage its resources optimally through pioneering change-making initiatives that a typical investor would feel too risky and averse to support, in particular since many of the initiatives supported by the foundation help to grow the field.

CAF is a pioneer in field development. CAF's objective is to raise awareness—in the United Kingdom as well as in Brazil, India, and Russia where it has offices or local partners—of the role philanthropic capital can play in catalyzing impact investing, particularly with high-net-worth philanthropists. CAF also has a strong voice when it comes to working with government at various levels, to help develop a better infrastructure of giving. CAF works with government to not only enable easier gift-aid[9] reclaim, but also assists in the government's understanding of the area of social investment. CAF has been approached by the UK Charity Commission to develop guidelines and communicate with charities and philanthropists about the principles of social investment.

The Omidyar Network has invested USD 611 million in the sector since 2004, and during this period it has supported a number of initiatives to develop the field. In partnership with the Stanford Social Innovation Review, it produced the thought-provoking "Priming the Pump" series of articles on scaling social impact via market-led solutions and social enterprise, and sponsors numerous networking events and support organizations, such as the Global Impact Investing Network, Avina, and Dasra (in India). Additionally, it has invested the Microfinance Information Exchange, Inc., Making All Voices Count, and the Alliance for Affordable Internet. Omidyar partnered with The Rockefeller Foundation and Avina Foundation to solicit the best innovations in infrastructure to build the impact-investing industries in Latin America and South Asia.

The Lemelson Foundation recognizes that the programs it supports will help provide evidence to inform policy in the future. The foundation hopes that by disseminating case studies and highlighting lessons learned it can effectively provide evidence that can help inform decisions with respect to new programs and resources aimed at promoting invention-based, self-sustaining, enterprises that serve the poor. Foundation grantees (including NESsT) are increasing their efforts to strengthen the local environment for social enterprise development, including building the capacity of local partners and local service providers. The ecosystem now includes not only regional governments, but universities as well, in a move to improve the capacity for invention, innovation, and entrepreneurship.

BBVA, through its Momentum Project, seeks to create a support ecosystem for the sector. Its entrance strategy in Latin America builds knowledge through case studies and knowledge sharing, particularly with local business schools. Business schools are implementers of the Momentum Project, thereby increasing their interest and capacity for integrating social enterprise into their academic curriculum.

RAF helps to build an ecosystem of successful entrepreneurs, investors, government officials, and other researchers (including the Romanian diaspora) already engaged in existing projects in Romania. RAF has also worked closely with the European Union (EU) to review programs and recommend policies based on its findings.

Citi Foundation is also committed to furthering the field of social enterprise. The foundation actively supports ANDE, the Aspen Network Development Entrepreneurs,[10] as a way to foster knowledge sharing to create jobs for low-income individuals. In Central Europe, Citi Foundation has also supported the development of many NESsT enterprise development tools so they could be disseminated to start-up social enterprises.

Finally, the Chilean government agency CORFO is now playing a significant role in developing the field of social enterprise in Chile. Its Innovation and Social Entrepreneurship Competition, launched for the first time in 2012, demonstrates the government's interest in this sector and its potential ability to mainstream the concept nationally. One of the challenges CORFO has faced with the program is the lack of awareness about the term "social enterprise" or "social business" (the phrase CORFO uses), and the perception that social entrepreneurship is the same thing as microenterprise. For the government to make a successful impact in the social enterprise sector, there must be consensus among different areas of civil society on the concept and it's potential. CORFO has the potential, with the scope and breadth of its programs, to significantly raise awareness about social enterprise, potentially providing a model for other governments in the region to replicate (e.g., in Brazil, SEBRAE, the agency for the promotion of micro and small enterprises, is contemplating launching a national social enterprise program).

CONCLUSIONS AND RECOMMENDATIONS

These pioneers—representing government/multilateral agencies, corporate foundations, family foundations, and HNWIs—recognize the need for patient capital, capacity support, tailored financial instruments, and development of the field and networks to facilitate pipeline flow. The social enterprise industry is generating increased interest from impact investors, though expectations for return may not yet match the reality of the enabling environments and support systems in Latin America and Central Europe. There is demonstrable need for pioneers such as these to pave the way for more entrants into the space. Many recognize the responsibility and challenges associated with such a position and continue to refine and rework their approaches to best serve the communities they work in, as well as provide models and lessons learned for future philanthropists.

Entrants in the social enterprise development sector should consider the provision of patient capital as vital to the lifeline of social enterprises. To nurture and sustain the long-term viability of any business, particularly in this delicate market, a pioneer philanthropist or social investor must realize that only with long-term vision comes long-term, sustainable social impact.

Additionally, entrants must consider the strategic importance of tailoring financial instruments to fit the needs of social enterprises. Organizations in the field need to creatively mix and effectively use grants, loans, equity, and their derivations (see chap. 8). Recognition of the challenges enterprises face with start-up costs, operational costs, and growth capital is necessary to provide creative methods of funding.

Equally, if not more, important to the provision of capital is the delivery of capacity support. Any business requires constant evolution in terms of business practices, management, technical know-how, and network building. At the early stage, it is critical. Pioneers demonstrate how to provide capacity support, whether directly or through intermediaries. Capacity building is a way to protect the philanthropic or impact investment, helping to create resilient social enterprises.

Further, entrants to the space must consider pipeline building through networks and investment partnerships. Pioneers, while willing to take risks, prefer to partner with other investors, incubators, or intermediaries to help build the "deal flow." Creating investor communities, disseminating information about social enterprise developments, and leveraging expertise from different sectors within the field will increase the flow of investable opportunities.

The development of the ecosystem is a process that pioneers emphasize. Some pioneers have engaged in applied research, or petitioned at the policy level to show lawmakers and other investors the importance of building a marketplace for socially driven businesses. It is not enough to only provide access to funding, because the success of this market depends on alleviating the many structural obstacles that social enterprises face but cannot overcome on their own.

There are pioneer philanthropists in all sectors, and they each have an important role to play in fostering a healthy pipeline of social enterprises. In Latin America, perhaps the sector that needs to be most encouraged is that of HNWIs and families, whose accumulated wealth has grown exponentially in the past ten years and who have a flexibility that allows them to pursue opportunities and varying levels of associated risk. Encouraging them to enter the sector by demonstrating pioneers as models and understanding their lessons and impact, will unlock resources to build the social enterprise sector in the region.

CASE STUDY 7.1   CORFO

Objective

CORFO is a government entity in Chile that was created in 1939 with the objective of developing and improving industrial capacity in Chile. Over the years, its principal objective has changed, and today it promotes entrepreneurship and innovation to improve productivity in Chile and achieve global leadership positions in competitiveness.[11]

Strategy

CORFO manages 50 different programs, including competitions and programs to support small and medium enterprises (SMEs) at different stages of development. For example, it has seed capital programs to provide early-stage funding for SMEs, as well as technology development and energy efficiency programs.

CORFO is a pioneer in the field of public sector donors because it is one of the few government agencies in Latin America to pilot initiatives that create a supportive environment for social enterprises, and because it has the capacity to catalyze SMEs (and social enterprises) at every stage necessary for their development. CORFO runs two programs that have had a positive impact—directly and indirectly—on the social enterprise sector: the Innovation and Social Entrepreneurship Competition and Start-Up Chile.

Innovation and Social Entrepreneurship Competition
CORFO has implemented this program to promote collaboration and support of social entrepreneurship. Social entrepreneurship is defined by CORFO as "the process or opportunity to create value for society, making a difference or impact in the community, either by creating products and services, or the creation of new organizations." CORFO's economic contribution can be as much as CLP 50 million annually (approximately USD 100,000), and can fund up to 80 percent of the total project. Projects must be implemented within a 24- to 36-month period.

CORFO is a pioneer government agency in Latin America in terms of creating the conditions that will support social entrepreneurship. Many Latin American countries have agencies that support initiatives for SMEs, and social enterprises can participate. However, given the particularities and high risk of social enterprises, they are disadvantaged in many competitions that are not exclusively seeking social impact. CORFO's program has a timeframe of up to three years, which gives the winning organizations the option to develop long-term projects. As chapter 6 described, most social enterprise donors in Latin America limit their funding to one year, often requiring recipients to reapply every 12 months, which may hinder or truncate a project due to lack of funding.

Start-Up Chile Global Entrepreneurship Competition
CORFO's Start-Up Chile aims to make Chile the Latin American center of innovation and entrepreneurship. The strategy for achieving this goal is to attract the best entrepreneurs to Chile to carry out their projects. The program provides participants seed capital and work visas to develop their projects in Chile. Though not specifically directed at social enterprises, Start-Up Chile has incubated a number of businesses pursuing a social impact.

Financial Instruments

CORFO primarily uses grants and loans to provide financial support, and these are divided among various programs. Importantly, each CORFO program has a clear objective, and there is a grant related to each program and its objective. There are other cases in which CORFO uses equity, but most of its actions and contributions to business organizations are microcredit support, grants, and soft loans.

Initial Findings and Challenges

As a recent entrant in the social enterprise field, CORFO is researching the sector and learning by doing. It intends to expand the government's presence in this sector, as it feels that social enterprises can help the national economy. In this sense, the Innovation and Social Entrepreneurship Competition is the first step of the Chilean government toward assisting intermediaries, such as incubators, capacity builders, and investors, develop the conditions for a vibrant social enterprise sector. CORFO does not rule out the possibility for new initiatives in the future that could complement this program, possibly in alliances with private companies and/or impact-investment funds.

The goal of the Innovation and Social Entrepreneurship Competition is to bring business entrepreneurship closer to social initiatives, with the aim of putting Chile at the forefront of this sector in Latin America. To achieve this goal, CORFO, in coordination with Chile's Ministry of the Economy, has completed a number of studies to obtain an overview of social enterprise in the country and to understand the actors in the sector, the opportunities for government action, and the potential impact generated by the government.

Of the challenges CORFO has faced with this new program and its approach to the social enterprise sector, two in particular stand out:

1. *Creating measurement instruments:* CORFO has recognized the need to create new assessment tools to measure different aspects of social enterprises, including social impact, growth capacity, and the generation of new market niches. This is one of the main challenges CORFO has faced, because as a state agency it must have empirical data to continue the program.
2. *Creating coherent terminology:* Another challenge CORFO has faced during the implementation of this program is a lack of awareness about the term "social enterprise" or "social business" (the phrase CORFO uses). This lack of knowledge is directly related to questions about what a social enterprise does, and how it operates as an entity and within the market system. From CORFO's first-year experience with the program, there was a tremendous lack of awareness about the term in all sectors, from universities to civil society entities.

CASE STUDY 7.2   HALLORAN PHILANTHROPIES

Objective

Halloran Philanthropies' mission "is to inspire, catalyze and accelerate sustainable social interventions that seek to raise the level of human well-being, while respecting the cultural diversity and ecological integrity of present and future generations."[12]

Halloran Philanthropies was established with the belief that business can be one of the most powerful drivers for positive social change by stimulating the economy, creating meaningful jobs, and providing products and services that positively impact the lives of the people living at the bottom of the pyramid. It invests in outstanding entrepreneurs implementing catalytic initiatives that address inequality and structural poverty, and foster the well-being of communities.

Strategy

Halloran Philanthropies recognizes social entrepreneurs as powerful catalysts who transform the way the world does business. Therefore, it supports investment in catalyzing change-making solutions to create and accelerate positive social change. Halloran's strategy relies primarily on utilizing its resources and network to support the advancement of social innovations and sustainable enterprises.

Halloran Philanthropies has a history of making leading-edge, high-impact grants in very early-stage enterprises and initiatives such as B Corp and SOCAP, to help establish key infrastructure for the overall development of social enterprise. Halloran believes it develops pioneering, change-making initiatives that a typical investor would feel too risky and averse to support.

On the investment side, Halloran has developed a close relationship with a small core group of fund managers, coinvestors, and entrepreneurs who have been crucial for Halloran as it refines and identifies its role in the impact-investing field.

Areas of Operation

Halloran works primarily in Mexico, Colombia, Brazil, India, and the United States. It supports the development and advancement of business solutions for poverty alleviation primarily through income generation, education, health, and housing.

Financial Instruments

Typically, the type of capital deployed is decided in partnership with the investee after the opportunity has been analyzed. Halloran's investment size ranges from USD 50,000–500,000. Halloran utilizes grants for operational support of high-impact accelerators, development of innovative products and services that enhance the capacity of social enterprises and build the field, and seed funding (USD 15,000–50,000) for social enterprises for idea development, proof of concept, and the fine-tuning of business models. Halloran offers bridge loans and equity investment when applicable. The foundation also sees an opportunity to support impact-investing funds, in the form of grant and direct investments.

Capacity Support through Field building

Start-up enterprises require a high level of engagement beyond funding and Halloran offers both financial and intellectual capital by providing access to its network, mentoring, and a global knowledge base. Moreover, it believes that early-stage incubators and accelerators can play a critical role in efficiently supporting these enterprises by validating and strengthening their business models to scale.

As Halloran's intent to concentrate resources in high-impact incubators, accelerators, and supporting organizations deepened, it also realized that it knew very little about the models and best practices of business incubators and accelerators worldwide. It has sponsored several gathering of accelerators and incubators in order to increase the impact of these intermediaries.

Halloran will also be working with Village Capital and ANDE in a comprehensive, open-source study of successful models for business incubators and accelerators for small and growing businesses (SGBs) in emerging markets.

In parallel to initiatives that strengthen the ecosystem and help disseminate knowledge and best practices, Halloran provides operational support to a number of incubators, accelerators, and supporting organizations such as Echoing Green, Unreasonable Institute, Buckminster Fuller Institute, Village Capital, Dasra, Villgro, Artemisia, Idesam, Village Capital, and Hub Oaxaca. Halloran recognizes the great value of an engaged approach to capacity support, and as it gains experience, it develops different models to address early-stage enterprise needs.

Exit Strategy

Halloran supports start-up initiatives that aim at becoming sustainable. However, it understands that in order to reach the poor, social entrepreneurs are working against the odds of profound market and government failures. Even when core operations no longer need to be subsidized, social enterprises still need philanthropic capital in order to continue innovating and scaling their impact. Therefore, each exit strategy is decided on a case-by-case base, taking into consideration the opportunity at hand and its potential for impact.

CASE STUDY 7.3   THE LEMELSON FOUNDATION

Objective

Prolific US inventor Jerome Lemelson and his wife, Dorothy, founded The Lemelson Foundation in the early 1990s on the belief that invention and invention-based enterprises have the power to improve people's lives.

Strategy

In the United States, the foundation supports an ecosystem that takes ideas from invention to enterprise, with the goal of launching businesses that will strengthen the US economy. In developing countries, the foundation supports inventors and entrepreneurs whose invention-based businesses create products that address basic human needs or increase the income of the poor. To date, the foundation has donated or committed more than USD 175 million in grants and PRIs in support of its mission.

Areas of Operation

The Lemelson Foundation supports programs that inspire youth to become inventors; stimulate and provide invention and entrepreneurship education; and support the launch, incubation, and mentoring of invention-based enterprises. The incubation work consists of providing early-stage support to inventors to build investment-ready, self-sustaining, invention-based businesses by promoting an iterative process (powered by user-centered design). The process requires an appropriate technological invention, a well-defined understanding of a problem integrating user context and needs, and a business proposition that can become self-sustaining.

The Lemelson Foundation believes its comparative strategic advantage is in "early-stage, invention-based enterprises on the path to self-sustainability and scale." It has a clear approach for launching enterprises, which is to support early and take big risks.

Financial Instruments

The Lemelson Foundation works with different methods of financing, including grants, loans, equity, and loan guarantees. The foundation views mixed financial instruments as key to serving early-stage needs, recognizing that donors and impact investors should become more creative in deploying capital. The sector is evolving, but a point of inflection where a large number of donors and social investors use tailored financial instruments has yet to be reached. It is the foundation's hope that its tolerance for risk and willingness to explore new types of financial instruments will help to inform the path forward for the sector. The Lemelson Foundation will continue to monitor the development of new financial instruments and innovative tools that will help the field.[13]

The foundation is also supportive of the creative use of grants to explore what works best. There are advantages, for example, to partnering with 501(c)(3) organizations, such as NESsT, which can enter emerging market countries and create funding vehicles to repackage philanthropic capital into investments. Strategic partnerships can help to deepen impact through creative application of financial instruments.

Capacity Support

The Lemelson Foundation sees capacity support as a critical part of getting organizations to reach self-sustainability. With capacity support, organizations and social enterprises can exist permanently as "agents of change" in the ecosystem in which they operate, becoming role models for both public and private sectors. Therefore, capacity support is linked to developing local competencies and the ecosystem. Realizing the dearth of critical technical as well as management support in the region, the foundation views the capacity building of developing country institutions as necessary for launching enterprises.

Early Stage

The Lemelson Foundation focuses on early-stage incubation. It has observed that critical needs—for ideas, people, teams, validation of enterprises, and funding—exist in this stage. As a moderately sized foundation, it believes it can tackle the early-stage challenges more effectively, as it observes that the size of many "deals" in the field fit a certain size of funder as well. The Lemelson Foundation has developed a niche in validating investable portfolio enterprises that can then be taken to scale with the support and investment of others.

Field Building

The regions in which the foundation works have many common challenges, not least of which is improving the educational context both at the policy level and at the curriculum level. The foundation supports the National Collegiate Inventors and Innovators Alliance (NCIIA), which is comprised of nearly two hundred colleges and universities in the United States. Each year it engages more than five thousand student and faculty innovators and entrepreneurs to help them commercialize their invention or innovation ideas. In developing countries, the foundation is supporting efforts to inspire young people toward science- and technology-based enterprise careers and to help foster support for invention-based technology enterprise that serves the poor within the public sector. In Peru, regional governments have created programs to foster innovation by sponsoring Regional Science, Technology, and Innovation Weeks in Cusco, Puno, and Cajamarca.

Case Study 7.4   Shell Foundation

Objective

Created in 2000 as a UK charity, its aim is to develop, scale-up, and promote enterprise-based solutions. The Shell Foundation acts as an investor, identifying financially sustainable solutions (self-sustainability is a goal).

Strategy

Shell Foundation's strategy can be summarized as follows:

- Commit USD 16 million per year, but leverage much more from strategic partners and investors.
- Use know-how and value-added resources from within the company—people, knowledge, and infrastructure.
- Operate with a "business DNA" and guide social enterprises with market principles, driven by Shell Foundation staffs who help with business models and business thinking/discipline.

- Adopt an "enterprise-based" approach using grants like an investor to encourage "propoor" innovation driving down costs and increasing benefits. The foundation sees a role for "angel philanthropy," and the acceptance of patience, flexibility, and high risk.
- Look for genuine long-term commitment on the part of the social enterprise management. The management team should have prior experience in the relevant market or issue. To find the right teams, it is imperative that the foundation have people on the ground.

Shell Foundation's approach[14] in establishing a social enterprise takes the following steps:

1. *Incubation*: Identify challenges with potential enterprise-based solutions and incubate ideas actively.
2. *Pilots*: Test approaches to gain firsthand insight into market and the challenges facing entrants.
3. *"Prove the concept"*: Use partnerships, resources, and knowledge of the market, facilitate the scaling of an enterprise, or form a new organization based on evidence from pilots.
4. *"Spin-off"*: Spin-off a financially viable (self-sustainable) entity to the outside. Shell Foundation hopes these entities have commercial financial support, increasing viability for scaling and replication.

AREAS OF OPERATION

Shell Foundation operates in four continents, with a stronger presence in India and Africa. In Latin America, the foundation is looking at Brazil and the Andean region for transport initiatives, like the Embarq, which has been quite successful in Mexico. The foundation is looking to scale and expand into Latin America. Replication of existing, successful initiatives is a formula Shell wants to explore, as an alternate to starting from scratch in relatively new territory. The foundation sees partnership with regional entities as key for developing a bigger presence in Latin America, with particular attention to shared approach and shared learning.

The foundation manages six programs:

1. *Aspire*: Helps SMEs in Africa access growth financing, in partnership with Gro-Fin. Shell Foundation targets enterprises seeking USD 50,000 to USD 1 million.
2. *Breathing Space*: Tackles indoor air pollution by marketing and designing new cookstoves that reduce toxic emissions and use less fuel. The foundation provides USD 3.5 million.
3. *Trading Up*: A bridging entity that connects major retailers with developing world producers. Shell Foundation forms partnerships with retailers and provides small producers with seed capital, business mentoring, and advice on product development and supply chain management.

4. *Embarq*: Sustainable transport initiative in Mexico City that promotes solutions to urban mobility, increased accessibility, and decreased pollution and transit times.
5. *Excelerate*: Delivers energy services to the poor in India and Bangladesh. Shell Foundation provides skills and finance to local entrepreneurs and assists start-ups to provide affordable modern energy services. The foundation also partners with Indian financial institutions to develop smart financing options for the poor.
6. *Climate Change*: A series of climate change initiatives are currently being developed.

The foundation's timeframe for scaling social enterprises is five to seven years. To start scaling, the enterprise must have a measurable large-scale development outcome, a multiple country and/or regional operation, earned income derived from the market, measurable leverage that matches or exceeds the foundation's grant contribution. The foundation measures its success in terms of scaling social enterprises. It has a 65 percent success rate of scalability, a 19 percent rate of successful launches without scalability, and a 16 percent rate of social enterprises that failed to achieve objectives.

Financial Instruments

Currently, the predominant instrument (85%–95%) is grant making, though the organization is expanding beyond grants and including loans and guarantees. Shell Foundation will not provide 100 percent of the financing. It works with external strategic partners who deliver and manage initiatives, and if possible also make the financial investments. In larger programs, Shell Foundation tends to take an active role in governance. Shell Foundation views the impact-investor market as risk averse, and the foundation provides loan guarantees to offset risk and make social enterprises more attractive for investment.

Capacity Support

Shell Foundation's capacity support includes business advice, market access, and governance support to complement its grant making. The foundation values codeveloping, learning, and testing business plans, understanding markets, spotting areas of deficiency, and progressively playing a role at the governance level. The foundation personnel are very involved with management support and are a predominant source of advice.

The Shell Foundation has started initiatives such as an intern program with Oxford University, and also seeks help from its corporate parent, which allows it to harness pro bono skills (particularly in areas such as marketing, branding, and supply chain management). Third-party capacity support is considered if the expertise needed is outside the competencies of foundation and corporate staff.

CASE STUDY 7.5   BBVA MOMENTUM

Objective

BBVA Momentum's mission is to contribute to developing social entrepreneurship[15] in Spain by implementing a support program and ecosystem so the most promising social enterprises can consolidate, grow, and scale their impact.

Strategy

BBVA's Momentum Project[16] is a pioneering initiative in Spain to help social enterprises that need assistance consolidating. The program provides training, advice, and support to improve the enterprise's social and economic impact. Cooperation and knowledge sharing among entrepreneurs that lead the enterprises is strongly encouraged. Each edition of the Momentum Project lasts one year and involves ten participants selected on the basis of the enterprise's viability, impact capacity, and growth potential.

The program calls for companies that are operating and have 2–3 years of experience, EUR 100,000 in turnover, at least 2 employees, an innovative approach to social change, and evidence that the business will create social impact. At least 51 percent of income must come from business operations—sales of products and services—which can be difficult for an organization dependent upon grants and donations. But BBVA believes that the program will help them become sustainable.

BBVA partnered with two academic institutions to manage the program: Santa Clara University (California), which runs an incubator program and The Escuela Superior de Administración y Dirección de Empresas (ESADE) (Barcelona), a highly regarded business school in Spain responsible for the training and capacity side of the program. The objectives include

- identifying and supporting social entrepreneurship in Spain;
- supporting the consolidation and development of those enterprises that provide effective and scalable solutions to social and environmental challenges;
- creating a supportive ecosystem for social enterprise;
- fostering the collaboration and exchange of knowledge among entrepreneurs, students, and managers for the cocreation of social and environmental value;
- generating knowledge related to social enterprise;
- inspiring the rest of society through disseminating the achievements and experiences of social entrepreneurs;
- fostering replication of the Momentum Project in other countries and regions throughout the world; and
- encouraging the participation of investors in funding social enterprise.

In 2012, BBVA decided to launch the program in Mexico and Peru. The bank sees opportunities in countries they are already operating in because of the strong networks and excellent market knowledge they have developed. Chile and Colombia are on the horizon of BBVA's overall regional strategy, and these countries will become part of the portfolio in the future.

The ecosystem formed by the Momentum Project includes students and graduates from ESADE, directors from BBVA and other relevant partners, and the entrepreneurs. BBVA believes that this ecosystem supporting social entrepreneurship will only grow richer with each edition of the Momentum Project.

Areas of Operation

BBVA's Momentum Project includes the following areas of operation:

- Mentor the elaboration of a development plan for the social enterprise.
- Support for access to financing—participants present development plans to potential investors on Social Investment Day.
- Increased visibility of the participating social enterprises and of the sector.
- Intensive training at the ESADE campus in Sant Cugat (Barcelona) during which professionals from ESADE provide basic knowledge on business administration, financials, communications, and so on. A team is created for each entrepreneur formulated by a mix of BBVA personnel and outside experts based on the social enterprise sector.
- The teams then present plans to potential investors and request funding.

Financial Instruments

Initially, the Momentum Project intended to only introduce the social enterprises to financing clients and match them. During the development process, BBVA presented the program and its participants to the risk capital and commercial lending area within the bank, and interest was expressed in possibly expanding the program. This sparked the idea for BBVA to create a fund within the bank to finance these ventures.

BBVA faced difficulty creating a fund for the Momentum Project because of the current regulatory system (bank regulations often make it impossible for them to invest in social enterprises). Instead, the bank invested EUR 3 million in a newly created limited liability company, which then gave loans to the six companies that made the final cut in the Momentum Project. The terms included low interest rate loans, interest-only payments for the first four years, and a loan term of eight years. In general, the program embraces "soft" loan terms, including no requirement for personal guarantees.

Social enterprises in the program—like most early-stage social enterprises—cannot access the regular capital market because of their risk profile. The investment required ranges from EUR 100,000 to EUR 1 million, and commercial lenders generally would not offer soft terms. BBVA has implemented a monitoring system to understand how the social enterprises are performing. It requests information on a monthly basis, plus a biannual review of the social impact using indicators that the Momentum Project adopted from industry standards (such as the Impact Reporting and Investment Standards (IRIS).

Capacity Support

The bank believes they are pioneering the way for other commercial banks in that they offer value-added services—risk assessment, money management, mentoring, and strategy—to early-stage social enterprises. Their internal structure and capacity support-building services go beyond the traditional sense of corporate social responsibility, and internally, BBVA sees this as a new type of business, not just goodwill. In fact, by 2015, they expect to have nearly three hundred employees volunteering their time toward developing this new key business unit.

Currently, the director of Global Risk has a team devoted to risk assessment of social enterprises—they analyze these businesses in the same way they do normal businesses. They perform due diligence under the assumption that BBVA would only support successful operations.

Involving Bank Clients

Additionally, in the private banking department there are new conversations with their clients about social enterprise as an investment. BBVA observes that long-term clients are now demanding a different type of investment. As a result, BBVA is cultivating this program to meet the social investment interests of HNWIs, family offices, and family foundations.

Still, BBVA has proceeded with caution in terms of program marketing for investors. As of the publication of this book, the framework for returns included interest-only payments for the first four years (2% for first and second years; 4% for third and fourth years), and the annual payment of 25 percent of the principal in each year from fifth to eighth years.

CASE STUDY 7.6   RAF

Objective

The Romanian-American Foundation aims to support civil society initiatives with a business-like approach, which we are confident will bring added value. We are here for the long term.

Roxana Vitan, executive director, RAF[17]

RAF was founded with the vision of creating a sustainable market economy in a democratic community. RAF seeks to strengthen and provide access to such a market for all segments of the Romanian population. It has utilized its strong ties to the United States, as well as business networks within Romania to develop entrepreneurship, cultivate education, and promote the importance of philanthropy in increasing the visibility of innovation in Romania.

Strategy

The foundation partners with public, private, and nonprofit leaders in Romania and the United States who are committed to entrepreneurship and education. RAF has identified creative partners and program managers to be catalysts for change, often civil society organizations (CSOs) or enterprises that implement programs aligned with their mission. RAF provides them grant funding. RAF has a long-standing relationship with NESsT based on their requirements for an intermediary that can provide an integrated, multilevel, long-term approach to expanding RAF's portfolio. They believe long-term impacts result from sustainable mentoring, evaluative processes, and focused approaches.

At the present time, the foundation funds programs by invitation only. Prospective partners and program managers are sourced by program officers and invited to work with the foundation team. The RAF team aids invited partners in preparing proposals and business plans for submission to the board of trustees for approval. Organizations that have been asked to submit proposals will have gone through a three to four month process of vetting and due diligence performed by the RAF staff. The board of directors approves grants three times in a year. The due diligence process includes a concept paper, a full application, a signed agreement, and monitoring and evaluation during the grant term.

Areas of Operation

RAF focuses on increasing capacity in terms of entrepreneurial skills and building access and reputations. In addition to supporting the NESsT Social Enterprise Portfolio in Romania, the foundation has two entrepreneurship programs.

Rural Entrepreneurship Program

In Romania, rural social enterprise represents a very important opportunity: an estimated 50 percent of the Romanian population resides in rural areas and 30 percent works in subsistence or semisubsistence farming. It is evident that consumers are interested, willing, and can afford to pay for premium products from rural areas and farmers. RAF has designed a program that involves several partners to address this opportunity, and is piloting an intervention model to stimulate rural producers' associations.[18]

RAF will provide training and advisory services to improve the abilities of small and semisubsistence farmers to register and organize as rural producers and to enhance their knowledge to access capital to expand their farms. RAF believes this program can impact 800 farmers trained in 40 rural areas throughout Romania. Further, through the help of at least 15 local advisors to provide further technical assistance, an estimated 400 farmers will benefit from exchange visits to learn about successful associations. RAF expects to provide local advisory services to over 1,500 farmers.[19]

Green Entrepreneurship Program

With many protected nature sites, inhabitants of these areas are often prohibited from developing industry, but can offer ecotourism. RAF believes incubators and accelerators for this sector can help scale businesses. It has been able to support organizations in the main ecotourism regions of the country. RAF works with one partner that has been funding community development and nature-related tourism for more than ten years. This partner has identified the most promising organizations to be invited into the program. Each of them received technical assistance and support to develop business plans and a start-up fund of USD 50,000.

Through this program, RAF has supported seven green, community-based social enterprises in economically disadvantaged communities. RAF firmly believes that income-generating activities add socioeconomic value to the local heritage and can be a sustainable tool for long-term conservation and local development. The first round of funding created 350 local jobs and aggregated 64 local producers. RAF seeks to have greater impact by launching a new round of funding and readjust its interventions based on the findings of the first round.

Financial Instruments

Although RAF is more formally a foundation that promotes the use of grants, their strategy also allows for experimentation with loans, often referred to as repayable grants, and the traditional grant. Currently, with its USD 3 million fund, the foundation has experimented with offering soft terms (often 0% interest rates). RAF believes that innovation with financial instruments helps partners create capacity and discipline, but has the additional value of providing more visibility to leverage EU-level funding for social enterprise development. Though there are many EU funds (described in chap. 3), timing and cash flow can often present barriers to organizations. RAF recognizes this, and often provides bridge financing for partners with repayable grants. However, RAF envisions an exit strategy in which partners reach sustainability and no longer require RAF financial support.

Capacity Support

RAF works very closely with all partners in order to be sure they are on the right track in terms of market demand and to measure impact. Alongside its partners, RAF staff visit the social enterprises to conduct thorough discussions with the entities as well as the final beneficiaries and to provide feedback and contribution in terms of capacity support. RAF's entrepreneurial program staff possesses a high degree of experience in the social sector. They, along with appropriate partners, can provide marketing and communication products such as ecotourism guides or crowd-funded initiatives to help organizations in need.

Field Building

RAF works with the government to change the environment for rural entrepreneurship by giving feedback and using lessons learned from their experience with farmers and local communities. The Rural Entrepreneurship program run by RAF is an example of how the foundation's work influences government policy. RAF and the Center for European Policies produced reports on the importance of developing small funds to serve rural-community business development, and which ultimately led to provide recommendations related to rural microlending at the EU level. RAF sees itself as a facilitator—an organization that liaises on behalf of an important sector to the Romanian economy. They believe that government, agencies, and the organizations themselves must "own" the entire process. RAF catalyzes interest, facilitates change, and helps to connect enterprises with the right partners in order to build success stories, which then help to fortify the marketplace.

8

THE (STAIR)CASE FOR MIXED FINANCIAL INSTRUMENTS

INTRODUCTION

The social investment[1] capital market hardly exists in either Central Europe or Latin America. There are very few financing instruments available for social enterprises to fund their start-up, consolidation, and growth. Grants have been the only source of funding for decades, and even grants have grown scarce, as private foreign donors have disappeared and local philanthropic sources have not stepped in to take their place. Social enterprises in emerging market countries remain dependent on funds from European Union (EU) and other foreign governments, which come in a variety of forms and support the enterprises at each stage of their development.

Alternative financing instruments have not caught on partly because many social enterprises fail to understand them. The majority of such enterprises have grown out of the nonprofit sector, which is entirely accustomed to grant funding and is suspicious of alternative instruments such as loans. It is also a supply problem, as banks and investment funds have not considered social enterprises as a business opportunity, in part because of the small size of the sector, and have therefore mostly ignored them. Impact-investment funds have attracted much attention and capital, but are rarely interested in early-stage social enterprises.[2] The financial markets have neither developed new instruments specifically for social enterprises, nor have they offered them the existing instruments that are available to other small businesses. Suspicion and lack of understanding is found just as much on the supply side as on the demand side.

Due to this market gap, social investors and support organizations have been encouraged to develop their own financial instruments in order to help grow social enterprises they support and contribute to an early-stage development of the social investment market. This has played out in more sophisticated capital markets (such as the United Kingdom or the United States) where some of the most innovative and successful financing schemes for social enterprises—such as social impact bonds[3]—originated in the philanthropic and social investment communities. However, these success stories have typically followed an approach of crafting tailor-made solutions to specific problems, which has not only worked

well for the enterprises being served but has also meant that standardized financial service offers have been slow to appear (loans are the only possible exception). Most of these financing instruments have only recently passed a pilot phase
and are just now being introduced to the market, especially in Central Europe
and Latin America. Social banks, venture philanthropy funds, and other social
investment funds have yet to emerge in large numbers, much less a widespread
acceptance of special financing products for social enterprises. Demand is growing, so adequate responses are needed urgently to address access to appropriate
finance needs for social enterprise development. Funds and banks must promote
the use of appropriate financial instruments, but at the same time take on the
responsibility of risk associated with the early stages of market entrance.

THE SPECTRUM OF FINANCIAL INSTRUMENTS

There are a number of mixed financial instruments, including grants, loans, guarantees, quasi-equity (see box 8.1 for definition), equity, and any combination
of these. Having access to finance means not only that money is available for a
social enterprise, but also that it is available in the form that is most appropriate
to its business model and development stage. The "funding staircase" developed
by Charity Bank, a specialized loan provider to charities in the United Kingdom,
demonstrates this point (see diagram 8.1). In step one, start-up social enterprises need a lot of development support and skill building and relatively modest amounts of money for planning in order to make them investment ready,[4]
that is, able to absorb larger amounts of financing in the future. The next step
requires seed capital, best provided in the form of grants and further capacity-
building support, both of which are needed in order to consolidate the new
social enterprise. As the enterprise grows and matures, moving up the staircase, it

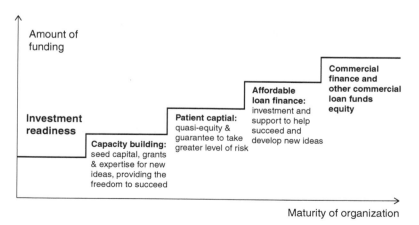

Diagram 8.1   The funding staircase.
Source: Charity Bank, UK, 2011.

needs larger and larger amounts of capital, which in turn requires new financiers. Initial supporters are often unable or unwilling to provide large amounts of grant financing for growth and to take higher risks. This step requires patient capital, often in the form of quasi-equity or equity, which requires specialized providers. With patient capital, an enterprise can achieve sustained growth, which will make it eligible and desirable for commercial financing in later steps of the staircase.

Social enterprises move up and down this staircase and can ideally find partners at each step along the way to help them design the best financing mix. In Central Europe and Latin America, some innovative financiers have served social enterprises at various steps on the staircase, providing a combination of financing instruments in order to fill the funding vacuum that prevent enterprises from advancing up the staircase. Providing such a variety of financial instruments is difficult and only seems possible for funds whose performance is measured on social rather than strictly financial return. In order to realize that social return, they supplement the funding with technical assistance or capacity building, which also makes the funding more effective.

As an early-stage social enterprise development intermediary, NESsT is providing financing and capacity-building in the first three steps of the funding process, and recently started piloting the fourth step (affordable loans) in order to develop successful models for further investment. NESsT's assessment of the social enterprise financing landscape found inadequate provision of financial instruments[5] in the regions where it works, which motivated the organization to invent and pilot financing schemes in its enterprise portfolio. While doing so,

---

Box 8.1 Financial instruments: Definitions

Grants: The best-known and most widespread form of financing for social enterprise (and NPOs). They are nonrepayable and can be provided multiple times.

Loans (debt): Repayable forms of finance of varying structures, depending on the purpose (investment vs. working capital) and the provider(s) of the loan finance. Loans carry interest, which has to be paid to the lender on a regular basis, often along with regular installments of the principal (initially borrowed amount).

Guarantees: Promises of payment to support debt-financing applications. The guarantor may guarantee the entire loan request or a portion only. The lender calls upon the guarantee when repayment by the debtor is late or never takes place. Guarantees are used to facilitate loan finance from third-party lenders.

Equity: Financing in exchange for shares, or partial ownership, of the social enterprise. To obtain equity investment, an enterprise must have the appropriate legal form (usually a company). The investor has voting rights and a certain level of control, and may receive dividends if the social enterprise generates profit. The investor can get the initial invest-ment back if he/she later sells his/her shares in the company.[6]

Quasi-equity: Quasi or soft equity is a special form of financing for social enterprises that fills the gap between a grant/loan and equity. It "has equity-like qualities without conferring ownership rights to the inves-tor." Forms of quasi-equity include use of underwriting, royalty share finance, repayment of loans based on results, and repayable or recover-able grants. It should be noted that some current definitions of qua-si-equity also embrace use of subordinated, unsecured debt as well as social impact bonds that are provided upfront capital tied to expected results of a specific social initiative."[7]

NESsT has been educating social enterprises about the importance and use of different financing instruments, as well as educating potential financiers about the sector and its investment opportunities.

The staircase approach should not be interpreted to mean that grants are use-ful only at the beginning, in the start-up phase. NESsT's experience shows that grants are instrumental for more mature social enterprises as well, enterprises that need to invest in infrastructure, additional human resource capacity, or intan-gibles such as promotion or brand building. Grants are important for consolidat-ing, proving the social enterprise concept, and readying it for future investment. Effective grants management helps build trust and make other financing instru-ments possible. When NESsT provided a grant and loan combination to one of its portfolio social enterprises, Kék Madár, in 2010, the USD 30,000 grant made the purchase of a new building possible, and helped unlock approximately USD 230,000 in EU funding for the expansion of the business. (See further details in the case example.)

In many cases, however, grants are not adequate for social enterprise develop-ment, because they may be too small, for too short a time period, of restricted use, or delayed in disbursement. Social enterprises therefore need more flexible instruments to be able to manage their finances and business effectively.

THE ROLE OF DEBT FINANCING IN SOCIAL ENTERPRISE STRATEGIES—MAPPING THE LANDSCAPE

Demand

The demand for debt finance has been on the rise among social enterprises in Central Europe and Latin America since the early 2000s:

- They have been facing a growing funding gap due to the withdrawal of tradi-tional funders from the region and the lack of significant local philanthropy.

- They need larger amounts of money in order to finance start-ups and growth.
- They need unrestricted financing.
- They need funds that can supplement the grants they manage to raise.

NESsT's survey-based research[8] of its Central European[9] portfolio revealed that although most organizations still prefer grant funding, half of the surveyed Central European CSOs already considered applying for a loan, 29 percent did apply for a loan, and 25 percent already took a loan. These were typically bridge loans to cover temporary gaps between income and expenses related to activities and projects, for which a grant was approved or a contract signed but funding was not yet provided. Amounts ranged from EUR 10,000 to EUR 100,000.

CSOs that obtained loans got them from commercial banks where they had personal contacts and thus a better chance of getting their application approved. They said that the biggest challenges in the lending process were filling in the required documentation and meeting the bank's criteria. This is not surprising, as loan applications and risk assessment frameworks in banks are designed for the business sector. They are standardized, have little room for specifics, and contain complex language that social enterprises find difficult to understand due to lack of expertise. The conditions of these loans in most cases were market conditions, which social enterprises find challenging. Collateral was a typical concern, but high interest rates, additional costs, and no adjustment to social enterprise specifics were also listed. These obstacles are why organizations have perceived bank loans as too risky and have avoided them altogether.

Concerning their future plans, half of the social enterprises surveyed in Central Europe said they would consider applying for a loan and 90 percent said they would welcome a newly established specialized loan fund. Interestingly enough, the purpose of the loan would be mostly enterprise expansion, equipment purchase, or working capital, as opposed to bridge loans for existing programs. In order to implement these plans for future projects, social enterprises said they would prefer loans of EUR 10,000–100,000 for a period of at least 3 years, and said they would appreciate technical assistance from the lender or a support organization during the loan application process.

NESsT commissioned research about debt financing of social enterprises in Latin America,[10] and confirmed many of the above challenges, while also showing that

- despite the presence of a microfinance sector and the apparent openness of banks to offer loans to social enterprises in the region, few actual experiences of social enterprise lending exist;
- organizations that have access to public or private sources of funding are not interested in loans and thus do not develop strong banking relationships;
- other organizations/social enterprises that are in need of bank finance don't receive it, because they do not meet the banks' risk assessment criteria, including adequate governance structures and clear and transparent financial records;

- often, social enterprises in need of bank finance are not able to demonstrate sufficient repayment capacity or collateral;
- social enterprises often lack experience in dealing with banks and specifically with loans and they often need to be prepared for financing by better integrating their social programs with enterprise activities, and overall further professionalizing their financial systems; and
- CSOs have diminished creditworthiness because of restrictions imposed by donors, such as restrictions on asset accumulation, profit generation, and so on.

Supply—Loan Funds

NESsT's research found that specialized loan funds catering to social enterprises are the exception rather than the rule in Central Europe. These funds mostly provide bridge loans for NPOs and offer relatively small amounts in the short term. Of the three specialized loan funds that were identified in the five countries surveyed, all offer bridge loans (secured by an EU grant or a contract) and two offer loans to develop social enterprises. The typical amount is rather small, ranging from EUR 1,600 to EUR 40,000, and the term is almost always 12 months, with one exception where 36 months is also available. Interest rates are close to or above market rates. The funds require a cash-flow plan or business plan with a detailed application form. None of them offers any capacity building or education on loans to social enterprises. Since those services may not fall under their mission, it makes doing business with them much more difficult, as their clients lack experience and need advice about how to deal with debt and how to determine whether they are ready to take on a loan. This is an absence that almost nobody has been willing to fill. It is problematic, as it hinders the further development of social enterprises, as well as the market for social enterprise lending. The loan fund described in box 8.2 is one of the more innovative funds available in Central Europe.

Box 8.2   TISE

Poland has an alternative provider of financing for CSOs and includes social enterprises. TISE[11] (Towarzystwa Inwestycji Spoleczno-Ekonomicznych SA or Society for Social and Economic Investment SA) is based in Warsaw and provides loans, financial services, consulting, and investment in order to facilitate the development of local initiatives for sustainable development, particularly in the social economy.

As part of its mission, TISE has actively been providing loans to nonprofit foundations, associations, entities in the social economy, and Small and Medium Enterprises (SMEs) since 2006. Loans can be used as bridge loans or for working capital and business development. Loan amounts start as small as USD 2,900. TISE has a very simple, client-friendly, and tailor-made approach to lending: documentation is simple, turnaround is fast, and the terms of the loan take into account individual borrower circumstances to the greatest extent possible. By February 28, 2013, TISE SA had granted 113 loans totaling about PLN 17 million (USD 5.2 million) to nongovernmental organizations and social economy entities.

TISE is 100 percent owned by one of the oldest and largest social-investment institutions in Europe, Credit Cooperatif, a cooperative bank active in France for 120 years.

The research in Latin America identified few alternative mechanisms that provide loan finance to social enterprises. Some are attached to development programs (e.g., the Social Entrepreneurship Program [SEP] of the Inter-American Development Bank [IDB], the Andean Development Corporation), while others are creative schemes to provide loans to CSOs based on their future cash flows. Some social enterprises that export products to Europe or the United States may receive trade finance from their importing partners, for example, from Root Capital or the Italian Etimos Consortium. There were only a few social or impact-investing funds in these four countries (see chap. 9 on early-stage impact investing), and the alternative loan funds that did exist tended to charge higher interest rates and provide funding to more traditional social activities such as education, health, and housing.

As described in box 8.3, the SEP-IDB program is uniquely focusing on development of social enterprise, offering both financing and technical assistance at the regional level. However, based on the average levels of funding provided, they are not focused on early-stage social enterprise, with average loans of USD 500,000 and loan/technical assistance packages of USD 800,000. According to Dieter Wittkowski, the director of the program, "while there is no official minimum loan amount, we usually do not make loans of less than USD 300,000. Although there are some exceptions if a project really interests us because of its innovation, social impact, etc. This is because it takes the same amount of work, steps, time, etc., to do a small project as a USD 1 million loan, and we simply try to be as efficient as possible in placing our funds. The SEP usually has about USD 10–12 million annually that we approve and our average project size (loan and donation) tends to be around USD 800,000."

In the case of SITAWI, the Brazilian loan fund described in box 8.4, the loan funding to CSOs and social enterprise is at lower amounts, ranging from USD 50,000 to USD 200,000. However, the organization considers itself as lender to more mature enterprises and does not provide capacity support with its loans, looking to the enterprises themselves to prove that they have access to this support from other sources.

Box 8.3   SEP-IDB

SEP[12] of IDB provides financing through local partner organizations to individuals and groups that generally do not have access to commercial or development loans on regular market terms.

Working through production intermediaries, such as CEPI Cafe (Central Piurana de Cafetaleros, Peru)[13] and ASOPROF (Asociacion Nacional de Productos de Frejol, Bolivia),[14] IDB offers loans and grants to private, nonprofit, and governmental organizations that provide financial, business, social, and community development services to disadvantaged populations. The SEP offers approximately USD 10 million in financing each year to projects in 26 Latin American and Caribbean countries.

The SEP supports projects that finance entrepreneurial solutions to poverty in two main areas:

1. *Rural business* (including production, processing, marketing, and value chains): These projects target rural micro and small producers from marginalized communities, with the purpose of providing
   a. access to finance with the support of innovative financing mechanisms; and
   b. access to national and international markets through value chains that link small-scale enterprises with larger ones.
2. *Provision of basic services* (including support to private alternative providers of education, health, potable water, and electric and/or renewable energy, among others): The projects being financed are pilot initiatives and social projects with business approaches that can be scaled up, thus achieving a demonstrative effect.

The SEP grants low-interest loans of up to USD 1 million; the average size of long-term loans is USD 500,000. In addition, the program offers technical assistance grants of up to USD 250,000, which are allocated to the development and strengthening of innovative institutions. SEP uses its resources strategically and funds a limited number of representative projects; such operations must be capable of promoting learning between countries or of being emulated in other parts of the region.

Box 8.4   SITAWI[15]

SITAWI is a privately founded NPO with the mission to develop financial infrastructure for the social sector in Brazil. SITAWI creates financial products tailored to the needs of social organizations. Its goal is to support the expansion of projects in areas such as employment and income generation, environment, health, culture, and civil rights.

SITAWI's two main products are social loans and social fund management. Loans range from USD 50,000 to USD 200,000, with interest of approximately 1 percent per month (below market rates in Brazil). SITAWI's investors do not receive a financial return, which is how the fund manages to keep the interest rates on its loans fixed and very low.

When selecting clients, SITAWI gives preference to existing operations with direct social and environmental impact. SITAWI does not provide business-planning support to start-ups, but it does consider among the selection criteria the potential borrower's willingness to incorporate management advice, allowing them to leverage SITAWI's expertise. Additionally, SITAWI only lends to social enterprises that do not have access to credit from development agencies.

According to SITAWI, there is more demand for their services than what they can supply. In the period 2009–2011, they disbursed 11 loans to 9 organizations. The cumulative lending amounts and people served are as given in table 8.1 below.

Table 8.1 Cumulative lending amounts and people served by SITAWI in 2009–2011

	2009	2010	2011
Lending (*social loans*) (*USD*)	270,000	608,000	983,000
Number of people reached	2,000	11,000	15,000 (cumulative)

Supply—Commercial Banks

Mainstream financial institutions are another potential source of debt financing for social enterprises. However, even though banks in the United Kingdom and Western Europe have already put the social enterprise sector on their radar screen, lending to the sector is still problematic. There is often a mismatch between demand and supply, and lack of information or risk perception makes banks cautious or raises the cost of funds.

In Central Europe, banks and microlending programs that cater to businesses with loan needs averaging USD 25,000–200,000, similar to those in the NESsT portfolio, do not consider social enterprises eligible given their organization status (NPO or owned by a NPO) and/or lack of collateral. Several commercial banks have an explicit policy not to lend to CSOs, which extends to social enterprises operated by CSOs. Some banks do not have such a policy and make some of their regular loan products available to NPOs, and may offer tailor-made loans based on long-standing individual relationships if the CSO/social enterprise is an account holder. Once the loan is granted, conditions tend to be similar to conditions offered to SMEs. However, in some cases, SMEs are eligible to obtain government-subsidized loans with more favorable conditions, which are not available to social enterprises.

Banks always require collateral, which can be a major impediment for social enterprises. Typically, the only way for social enterprises to borrow from banks is to secure the loan with a personal guarantee or mortgage provided by the executive director of the CSO. This is the way financial institutions cover the perceived risks of social enterprises, which they usually know very little about and which they do not have the methodology to assess. Recently, a commercial bank interested in lending to social enterprises stated that they intend to put their social enterprise clients in the same portfolio as the state-owned oil and gas company of Hungary, since the only thing that matters is that they should be financially viable businesses.

Access to start-up financing is a very big impediment in emerging market countries where social enterprise is a nascent sector. Most banks in Central Europe do not consider social enterprises a big enough target group to approach or to develop special loan products for, particularly during a recession when most of their clients are cut off from borrowing. Had this chapter been written in 2008, it might have provided a more optimistic view of involving banks in social enterprise lending initiatives. Currently, this seems fairly unrealistic, so the need for alternative lenders/funders is even greater.

NESsT's research in Central Europe also identified several failed initiatives whereby banks tried to develop loan products for NPOs. Flawed risk assessment methods and a lack of information on the part of the banks, as well as a lack of repayment potential on the part of the NPOs, prevented these initiatives from succeeding. NESsT has not found any significant attempts to create a loan product specifically for social enterprises.

The fact that social enterprises are not considered creditworthy definitely presents a challenge even in environments where banks seem to be willing to offer them loans. NESsT's Latin America research found that in theory banks were more willing to lend to NPOs than their Central European counterparts, and CSOs that had developed efficient management and demonstrated capacity to generate funds to repay loans could obtain debt financing with the same conditions as any other company. However, even a loan under what could be considered normal conditions is problematic, as market conditions often hinder start-up or development of early-stage social enterprises due to the "social costs" attached to their activities. Bank staffs who were interviewed did not seem to take this under consideration. They also had serious reservations about the creditworthiness of their social enterprise clients. They believed these clients lacked convincing business plans or cash-generating mechanisms, transparent financials, good governance structures, and collateral, the latter often due to donors' restrictions on CSOs accumulating assets.

Insufficient cash-generating potential is a contentious issue, given that many social enterprises never promise to produce high financial returns due to their focus on social return or the limited productivity they may have working with disadvantaged employees. This is one of their limitations when seeking nongrant financing, as lower or zero financial returns make them unattractive to financiers that offer market capital.

Insufficient collateral points to a problem in the general funding scheme of social enterprises, namely the position of donors. Donors send mixed signals by often penalizing cash-generating activities, such as product and service sales (see examples in chap. 3 on EU policy). They often restrict asset-building efforts by social enterprises/CSOs and they frequently do not support long-term sustainability plans, which include social enterprise development. With these conditions, donors limit the potential creditworthiness of social enterprise and CSOs.

In Latin America, banks tend to exclude certain fields of activity, such as human rights or addiction issues, from both their lending and their philanthropy. They prefer to donate to traditional sectors, such as education or production in rural areas. Some banks that NESsT surveyed mentioned a reputational risk, for example, if a social enterprise borrower went into arrears. The bank feared they would be unable to follow standard bank procedure and take the collateral, which might lead to a public outcry. So they prefer to avoid such a risk altogether. Several Central European banks solve this dilemma by putting social enterprise in their corporate social responsibility (CSR) or philanthropic portfolios, preferring to give grants or sponsorship. This way they can say they are separating two portfolios with very different risk profiles: a loan (business) portfolio and their CSR portfolio (with 100% risked capital). While an increase in the amount of available grant sources is certainly beneficial, it also deprives social enterprises of a fair chance to get experience with debt financing and to prove themselves as viable and bankable businesses.

While most banks are still not interested in social enterprise finance and no significant new investment or loan funds have been established, the landscape is slowly changing. Social enterprises as well as financiers are becoming more aware of a potential market niche. A major Central European bank launched a program in 2010 to promote its social enterprise finance facility, which they claimed was a EUR 1 million investment. The announcement was heavily promoted, and included a road show with Muhammad Yunus,[16] making the concept of social enterprise and its successful examples better known in the region. Unfortunately, the loan facility itself has yet to materialize, or at least no deals were made public. The bank's subsidiaries in some countries set up their own team and launched their own lending programs, trying to identify and capture creditworthy social enterprises. But the efforts were few and forced, rather than responses to real needs and financing of sustainable business models. The bank offered mostly commercial rates, no accompanying grant funding, concrete business development, or mentoring support. It is believed that the bank lacked resources, knowledge, and commitment to really enter the social enterprise finance arena and remain there as a long-term active player. The financial and profit focus of the bank ran counter to the requirements of social finance, which is why the program apparently has not reached its goals.

In Hungary, there have been attempts to set up a private loan fund by a consortium of smaller organizations, as well as a new ethical (and green) bank initiative,[17] whereby an existing cooperative bank launched new products to finance environmentally and socially responsible businesses, among them social enterprises. They have involved environmental and civil society experts in the credit committees, and promise to spend HUF 1 billion on the new loan products that will offer favorable conditions to preferred social and environmental projects. These initiatives have not gained a lot of visibility yet, but they are welcomed by the sector, as they promise to fill in major gaps in the financing spectrum.

The Role of Intermediaries

The role of intermediaries in the social finance[18] landscape is critical when considering the challenges currently faced by social enterprises. Intermediaries can find and link lenders and borrowers by providing information, expertise, and education. In some situations, intermediaries are well positioned to provide guarantees for loans offered by more risk-averse mainstream lenders. This is a function that government guarantees could also perform, if they included social enterprises among the eligible entities.

Intermediaries, which oftentimes are simultaneously support organizations or incubators, can help make social enterprises ready for debt financing or for impact investment by providing capacity building as well as tailor-made financing packages including grants at the early stages. In addition to building the capacity to run the business, intermediaries often facilitate the organizational development process to help social enterprise borrowers integrate their activities, strengthen their governance and organizational culture, and make them more attractive candidates for lending as well as investment.

The Latin America research sheds light on the need for better integration of the social enterprise activity and the rest of the organization in cases where the social enterprise is a subsidiary of a NPO. Potential lenders complained that a major impediment is the institutional weakness of the loan applicants and the lack of transparency in structure as well as activities. Alternative loan funds and social finance initiatives may have recognized that experienced social enterprise support organizations are valuable, yet most of them are not willing to allocate funding for such services. The entry of new actors with resources and experience in financial instruments presents an opportunity for developing new financial products that combine fresh ideas with tested methodologies.

Experience in Using Mixed Financing Instruments

NESsT Pilots

Based on its research, NESsT responded to the market gap. Four years ago, it initiated a few alternative financing pilot programs with its social enterprise portfolio to address their specific financing needs. The experience of the pilots showed the importance of having an in-house alternative financing facility to provide an appropriate mix of financing. It also showed the need to work with willing partners to facilitate the placement of their money, while at the same time adding the capacity building and support necessary to make the transaction a success. NESsT also observed that by piloting loans and other forms of investment, the organization was encouraging others to follow in its footsteps. From the start, NESsT hoped these pilots would demonstrate models leading to a stronger enabling environment and a more diverse social finance market.

Table 8.2 below shows a summary of the NESsT pilot cases to date. The amounts, terms, purposes, and financing instruments vary according to the organization's need. NESsT provided two loans directly, one for infrastructure development and one for working capital, while nine loans were offered to start-up technology enterprises through a partner, a microfinance institution. In 2010, NESsT guaranteed two loans (bridge and working capital) that were extended by TISE, a social economy finance fund (see box 8.2 above). In 2010, NESsT made its first equity investment in Fruit of Care, a social enterprise that markets and sells high-quality gift items made by people with intellectual disabilities (see more on this case in chap. 5 on scaling). In total, this amounts to close to USD 200,000 in investment.

Case Study 8.1   ADV—Bridge Loan

ADV is a Romanian foundation set up in 2002 in Iasi, whose mission is to ensure that people living with HIV/AIDS in Romania have access to the key services and support they need to improve their quality of life (see more detailed example in chap. 3). With NESsT's help in 2007, ADV launched a social enterprise to train and employ youth with HIV/AIDS. Util Deco is a sheltered workshop[19] that provides business support services, such as photocopying and binding, and creates and sells quality handmade products, such as textiles, paintings, glassworks, postcards, agendas, and calendars. In 2010, ADV needed bridge financing of EUR 100,000 for an ongoing EU-funded project on social enterprise development. NESsT collaborated with TISE from Poland to provide the financing to ADV with tailored conditions: an acceptable interest rate and a repayment schedule that matched the project cycle. No collateral was required, but NESsT guaranteed 20 percent of the disbursed amount, based on its knowledge of ADV as a portfolio member and on a thorough analysis of their EU project and organizational cash flows. This guarantee unlocked debt financing for ADV.

The key risks identified were the unpredictable reimbursement schedule by the Romanian government, which could upset cash flow and cause repayment delays, and possibly lower than projected revenues from the social enterprise, which would have reduced the other source of repayment. In order to mitigate these risks, NESsT decided to continue working closely with ADV and monitor their organizational financials regularly. ADV has been paying the interest on schedule and is in its second year of the three-year loan term. TISE has not needed to call on the NESsT guarantee.

Table 8.2 NESsT pilots in loan finance, guarantees, and equity investment, 2010–2012

Organization	Amount	Instrument	Provider of funds	Term	Purpose	Analysis	Status	Comment
Kék Madár (Hungary)	USD 55,000	Loan	NESsT	6 years	Infrastructure investment for scaling	Growth business plan, performance management tool	Annual repayment on schedule	Combined with grant
Fruit of Care (Hungary)	USD 20,000	(Owner's) loan	NESsT	6 months	Working capital: inventory	Business plan, performance management tool	Rescheduled	
Welldorf (Hungary)	EUR 4,000	Guarantee	Third party: TISE	3 years	Working capital	TISE format, cash flow	Rescheduled	Loan: EUR 20,000
Alaturi de Voi (ADV) (Romania)	EUR 20,000	Guarantee	Third party: TISE	3 years	Bridge loan	TISE format, cash flow	Quarterly repayment on schedule	Loan: EUR 100,000
Affordable Technology (9) (Peru)	USD 64,000 in total	Loan (no grants)	NESsT	18 to 40 months	Investment and working capital	Cash flow and analysis by Popular SAFI	2 repaid, 1 in arrears, and 6 repaying on schedule	Through third party: Popular SAFI; lessons learnt
Fruit of Care (Hungary)	USD 2,000	Equity	NESsT	Indefinite	Founding capital	Business plan	40% ownership	Combined with grant

Case Study 8.2   Kék Madár—Infrastructure Loan and Grant

Kék Madár is a foundation established in 1997 with a mission to create economic and educational opportunities for people with intellectual and physical disabilities. It provides job training and temporary employment, to help its clients transition to full-time employment and independent lives. In 2006, Kék Madár approached NESsT and started the business planning process for a restaurant. This restaurant would train and employ people with intellectual disabilities, and would offer a nutritious dining alternative to customers. With NESsT's capacity building and financial support, the restaurant (Ízlelő) was launched in May 2007 and entered the NESsT incubation portfolio.

In 2009, Kék Madár approached NESsT again, this time with an ambitious plan to quadruple the restaurant from 25 to 100 seats, with 60 seats serving 150 daily customers and 40 seats in a separate space for catering services. However, the enterprise needed significant funding to purchase a neighboring building for the Kék Madár offices, which would then unlock EU funding to pay for the expansion and refurbishment of the restaurant. The business plan demonstrated that there was a clear market demand for dining and catering. The foundation's executive director is an exceptional, committed leader who won the "Most Inspiring Woman of the Year" (business category) award by a Hungarian women's magazine. Kék Madár had a solid track record and a history of winning and strategically implementing significant grants. These factors carried a lot of weight when NESsT decided to offer a loan to support the growth of the business.

Kék Madár received a grant and loan combination totaling USD 85,000 (USD 30,000 grant and USD 55,000 loan) for the purchase of a new building. This financial investment has been accompanied by about USD 60,000 worth of capacity-building support; an essential part of the NESsT package. Kék Madár had not been eligible to obtain bank financing unless the director agreed to use her home as collateral. The USD 30,000 grant decreased the overall loan and kept the payments within the financial growth projections. Repayment would be made through six annual installments with NESsT receiving a 3 percent interest rate contingent on business revenues. The loan was backed by a mortgage on the newly purchased building, standard practice for real estate loans in the social finance sector. The conditions were jointly determined by NESsT and the foundation in order to ensure the best loan solution to Kék Madár's need. The term was long enough to take into account the refurbishment period and the relaunch of the restaurant. This was also an advantage when the processing of the government grant was delayed by two years. NESsT decided to request a modest transaction fee and made it payable in installments, depending on the business performance (revenue) of the restaurant, in order to provide flexibility for the management.

This was the right instrument to use in the Kék Madár case, and supplementing the loan with a grant helped to determine the optimal level of debt that the organization could comfortably take on. Kék Madár is on track with repayments and plans to reopen the larger and renovated restaurant in June 2013. It also plans to help launch five new similar restaurants in the next five years.

Case Study 8.3   Popular SAFI: Start-up Grants and
Loans to the Affordable Technology Portfolio

In order to offer financing to NESsT's start-up affordable technology portfolio in Peru, NESsT was advised to set up an investment fund managed by a local microfinance institution. The concept was to provide loan financing for the start-ups, given the for-profit nature of the social enterprises that would be established (several started out as family businesses or sole proprietorship structures).

The long-term goals of the technology social enterprise initiative were to accompany promising technological innovations through the business planning, incubation, and growth phases with adequate financing and capacity-building support. Much like the funding staircase presented at the beginning of this chapter, NESsT planned to provide program participants with grants in the planning stage, then grants and loans in the incubation stage after the social enterprises were launched, and eventually offer them a whole range of financing options, including grants, loans, and equity in the scaling phase.

Popular SAFI,[20] an investment fund founded in 2006 with considerable experience in providing working capital and other loans to SMEs, was selected to manage NESsT's investment fund. An assessment of financing options for higher-risk investments in Peru recommended that NESsT separate the lending role from the capacity support role to avoid confusion and reduce the chances of subjective decision making in the lending process. Popular SAFI became the lender and NESsT kept only the capacity and portfolio manager roles. Popular SAFI's responsibilities included assessing business risk, structuring the deal and the corresponding collateral, establishing the loan conditions, providing the cash to the borrowers and receiving repayments, administering each individual loan, and providing progress reports to NESsT. The loan terms were established with NESsT, taking into account the circumstances of the borrowers as much as possible. As a result, they were more favorable than terms in the microfinance market in Peru.

Three years into the program NESsT realized that loans may not have been the best tool for technology social enterprises of this type, as their repayment capacity had been weakened by the types of problems typically faced by technology start-ups: delays in producing a prototype, delays in obtaining the necessary certification, difficulties in starting the commercialization of the product, and low level of sales capacity of the newly created enterprises. It appeared that some of the businesses were overburdened by debt, although they all did their best to continue paying the interest due, according to either the original payment plan or a rescheduled one. In the next round of financing, NESsT will consider more grant funding for start-up technology enterprises to provide them with the necessary breathing space at the beginning.

Of the nine loans provided to the first round of innovators, two already have repaid their loans, while six are repaying on schedule and only one is in arrears. This is a very good result, which shows that despite the start-up difficulties, social enterprises were able to deal with the loan conditions. The flexibility shown by Popular SAFI to reschedule for those struggling reflects a patient capital approach and should result in more loans that are eventually repaid.

Social Finance in the United Kingdom - Charities AID Foundation (CAF)

CAF[21] is a UK-based charity with the mission of motivating society to give more effectively, and helping to transform lives and communities around the world. CAF operates globally with affiliates in the United States, Australia, Bulgaria, Brazil, India, Russian, South East Asia, and Southern Africa.

CAF has several related entities that serve the financial needs of NPOs. One of these affiliates, CAF Venturesome, works with philanthropists who provide donations and investments for it to invest in its loan funds. In most cases, the social investment is recycled back to the funds, but in some cases, the investor receives a financial return. CAF Venturesome was set up in 2002 to provide affordable financial support to charities, social enterprises, and community groups when grants may not be available and access to traditional financial institutions is difficult. It offers three to five-year interest-bearing loans between GBP 25,000 and GBP 250,000 to help NPOs and social enterprises meet their financial needs, whether for bridge loans, working capital, or other needs. CAF Venturesome currently manages GBP 13 million. Since its inception, it has offered GBP 30 million in loans and supported 360 charities and social enterprises. CAF Venturesome is a leader in new social investment market developments, including payments by results. CAF Venturesome manages the following four funds:

- The Community Land Trust Fund provides needed funding to community land trusts that offer affordable housing in areas that are often underserved by other low-cost housing providers. The financial capital is for both predevelopment and construction phases, filling gaps not covered by commercial development financing.
- The Innovation Fund is set up to test new and innovative financial mechanisms, such as loans or quasi-equity that are paid back by a fixed percentage of future revenues, or social impact bonds that provide up-front capital tied to the expected results of a specific social initiative.
- The Development Fund supports charities and social enterprises that are in a critical development stage and might need rescuing or transitioning to a new business model, or are in a period of high growth.
- The Social Impact Fund provides low-risk capital, such as bridge loans, for organizations that are waiting on funding from a donor and need to start spending on the project, or working capital that will be paid back over a longer period of time.

Loans provided by CAF Venturesome range from low risk to high risk. Bridge and working capital loans are lower risk, and are never more than five years (usually three years). However, higher-risk loans are used for consolidating NPOs or social enterprises that need to streamline processes or for growing those that are ready for rapid growth. Below are two organizations that CAF Venturesome finances: the first to provide a working capital loan and the second to enable the organization to consolidate its operations.

Case Study 8.4   MidiMusic—Working Capital Loan

MidiMusic[22] provides an excellent example of a small social enterprise that needs the type of loans offered by the Social Impact Fund—namely, bridge loans and working capital to carry them through a short-term cash-flow crunch. These cash flow problems are often created by delays in receiving promised revenue, sudden, unexpected changes in revenue or expenses, or by reimbursement-only grant awards that require significant up-front outlays of cash.

MidiMusic provides space and services to help children, adolescents, and young adults become inspired by music and the creative industries. It works with children and adolescents in struggling parts of London, offering music classes, after-school clubs, and counseling. Its target groups include the unemployed, children with learning disabilities or mental health issues, and foster children. The services are free or at an affordable cost, due in part to MidiMusic's partnerships with local governments that provide funding for the services via direct grants or fee-for-service arrangements. More than 50 percent of MidiMusic's revenue comes from local government funding.

When some governments had to cut back services in 2012, MidiMusic was able to diversify funding and continue programs, but faced challenges in maintaining adequate cash reserves. It approached CAF Venturesome for assistance. After assessing the organization's finances, assets, and strong social impact, Venturesome decided that MidiMusic would be able to diversify and expand its fundraising and repay the loan. The organization also owned a surplus asset (with a higher value than the loan) that it was selling, which could act as collateral.

Through the Social Impact Fund, the social enterprise borrowed GBP 36,000 for a three-year working capital loan. Interest rates are slightly higher than what a commercial bank would require of a business. At the time of writing this book, MidiMusic is growing and diversifying its fundraising base, and it is on target with its fundraising goals and current with its loan. For MidiMusic, the loan has allowed the organization to more comfortably pay staff and other expenses while diversifying its revenue model, and continue services that benefit thousands of children annually.

Case Study 8.5   KIDS—Consolidation Loan

In 2007, after nearly 40 years of pioneering services for thousands of children with disabilities, their families, and young people, KIDS[23] was in a very serious cash-flow bind. It no longer had sufficient cash reserves to fund operating losses, and its bank would not extend new credit. KIDS turned to Venturesome—perhaps the only financial institution that would entertain a loan—and within three weeks had secured this financing.

KIDS was established in 1970 by John Mulcahy, a teacher concerned about the development of a child with a disability in his class. The organization started providing trips for children with disabilities, and expanded into respite services, child care, transportation, playgrounds, and after-school care. KIDS provides services that directly meet their needs. Its programs reach thousands of children who are often excluded from the opportunities available to other children. KIDS' budget is about GBP 9 million, with nearly 90 percent of its revenue from local government payments for specific services.

When KIDS approached Venturesome, it did so with a well-thought-out turn-around plan created by a new CEO and a talented group of trustees. Venturesome staff analyzed the plan, saw that it had strong opportunities for growth, and increased impact despite a challenging economic environment. Based on this assessment, Venturesome extended an unsecured, 5-year GBP 250,000 loan to KIDS. KIDS used the infusion of capital to end unprofitable contracts, close some programs, diversify its revenue, and initiate new "profitable" contracts and programs. It improved its management of costs, and it exceeded its fundraising targets. At a time when many social service providers were shrinking, KIDS actually expanded the number of clients it served. KIDS was so successful that it repaid the loan after only two years.

Although this short-term loan was large and risky, Venturesome had done its financial due diligence. Perhaps most importantly, it was impressed with the CEO and the management team, and it fully understood the social impact KIDS would continue providing. "KIDS owes its existence to the support of Venturesome at a critical moment in the charity's development. After two years of stability, KIDS is now growing fast with an increase of income year on year of 18%. Without Venturesome none of this would have been possible," shares Kevin Williams, chief executive of KIDS.

What Is the Best Way to Provide Debt Financing to Social Enterprises?

These cases show that mixed funding packages disbursed over several years and linked to performance are best. In almost all of the NESsT cases, grant financing prepared the social enterprise for stepping up to the next level of funding, and in some cases a loan or equity investment was directly combined with a grant to make it more effective. Fruit of Care, for example, needed a small amount of equity to help set up a nonprofit limited company, as well as a grant investment for the initial institution building of the start-up company. With Kék Madár, a mixed package of a grant plus a loan with soft terms (but with collateral) spread the risk and enabled the social enterprise to grow significantly. Continuous capacity building, such as NESsT's support of Kék Madár, is the best way to accompany financial investments to lower risk and to build bankable and investable social enterprises.

In the case of Welldorf (see Table 8.2) and ADV, the loans guaranteed by NESsT helped them achieve their business goals, consolidate the social enterprise, and prepared them for exit from the portfolio. Welldorf used the loan for building inventory and staff, thus strengthening its operations and aiding cash flow to prepare for exit. ADV's guarantee, as shown, was for a bridge loan to help the social enterprise move forward with a project investment while waiting for donor funding. The social enterprise's track record and cash flow, demonstrated to TISE and NESsT that it would pay back the bridge funding.

Social enterprise debt financing often needs to carry soft conditions, which can mean lower interest rates, as was the case with the affordable technology portfolio in Peru, or individualized repayment schedules as was the case for the bridge loan offered to ADV. However, if the organization has strong revenue but needs financing to reorganize and improve efficiency, as was the case with KIDS, a higher interest rate appropriate to the risk still worked for both parties. MidiMusic had working capital needs typical of many businesses, but it could not obtain a commercial loan or line of credit. CAF analyzed its finances, and understood that it could pay back a loan.

Debt finance, however, is usually not appropriate for start-up social enterprises, unless the loan carries very soft conditions and the lender is very patient. Social enterprise start-up success statistics fit this general trend. Social costs of the enterprise, costs incurred by the social side of the business,[24] are an additional burden and need to be considered when analyzing loan readiness. Careful due diligence needs to be conducted and capacity building needs to be provided to prepare the enterprise for the loan. Many also take much longer than expected to go beyond the start-up phase, and therefore could potentially need additional debt financing. Adding grants to the financing package for start-up technology social enterprises in Peru was a key lesson in this respect.

Developing a social enterprise is new to many of the people who launch them. Organizations unaccustomed to operating a business are cautious when doing so for the first time, and are therefore reluctant to take on debt right away. Unless the social enterprise is a business that has mass-market potential, is replicating an already functioning model, or has relatively low social costs, it is not recommended to finance it with debt in the start-up phase.

These examples show, however, that social enterprises are becoming increasingly strategic with the use of various financing instruments, and that they understand they need to use scarce grant funding wisely, for development purposes. If they have stable cash inflow and a realistic growth plan, loans can be used to finance ongoing operations, human resource capacity, and new systems as well as longer-term investments in infrastructure.

Equity Investments in Social Enterprises

Equity investments continue to be the least common form of financing for social enterprises, not only in Central Europe and Latin America, but in more developed markets as well. According to the European Venture Philanthropy Association (EVPA),[25] grants are still the primary instruments used by its members.[26] In the 2011–2012 survey, the percentage of funding in the form of grants was 65 percent, although 10 percent less than the previous year.[27] And, "equity and quasi-equity represented 15 percent of the total funding, an increase from the 11 percent in 2010. Debt instruments have doubled their proportion of total funding since 2010, accounting for 18 percent in the last fiscal year," the report states, and adds that organizations are using a selection of financing instruments, "suggesting that tailored-financing is becoming a reality."[28] The impact-investing fund described in box 8.5 provides a good example of the use of equity to invest in social good.

Box 8.5   Social venture fund: Using equity for social ends

The investment approach of the Social Venture Fund, Germany,[29] is to use the fund's capital for the most effective social impact by focusing on financing the growth and expansion of already proven and successful social businesses. "The Social Venture Fund invests in social enterprises which have innovative and entrepreneurial driven solutions for urgent social and environmental challenges. The Fund provides support when it is not possible to acquire traditional sources of capital. Therefore, the Social Venture Fund closes a financing gap and acts as a catalyst for the comprehensive distribution of creative ideas and solutions. The Social Venture Fund's goal: preserve and recycle invested capital for future investments."

One of the investments made by the fund is VerbaVoice, a Munich-based social enterprise that invented a mobile solution to transfer voice into text for hearing-impaired people in almost real time. By selling their unique system for the visualization of speech, they help approximately 300,000 hearing-impaired people in Germany.

The Social Venture Fund invested EUR 500,000 in the market entry of VerbaVoice in Germany, while Bayern Kapital provided the remaining part (EUR 240,000) of the total estimated EUR 750,000 financing need.[30]

The research in Central Europe and Latin America confirmed the lack of equity funds that would invest in social enterprise. This may change rapidly in Europe in the coming years, given the recently approved European Social Entrepreneurship Fund label, which could help to leverage private and public capital toward social enterprise investment (see chap. 3 for more detail). Equity investment in its current form and in the current markets faces several challenges, which are widely discussed in social investment circles worldwide.

First, there is a lack of investable opportunities, partly due to the small pool of investees, and partly because of the mismatch in size of the investments and investees. A lot of investors are looking to place large amounts of capital that the majority of social enterprises are not yet ready to absorb. The "mid-market" investment offer is hard to find, so investors leave without investments, while social enterprises do not manage to raise the capital they need.

The large size of desired investments may be a result of high return expectations. Many equity investors are looking to place large amounts because this is how they expect to cover their costs and receive a financial return that they find acceptable. However, the majority of social enterprises, particularly early-stage ones, are not able to offer high financial returns even on smaller amounts of capital, so there is a mismatch in the market. Equity investments appear to work best in those cases where the investor's focus is primarily social return and where the financial return is of secondary consideration.

In addition to the size of the investment, the expectation of a financial return is also a challenge. Profitable social enterprises are often legally not allowed to pay dividends to their shareholders; financial return can only be realized upon selling one's shares. At the moment, there are no secondary markets presenting exit opportunities for current equity investors, since the industry is still very young. Equity investors are therefore cautious, waiting for the development of the market, which will present more options for successful exits. A third challenge for impact investors may be that because they are looking for a financial return, even if it is modest, they consider it another funder's job to make sure that the social enterprise operates successfully—in other words, they are not willing to pay for capacity building or start-up costs. Without these services, however, most social enterprises will fail during the early phase of development.

The legal and economic environment also presents major obstacles to equity investment in social enterprises. In some countries, it is simply forbidden, and other countries lack the sophisticated market mechanisms or frameworks that allow it to happen. The most developed social investment markets, the United Kingdom and the United States, are also facing challenges to social equity investments. Exit opportunities are limited and investments stay in portfolios for longer periods of time than expected. In the past decade, governments in these countries sometimes provided opportunities for exits on the part of investors. Government procurement contracts with social enterprises secured revenues that replaced investor capital. Today, this has become more difficult due to severe budget cuts. The use of grants and loans is still prevalent in many cases.

Finally, the nature of many social enterprises, namely their typical origin in the nonprofit sector and their subsequent nonprofit legal form (as a foundation or an association), prohibits them from legally taking equity. In order to overcome this barrier, social enterprises that are interested in long-term growth capital need to carefully design their structures and come up with investor profiles and criteria to accept external capital, but make sure that it is the right type of capital and has social return as its priority. This is an area where social enterprises need a great deal of capacity building and training, as they are moving in territory that is foreign to them. Investors, intermediaries, or government support agencies could all step in to provide the necessary support in this area.

The discussion of the above issues is very much on the agenda of the EU's Social Business Initiative, as its main goal is to attract private sector capital to the social enterprise sector. The European Commission recognized that the EU and its member states can do a lot in terms of regulations, incentives, and creating enabling environments in order to improve social enterprise access to investment capital. The plan of action described in chapter 3 provides more detail on policy initiatives that are being considered.

Conclusions and Recommendations

An analysis of the social investment landscape in Latin America and Central Europe, and NESsT's own lessons from its pilots and practical experience, confirm the findings of this book and demonstrate that grants, loans, and equity have very specific roles to play in the development of social enterprises and can be the key drivers to success.

The research conducted provides important evidence that demonstrates the appropriateness of providing debt finance because it helps finance the incubation and later expansion/scaling of social enterprises. Additionally, it leverages funds from third-party lenders to complement its grants. And finally, it helps professionalize social enterprises and makes them ready for debt financing and investment from the market.

Grants have a fundamental role in the mix of financing instruments. They provide critical funding for start-ups and new ideas: they pay for things nobody else is willing to pay for; they help build trust between social enterprises and donors; they help obtain proof of concept; they make other financing instruments more effective; and they can be extremely useful when testing new ideas once the social enterprise has consolidated. At the same time, grants do not always provide the level of influence to make necessary management and governance changes. Developing greater levels of influence, sometimes through equity investment, should also be considered.

The provision of debt financing and equity investments can be very challenging for several reasons. There are times when, in spite of meticulous planning, business cash flow does not allow for repayment according to schedule. Additionally, collateral or lack thereof to back up a loan can make the loan very difficult to execute. A more flexible approach is called for in such cases.

Determining the interest rate is not always easy and there needs to be a process that balances the need for soft conditions to prepare borrowers for debt, and to cover some of the costs of lending. The NESsT experience demonstrates that when done carefully, borrowers are able to repay softer term loans and transition to the commercial bank sector.

Equity financing is typically more time consuming than other methods and pushes investors to invest more resources in the social enterprise. Owners take on more responsibilities than a lender or grant donor does, who always remain on the outside of the social enterprise. Further, equity investors have more formal legal obligations and are responsible for the business operations of the company. Exiting from an equity investment in a social enterprise in Latin America or Central Europe currently can be very hard or impossible, due to the lack of buyers and a secondary market.

Given the identified challenges, there are a number of recommendations to investors and the social enterprise sector. Entrants to the field must realize that debt finance is needed at several stages of social enterprise development, starting with early incubation, for example. It follows that debt finance must be accompanied by capacity building in order to make the funding more effective. Those intermediaries and social enterprise support organizations play a pivotal role in matching supply with demand as well as in producing investment-ready social enterprises for interested lenders and investors. Naturally, such intermediaries need funds and resources to operate and further develop their investment-readiness programs.

The investment-readiness stage is critical, and lenders and investors should consider accompanying their financial investment with the direct provision of capacity support to the social enterprise, or providing that capacity support through an intermediary. Investment-ready social enterprises continue to need grant support for development purposes. And overall, expectations of financial return need to be reconsidered; lenders and investors in social enterprises must be ready to accept realistic (lower) returns in exchange for high social impact.

Furthermore, there are several gap areas for social enterprise incubators and intermediaries to fill. Smaller- and medium-sized social enterprises without a credit history but with repayment capacity could develop a track record through intermediaries by experimenting with loans when appropriate. Setting up a loan fund and continual lending would make a lot of sense for such first loans. Such a loan fund could offer products to social enterprises working in areas that banks are less likely to support, for example, human rights, democracy building, or environmental issues.

Additionally, innovative start-up social enterprises present interesting opportunities for incubators and intermediaries. They require much softer terms than what banks are willing to offer. They are not targeted by alternative financing entities, which actually charge higher interest rates and tend to focus on more traditional social issues, such as education, health, and housing. The new types of social enterprises could use loan guarantees, which could help them obtain debt finance from mainstream institutions. Finally, incubators in the field must realize that there exist unexplored opportunities to partner with funds and investment programs to help prepare social enterprises for alternative financing.

9

EARLY-STAGE IMPACT INVESTING IN LATIN AMERICA*

INTRODUCTION

Early-stage impact investors—those investing at the USD 250,000–500,000 levels during the start-up and early stage of business development—recognize the higher risks that usually accompany early investments in unproven markets. Unlike pioneer donors mentioned in chapter 7 and social investors in chapter 8, impact investments must always generate a financial return, and usually this return must come first. But, like them, they are a bit more patient than purely commercial investors, and are willing to provide longer financing and in some cases, even provide capacity support.

In this chapter, we share observations from discussions with 17 early-stage impact investors about their experiences of doing business in Latin America: their impediments, challenges, successes, and future plans. Of the 17 investors interviewed, 5 made investments within a single country and 12 invested in multiple countries. Early-stage impact investors operating in the region are relatively few. Those that do exist have just recently set up their funds, are starting their due diligence process, and/or have recently started making investments—early-stage impact investing in Latin America is just beginning.

The research also shows the critical role of incubators and accelerators in supporting social enterprises, recognizes some of the creative new ways impact investors are partnering with incubators, describes some of the new entrants to early-stage investment, and documents how impact investors are utilizing new investment vehicles to support social enterprises. The research has identified some of the political and legal challenges that this new class of investor faces, which builds a compelling argument for guides that will help investors to navigate the challenging tax, legal, and regulatory environments that they might come across throughout Latin America.

METHODOLOGY

The research process began with a list of 166 known active impact investors globally that are deploying capital to social enterprises. This list was compiled from NESsT's own contacts, third-party publications, desk research, and referrals. These investors were screened to determine what stage they participate in (start-up and early-stage enterprises), the size of their investments (USD 500,000 or less), and their locations (operating in one or more Latin American country). Following this screening, 34 investors were selected for further research. Seventeen of these were selected for in-depth research and interviews. Of these 17, a few operated outside of the investment size constraint, but after conducting interviews, NESsT ascertained a better understanding of the support ecosystem. Finally, this chapter includes four case studies that illustrate financial instrument innovation, policy challenges, capacity building, and pipeline issues.

LATIN AMERICA BUSINESS AND IMPACT CLIMATE— GROWTH BUT NOT WITHOUT CHALLENGES

Latin America presents an interesting environment for impact investors. From an investment perspective, Latin American economies have grown at a much healthier pace than the sluggish economies of the United States and Europe. According to the Economic Commission for Latin America and the Caribbean, Latin America grew by 5.9 percent in 2010, 4.3 percent in 2011, and is forecasted to grow at a rate of 3.7 percent in 2012.[1]

Achieving social impact requires impact investment and private sector solutions. Decades of dictatorships have left the region with a weakened civil society, wide disparities in wealth and income, and a lagging educational system. In fact, the education sector is both an opportunity and an impediment to success for impact investors. The Achilles' heels of most Latin American countries have been their education systems, which are consistently ranked as mediocre to very poor compared to the rest of the world in studies produced by groups like the World Economic Forum.[2] In studies ranking the top universities in the world, such as the British *Times* and *US News & World Report*, Latin America does not have universities ranking in the top hundred. This gap in higher education leads to a chasm in innovation: "When it comes to scientific research, U.S. inventors—many of them from major universities—register 192,000 patents a year, while all 33 Latin American and Caribbean countries together register only 21,000, according to the Ibero-American Network of Science and Technology Indicators, known by its Spanish acronym Ricyt."[3]

Despite the many social problems in the region and the need to strengthen civil society, many international aid organizations have moved away from Latin America due to greater needs in Africa or Asia, or due to constrained budgets. As an example, United States Agency for International Development (USAID), one of the largest foreign aid organizations, has exited both Panama and Costa Rica, and is in the process of exiting Brazil. Unlike in the United States, people in Latin American countries do not share a culture of giving to philanthropic endeavors. Some see impact investment as a way to sustainably strengthen civil society organizations (CSOs).

One potential obstacle for impact investors is the divided nature of the region. Instead of one continuous market like the United States, the European Union (EU), or India, Latin America is comprised of disunited countries, which all have unique policy and cultural environments. Compounding these factors is political risk—while democracy and transparency in government has vastly improved in recent decades, political unrest and shifts in government policies can negatively impact the climate for investment.

The interviews that were conducted illustrate the opportunities and challenges impact investors see in the region. Observations made by Fondo de Inversión Social (FIS) indicate that the private sector needs to fill the void of civil society and charitable organizations in Chile, for example. Yet investors, such as Pomona Impact, operate with a degree of hesitation given political risks observed over the last few decades in Central America and Ecuador. Corruption, or in some cases favoritism, create real barriers to entry that are often difficult to mitigate. Small Enterprise Assistance Funds (SEAF),[4] an investment management group that provides growth capital and business assistance to small and medium enterprises (SMEs) in emerging and transition markets, list macroeconomic conditions such as political instability and exchange rate volatility as the greatest challenge to successfully investing capital in early and growth-stage SMEs.

Historically Not a Priority Region—Currently Gaining Traction

For most of the international impact investors who focus on more than one continent, Latin America has not been a top priority. However, all of the investors interviewed for the research cited plans to increase their presence in the region over the next three years. Investors generally cited India as a top priority, then Africa, with Latin America as the third priority. KL Felicitas Foundation prioritized India because despite some antiquated policies, the country has a culture of entrepreneurship, with a developed social enterprise sector and huge potential to scale. Indeed, other well-known early-stage impact investors not approached for the research also elect to focus on India and Africa. First Light Ventures (the seed fund of Gray Ghost Ventures) is "doubling down" on India while the Unitas Impact Fund focuses on livelihoods businesses in Asia and Africa.

Invested Development noted interest in India despite the fact that impact investment in India has a lot of players, and is also interested in the entrepreneurial activity in Nairobi. The organization cited Latin America as a third priority after India and East Africa, though it anticipated making more investments in the region over the next three to five years. Accion Venture Labs mentioned India and East Africa as places where radically innovative social enterprise ideas emerge. They consider these areas "low hanging fruit," but still expect 20 percent of their investments to be invested in Latin America in the future. Eleos Foundation, for example, has commercial investments in India (E Health Point Services), Kenya (Sanergy), and Liberia (Liberty and Justice) and is now actively pursuing investments in Latin America.

Toniic, a global network that supports impact investors, cited India and North America as the most popular locations for deals, followed by Latin America, then Sub-Saharan Africa, and finally, Asia/North Africa. The organization has facilitated 23 early-stage impact-investment deals in total, with roughly 20 percent of its overall investment in Latin America. In addition, Toniic has plans underway to become more active in Mexico, Brazil, and Colombia, countries that incidentally have regulatory frameworks that are evolving to be friendlier toward impact investment for social enterprises.

Acumen Fund is now in the process of fundraising for investments in Peru and Colombia. The organization sees the countries as a natural fit to its expansion criteria and as having potential for a pipeline of investable social enterprises, given the mix of entrepreneurship, human talent, and significant inequality. The Global Business Fund recently opened a regional office in Lima.

Actors in the support environment for social enterprises (foundations, governments, development agencies, etc.) can speed up and stimulate Latin American social enterprise investment with incentives. Some examples of such incentives may include loan guarantees for Latin America focused portfolios, sponsorship of General Partner (GP) or portfolio manager salaries in various Latin American countries, or sponsoring/offsetting technical assistance costs for new funds' portfolios.

EXITS AND CAPITAL MARKETS

Among the top concerns for impact investors in Latin America is how an investor can exit. An exit occurs when investors receive the invested capital plus interest or profit through an event such as a sale or public offering of shares on an exchange. Investors across the board point to the relatively less-developed capital markets in Latin America compared to those in the United States as limiting exit options. For the most part, an exit in Latin America would consist of a buyout by a larger corporation, a buyout by the social enterprise management, or a successful repayment of loan obligations. Daniel Izzo of Vox Capital envisions that future exits for Vox will take the form of a strategic buyout by a larger corporation, but openly expressed concerns for how the mission of a social enterprise could be protected in such a case.

Tyler Gage, the president of Runa, a social enterprise that sells Ecuadorian guayusa teas and in the process employs and provides livelihoods for indigenous farmers in the Amazon,[5] shared concerns about preserving the social mission of Runa while accepting investment to scale. This concern led him to explore many different sources of funding. In 2012, Runa received a USD 500,000 equity investment[6] from the CreEcuador fund (an initiative of the Ecuadorian government):

> The Build Ecuador Fund (CreEcuador) plans to cash out of its investment in Runa in roughly six years, in order to use its earnings to make additional investments in sustainable businesses. However, rather than selling shares to a private investor, the Fund's vision is to sell shares to Runa's employees and the farmers Runa supports.

Runa will work to design programs for farmers and employees to buy shares back from the government, and thereby give farmers more direct investment in Runa's success.[7]

Monitoring cases like Runa over the next several years to document and highlight progress on exits could be crucial to the success of the sector in the region. Bringing attention to social enterprise buyback exits, follow-on investments, and acquisitions can potentially draw more investors to consider social enterprises in Latin America. Furthermore, documenting successes is especially important since most early-stage funds operating in the region are relatively new. The majority of funds interviewed for the research have small and growing portfolios, and some are still doing due diligence on their first deals. In a way, it is too early to evaluate the track record of impact investing in Latin America, and case studies will help to assess successes down the road.

Investors are using traditional investment vehicles such as debt and equity, as well as hybrids such as mezzanine debt. The latter option, specifically convertible debt, the use of debt that is potentially converted into equity upon repayment, is the most frequent option with early-stage social enterprises in Latin America.[8] Enterprises at this stage tend not only to have the cash flows to service traditional debt, but also have financing needs that are too small to permit the efforts and transaction costs that come with an equity investment. In addition, several impact investors cited the lack of exit opportunities as a factor in preferring convertible debt over equity.

Investors that represent foundations or nonprofits tend to be more flexible in pursuing the most appropriate vehicle to support the entrepreneur. These investors include Village Capital, KL Felicitas, LGT Venture Philanthropy (LGTVP), Eleos Foundation, and Grassroots Business Fund. Village Capital cited interest in an entrepreneur-friendly alternative to convertible debt, such as a revenue-sharing agreement. LGTVP uses equity, convertible debt, loans, and grants. The organization has also considered some sort of revenue participation and grant making equity—a form of investment that provides investors the right to convert a grant into equity to benefit from the potential upside of a sale or liquidity event.

Investors expressed a range of views on exits and the use of debt and equity. Exits can occur by the entrepreneur or social enterprise repurchasing the shares, or through a merger or acquisition by another company. New Ventures/Adobe Capital acknowledges that due to the lack of exit opportunities in Mexico, for example, utilizing pure equity investment would not be a suitable strategy; rather they consider mezzanine or convertible debt to be appropriate vehicles for social enterprise investment. Indeed, this observation is indicative of a growing trend— Pomona Impact is increasingly considering the use of mezzanine debt because it would not require a liquidity event. LGTVP pursues nonfinancial exits (i.e., where sustainability of the organization is the primary intent, often achieved by providing grant funding) along with financial exits. Because they support organizations with a range of financial instruments, they cited two exits where the grantee organizations in Latin America had become self-sustainable. These organizations were Escuela Nueva in Colombia and Fundação Pro-Cerrado in Brazil. The Central American Renewable Energy and Cleaner Production Facility (CAREC), a venture capital financing facility developed by E+Co, also has not used equity investments in their operations in Central America, citing a lack of exit potential. The fund had only reported using mezzanine debt, preferred stock, or traditional debt investments.

Grass Roots Business Fund also cited a preference for quasi-equity type vehicles that carry the benefits of debt and equity. The organization had one successful loan exit in Bolivia from the Fundación Innovación en Empresariado Social (IES Foundation), a Bolivian development institution that uses investment capital and value-added services to assist SMEs in Bolivia improve their sustainability and social impact. Inversor of Colombia invests primarily with equity, and envisions that exits will take the form of management buyouts (MBOs). They do not anticipate private equity buyout potential as that sector is still nascent in Colombia. Equitas Ventures of Argentina exited renewable energy social enterprise Agarrá la Palá (ALP) Group (USD 100,000 invested) through a sale with a 75 percent return.[9] Two of their investment loans are partially amortized—healthcare social enterprise Sistema SER (USD 40,000 invested) and inclusive enterprise RedActivos (USD 80,000 invested—80% amortized). Alternatively, SEAF sees exit opportunities in the form of a MBO or a strategic buyout by another firm. The organization has experienced four exits in Latin America to date: three in Peru and one in Colombia.

Among the most interesting and new innovations in social enterprise investment vehicles is Invested Development's efforts to pilot an impact investment factoring fund (see case study 9.1 on Invested Development).[10] Some of these investment vehicle innovations circumvent the exit dilemma entirely, offering a different approach from the traditional venture capital model.

At this point, little is known or documented on the success/failure of alternative investment vehicles for impact investors in Latin America. Monitoring, documenting, and disseminating information on the success of these alternative vehicles would inform investors and provide confidence in the use of the most successful ones, potentially attracting new investors to the region.

INCUBATORS AND ACCELERATORS—WIDENING THE PIPELINE FOR IMPACT INVESTORS

Research indicates a near unanimous sentiment that incubators and accelerators are a potential source of investment deals. Specific incubators and accelerators listed by investors as potential sources for deals include Agora Partnerships, New Ventures, Artemisia, NESsT, Ashoka, Technoserve, the Global Social Benefit Incubator (GSBI), and Wayra (mobile tech incubator sponsored by Telefonica). A few of the incubators/accelerators were universally recognized in interviews and oversubscribed in terms of investor interest. Arguably, these incubators and accelerators alone cannot deliver the pipeline for a region with close to 600 million people, and impact investors need a larger network of social enterprise incubators/accelerators.

Interestingly, there appears to be a blurring of lines between incubators/ accelerators and impact investors. New Ventures and NESsT are two incubators/ accelerators that are designing or launching their own impact-investing funds; Vox Capital is an impact-investing fund that launched Vox Labs, a fund intended for earlier stage projects. A condition for investment from Vox Labs is the participation in an accelerator program that will prepare the enterprise for a larger investment. This development demonstrates the need both incubator operators and investors see to increase technical assistance and capital to support early-stage social enterprises.

Outside of the incubators and accelerators, investors also cited their networks, entrepreneurs, industry events (like SOCAP and the Latin American Impact Investing Forum),[11] and various business-plan competitions for sourcing deals. Surprisingly, only three investors mentioned universities in any capacity, with two referring to them specifically as a potential source for impact investments. And as discussed in chapter 4, universities are already demonstrating that they can be a pipeline for impact investors through social labs, on-site incubators, as well as by fostering the educational foundation for entrepreneurs to build businesses, manage them, and prepare them for investment vehicles.

Investors build their pipeline of social enterprises in a number of ways. Pomona Impact cited Agora Partnerships as a source of two investments. The fund makes investments of USD 50,000–250,000, has made four investments so far, and has two to four investments in the pipeline. Additionally, Village Capital (see case study 9.3 on Village Capital) seeks both a local accelerator partner and a local capital partner. In 2011, the organization initiated a partnership with Artemisia that resulted in two investments, and explored partnerships with both Agora and New Ventures Mexico. Village Capital is also considering expansion plans in Mexico and Colombia.

Well-developed networks—relationships with entrepreneurs, events, incubators, and accelerators—are sometimes a preferred vehicle (to unsolicited requests) for finding business opportunities, as Vox Capital observes. Vox cofounder and general partner Daniel Izzo indicated that the organization has employees dedicated entirely to deal with sourcing and portfolio development. The organization looks to incubators from most Brazilian universities for technology- or intellectual property–related businesses, while it looks to accelerators for more developed businesses.

Invested Development cited the social enterprise investment network Toniic, business-plan competitions (both industry focused and university), and incubators as potential sources for deals. Invested Development plays an active role at events, in social networks, and at business-plan competitions. The organization's staffs offer their time as contest judges because they find that often the best enterprises don't necessarily rank first. Finally, they accept applications over-the-transom through Gust, and receive applications globally on a regular basis. LGTVP listed several incubators/accelerators, including New Ventures, Agora, Ashoka, and NESsT, as potential sources for investment as well as relationships with organizations such as IDB, Avina, and BiD. LGTVP also finds events like SOCAP and Latin American Impact Investing Forum as efficient opportunities to identify deals (1–3 investments a year). LGTVP also listed the Internet, volunteers, and LGT iCats Fellows as additional sources.

Accion Labs relies heavily on incubators for their India and East Africa work and anticipates that in order to be successful in Latin America it will have to find the right incubators there as well. In addition, the organization cited the potential for it to add value and later-stage investors can be a source of follow-on investment. Eleos Foundation seeks to forge strategic deal-flow partnerships with business-plan competitions, investor networks, incubators, and accelerator programs that position promising entrepreneurs for capital investment. At the time of this research, Eleos was actively searching for the right incubator/accelerator to partner with in Latin America. To that end, Eleos explored relationship building with ten incubators in 2012.

FIS discussed a gap in the early-stage pipeline in Chile (see table 9.4, case study on FIS). The organization works with incubator Simone de Cirene and is actively networking in Chile through formal relationships with organizations like Avina, as well as informal relationships with groups like Sistema B (Latin American version of B Corp)[12] and Fondo de Solidaridad e Inversión Social (FOSIS), a Chilean government agency aimed at poverty reduction (where FIS fund manager María José Montero participates on the advisory board). Montero also participates as a judge in various business-plan competitions. Additionally, Adobe Capital, after a 2012 launch in Mexico, plans to utilize the accelerator New Ventures for sourcing investments. The fund has raised USD 20 million to date and intends to invest in 10–12 social enterprises. New Ventures worked with over two hundred businesses and received over five hundred applicants in 2011. New Ventures also manages a directory called the Green Pages, a free listing for three-thousand-plus businesses in Mexico. Adobe anticipates a solid pipeline from the New Ventures' acceleration activities and the Green Pages. Further, Inversor of Colombia looks to make investments in social enterprises of USD 500,000–1.5 million. The organization lists several main sources for their pipeline: networking (mainly through founding members of the organization), working with corporations (to support low-income producers linked to their supply chains), and deals with organizations/incubators that are providing capacity support for entrepreneurs (like New Ventures Colombia, Endeavor, chambers of commerce, and social investment banks).

As discussed in chapter 4, not all incubators and accelerators have sustainable business models or sustainable access to funds. Supporting the work of these organizations to expand and multiply, as well as facilitating the emergence of new incubators focused on social enterprise, are ways to improve the entire ecosystem. This could provide more investable social enterprises and improve their quality, improve the performance of funds (which would have a larger pipeline to choose from), and finally, attract new investment due to the better performance of the enterprises and funds.

BUILDING CAPACITY

Investors have varying strategies for developing the capacities of the social enterprises they intend to help scale. Some look to incubators/accelerators, while others build skills internally through participation in strategic planning and by tapping their organization's networks.

Charly Kleissner, cofounder of KL Felicitas Foundation, Toniic, and Dasra Social Impact, said that social enterprises in emerging market countries need high levels of capacity building, more so than typical businesses, because they lack the formal training that is taken for granted in developed countries. In addition, Kleissner mentioned that since international investors lack proximity to their investments, it is important for the organization to have a local support network. In his view, most venture capital fund managers are geographically close to their investments so they can support them more effectively and monitor their performance. Indeed, it is NESsT's experience that private equity in Latin America is now restructuring its model to be more local and less dependent on portfolio/deal teams based in the United States. The trend is for private equity funds to set up offices directly in the region, as navigating the local markets (both legally and culturally) requires local presence. This also helps with deal sourcing. International impact investors should monitor the development of this localization of private equity in Latin America and consider whether it may be applicable to their future success in the region.

LGTVP cited a lack of financial and management acumen as one of the greatest challenges to scaling social enterprises. LGTVP finds that many of the enterprises are young and growing, yet lack management experience and need capacity building. LGTVP builds capacity in their portfolio investments through a hands-on approach that provides four hours a week with the social enterprise. This is possible through their iCats Program, which sends midcareer professionals to work for one year with an organization. The program currently has 30 iCat fellows, with aims of accommodating 50. Finally, over the years the organization has developed its own risk assessment, capacity, and performance measurement tools to help guide organizations.

As mentioned above, an additional trend has been the symbiotic development of some incubators/accelerators and funds. In some cases the incubator/accelerator is subsidizing the fund by absorbing the costs of the due diligence or technical assistance. For example, the partnership between New Ventures and Adobe Capital in Mexico will allow Adobe to benefit greatly from the network New Ventures offers, while developing the pipeline to grow the social enterprise industry in Mexico with the Latin American Impact Investing Forum. Additionally, Grassroots Business Fund is an organization that consists of a nonprofit and a for-profit investment fund. The nonprofit investment fund incurs most of the expenses associated with the investment sourcing and technical assistance provided to the enterprises. Currently, they have a USD 45–50 million investment fund, and an additional technical assistance fund of USD 10–12 million. The technical assistance is provided for by grants, and is funded mostly by bilateral institutions and foundations.

An alternative approach is exemplified by Vox Capital/Vox Labs (see case study 9.2 on Vox Capital). Vox provides active support and mentorship to its portfolio companies by taking a board seat in the social enterprise and participating in monthly planning meetings. Vox Capital divides its support for portfolio enterprises into three main areas: governance, strategic planning, and networking. Further, Village Capital has developed an innovative methodology for delivering capital to social enterprises that minimizes transaction costs and relies on finding strong incubator/accelerator partners. The organization partners with a local incubator/accelerator organization to execute an investment-ready training cohort for impact entrepreneurs (see case study 9.3 on Village Capital). The cohort methodology employed by Village Capital democratizes the delivery of investment capital as cohort participants determine among themselves the recipients of capital. The methodology relies heavily on strong relationships with incubator/accelerators like Artemisia.

Successful models of impact investors and incubators collaborating to provide early-stage capacity support should be documented and disseminated widely. These models demonstrate how both the investors and incubators' incentives can be aligned to share the costs and benefits of early-stage social enterprise development. Furthermore, one option for further strengthening capacity support in Latin America could be to help incubators and accelerators with a track record of successful social enterprise development set up early-stage impact-investing funds.

POLICY ENVIRONMENT FOR LATIN AMERICAN IMPACT INVESTING

Favorable Policy

Investment in social enterprises is beginning to occur across Latin America. However, at present there are only a few countries, such as Mexico, Brazil, and Chile, with policies that support the development of the sector (albeit in some cases indirectly). If investors interviewed for this research were benefiting from government policy, it was often only because of favorable policies enacted to support venture capital and private sector development. Adobe Capital and New Ventures reported government support as essential to the development of their impact-investment projects. They reference the Mexican government's Fondo PyME that has invested USD 8 billion in support of economic development, including support for accelerators and funds (in the form of investments or loan guarantees). Policy changes in Mexico have permitted a wide range of funds to take on pension fund investment, increasing the flow of capital to investment funds (not just those focused on social enterprise). Adobe lists pension funds, other investment funds, and family offices as investors, in addition to the Mexican government. Additionally, Inversor reported investment in their fund by the Colombian government, combined with private sector capital from institutions like JP Morgan, private offices, and foundations such as Halloran Philanthropies.

FIS mentioned that CORFO (the Chilean agency for the promotion of investment in innovation and entrepreneurship) was interested in investing in the FIS fund. FIS focuses on growth-stage enterprises, and although CORFO does invest in growth stage, it did not do so in this case. CORFO's policies support the growth of risk capital funds investing in traditional enterprises (not social enterprises, although this is changing, as discussed in chap. 7). Two specific initiatives are the F2 and F3 initiatives that match capital raised by fund managers two to one and three to one, respectively. The three to one match is reserved for projects deemed innovative by CORFO. According to research funded by the Kauffman Foundation on Chile and CORFO, "between 2006 and 2010 sixteen new funds were approved for additional total commitment of over USD 200 million. Of these, two funds were specifically focused in startups."[13]

The hand of the government can be witnessed in other cases as well. Vox Capital reported Brazilian government involvement in venture capital projects, but Vox itself has not received government support. The fund has one main partner and only recently has solicited additional investment. Additionally, as referenced earlier, the Ecuadorian government has become involved in investing in social enterprises with the CreEcuador[14] initiative. According to B Corp, "the fund is part of President Rafael Correa's vision for a Citizen Revolution (*La Revolución Ciudadana*)—Ecuador's dual mission of building a robust economy that competes in global capital markets, while also providing socialist-type government programs to support its citizens."[15]

The above examples demonstrate that government programs, laws, and regulations can play a significant role in catalyzing resources for impact investing in Latin America. Governments can play an important role in complementing impact-investing capital from the United States and Europe directed at the region. Successful case studies of government programs promoting impact investing in Mexico, Ecuador, and other Latin American countries should be publicized across the region to impact public policies and increase the enabling environment for impact investing.

Unfavorable Policies, High Transaction Costs

Although there are some pioneering efforts to create a more favorable environment for impact investing, policies continue to be an impediment. Some investors cited examples where policy sometimes worked in direct opposition to their objectives, or presented clear barriers to entry. Vox capital did indirectly benefit from government policy through one of its investments in affordable housing.[16] Village Capital experienced difficulties with regulations and taxes on foreign direct investment in Brazil. Vox Capital also experienced the same difficulties as Village Capital with regard to foreign direct investment in Brazil. To avoid paying excess taxes and bank fees with each foreign investment, Vox Capital set up a limited liability company (LLC) in the United States (Florida) that pools foreign investors to minimize transaction costs. Daniel Izzo of Vox Capital called the laws requiring investors to have a Brazilian bank representative "nonsensical" (see case study 9.2 on Vox Capital).

E+Co partner CAREC reported that it was difficult to establish a fund in Central American countries. They reported finding that an investment fund is often not a recognized structure in Central America and that policy is more oriented toward traditional banking. As a result and based on the suggestion of advisors, CAREC established a fund in the Cayman Islands, which has a large number of international funds, combined with legal support for investment funds.

LGTVP has had the benefit of being able to leverage LGT group's legal resources in several different countries. Still, the organization was presented, oddly, with the challenge of Colombian policy preventing it from investing in the form of a grant. Overcoming this challenge was difficult and involved working with many different levels of government. Like CAREC, LGTVP is a fund registered overseas, in Luxembourg as a Société d'Investissement à Capital Variable-Social Investment Fund (SICAV-SIF),[17] due to the country's investor friendly policies. Some LGTVP clients invest up to USD 5 million through this vehicle.

Influencing Investment—Investor Guides

One way to support impact investors with their efforts in Latin America is to create comprehensive "investment guides" for each country. These guides could advise potential investors on the different regulatory pitfalls or policy benefits that stem from investment activity in a particular country. Specific country investment guides could focus on topics such as tax environments, benefits and drawbacks of incorporating a fund, term sheet templates, legal guides, and resources. Additionally, guides could create benchmarks for valuating social enterprises in a particular country and the region. Research indicates that several investors, including Village Capital and LGTVP, possess a strong interest in this type of resource.

Latin American Impact-Investment Fund Managers—A New Class

As documented in the research publication by Monitor Institute and Acumen Fund entitled, "From Blueprint to Scale," a primary concern of many impact-investment managers is a "lack of (a) track record of successful investments."[18] This concern was not lost on the investors surveyed and many cited the risks associated with operating at the early stage. Many of the investors believe deeply in the potential for social enterprise and have staked their careers on the industry. FIS pointed out that, as the first impact fund in Chile, the greatest challenge is the need for a strong portfolio of social enterprises to prove the concept. In their view, investors vote with their dollars, and if they do not see potential for return, they may be hesitant to invest in the future. Vox Capital added that its greatest challenge is also developing Vox Capital as a success story and building a track record of success. Along the same lines, Village Capital's ultimate goal is to continue to invest in early-stage social enterprises, and build the track record and reputation needed to raise a for-profit fund targeted at early-stage social enterprises.

Case Study 9.1   Invested Development

Background
Invested Development is an impact-investment firm that invests in seed-stage, for-profit social enterprises with innovative solutions to poverty in mobile

Table 9.1   The Impact Factoring Fund: Repurposing old financial instruments for impact-investment innovation

Structure	Limited partnership
Investment Sizes	Equity from USD 100,000 to USD 1 million
Industry	Mobile technology for base of the pyramid (BoP)[a]
Geographies	Emerging markets—including East Africa, India, and Latin America

Note: [a]The World Resources Institute defines BoP as those with annual incomes below USD 3,000 in local purchasing power—approximately 4 billion people who live in relative poverty. Their incomes in current US dollars are less than USD 3.35 a day in Brazil, USD 2.11 in China, USD 1.89 in Ghana, and USD 1.56 in India. "The Next 4 Billion: Market Size and Business Strategy at the Base of the Pyramid," Executive Summary, World Resources Institute, http://www.wri.org/publication/content/7790.

technology and alternative energy (see table 9.1). The technologies they invest in must create an impact for the underserved in emerging markets, with a particular focus on Africa, India, and Latin America.[19]

One portfolio company of Invested Development is Frogtek, a for-profit social venture dedicated to creating business tools for microentrepreneurs in emerging markets. Frogtek develops software applications for small shops, restaurants, and other microretailers that can be run on mobile devices and are designed specifically for customers at the base of the pyramid. The Frogtek team is 25 people across Mexico, Spain, and Colombia.[20]

The Portfolio Company

Frogtek's innovative products, the Tiendatek Smartphone and the Tiendatek Tablet enable "mom-and-pop *tiendas*" or microretailers in Mexico and Colombia to significantly increase their incomes.[21] Before Frogtek, shop owners were left to manage inventory and expenses on paper, a solution that does not serve to optimize profits. Frogtek products allow mom-and-pop shops to have a point-of-sale tool to help them manage the business.

The Challenge

While Frogtek's products are truly innovative and serve financially underserved communities, they are typically out of the price range for most retailers, requiring that Frogtek extend credit for up to two years of financing. The delayed nature of payment for Tiendatek constrains the growth of the firm by shortening the sales cycle and tying up cash during a high-growth phase for the company. Invested Development witnessed this constraint to growth in different companies throughout their portfolio—with Frogtek and a renewable energy company offering solar solutions to customers off the grid in East Africa. They found that their portfolio companies operate in markets lacking consumer-financing solutions.

The Solution

In May of 2012, the firm launched "the Impact Factoring Fund." Factoring is a financial vehicle in which investors purchase the receivables of a business at a discount, absorbing the receivable. The concept of factoring is not a new idea, and has been used for centuries. However, this application to support social enterprise is a new concept. With the Impact Factoring Fund, Invested Development is piloting an approach that targets entrepreneurs for whom lack of financing is an impediment to rapidly growing the business, such as Frogtek. Invested Development sees the Impact Factoring Fund as a way to deliver working capital to businesses in their portfolio without follow-on investment and, if successful, the concept can serve as a way to involve other impact investors and has potential to exist outside of the Invested Development portfolio.

Case Study 9.2   Vox Capital, Vox Labs

Background

Vox Capital is a venture capital fund that helps reduce poverty by investing in innovative, high-potential companies serving low-income populations (see table 9.2).[22] Vox Capital injects capital and provides strategic advice and management support to leverage the financial results and social impact of these businesses.

Through its portfolio, Vox Capital aims to help create a Brazilian cluster of profitable, large-scale businesses with social impact, capable of attracting talent, innovation, and domestic and international participation. As a player in this cluster, Vox Capital intends to improve the lives of millions of low-income individuals in Brazil.

Vox Capital has made four equity investments and five convertible debt investments through Vox Labs.

The Challenge/Opportunity

Vox Capital is actively involved and "hands-on" in developing its pipeline of deals and mentoring the portfolio. Through its work, Vox Capital observed a gap in the social enterprise ecosystem in Brazil. Specifically, there was no investment support for early-stage social enterprises. Most likely, early-stage social enterprises carried a perceived risk with traditional private equity investors, and as a result of this perceived risk, there were no competing players emerging and responding to these opportunities. Vox Capital not only viewed this gap as a threat to its success and future pipeline of deals, but it also saw the gap as an opportunity for financial products.

Table 9.2 Vox Labs: Investing at the early stage, utilizing accelerators

Structure	Limited partnership (Brazil), LLC (US)
Investment Sizes	USD 1 million equity (Vox Capital) and USD 100,000 convertible debt (Vox Labs)
Industry	Businesses serving the BoP
Geographies	Brazil—all regions

The Solution
The solution to address this critical early stage need was Vox Labs. Vox Labs offers convertible debt investments to early-stage businesses, contingent upon their participation in a local accelerator like Artemisia. This will prepare them to be ready to assume larger equity investment from Vox Capital.

The Results
Vox Labs has now made convertible debt investments in three companies: CDI Lan, Banco Pérola, and Saútil. CDI Lan leverages a network of over 4,800 Internet cafés to offer BoP solutions in financial services and e-learning. Banco Pérola is a microcredit organization offering credit to young entrepreneurs in regions where financial services are scarce. Finally, Saútil provides free web-based health care information for the BoP in Brazil. In the first three months of operation, Saútil reached 60,000 users, USD 100,000 in advertising contracts, with 90 percent of users living below the poverty line.

Since the Vox Labs program began in Q4 2011, no Vox Labs company has received follow-on investment till the time of the research. In 2012, the advisory board and the investment committee for Vox approved an equity investment in Saútil, the first company supported through the Vox Labs program. Saútil will receive an equity investment via a hybrid model that includes convertible debt and support from the accelerator Artemisia.

Case Study 9.3   Village Capital

Background
Village Capital uses the power of peer support to build social enterprises that change the world. Inspired by the concept of the "village bank" in microfinance and peer support groups such as Young Presidents' Organization (YPO) and Entrepreneurs Organization (EO), Village Capital puts the hard tasks of building companies—criticism, strategy, feedback, and legwork—in the hands of entrepreneurs themselves (see table 9.3).[23] Village Capital organizes cohorts worldwide and runs education programs focused on intensive peer review. At the end, entrepreneurs assess one another, and do so in a collegial way. Entrepreneurs even sit in the investor's seat: the top ranked can receive precommitted capital from partner investors. In Village Capital programs, entrepreneurs leverage help from

Table 9.3   Legal and regulatory challenges: Brazil

Structure	Nonprofit donor advised fund
Investment Sizes	Convertible debt USD 75,000
Industry	Mobile technology for BoP
Geographies	Global—Brazil, China, India, United States, United Kingdom, Africa, and more

their peers—individuals rooted in practical experience—and gain a network of like-minded leaders to reach scale.

Village Capital's innovative model of democratizing early-stage impact investment has displayed impressive results. While no Village Capital cohort participants received institutional capital prior to the program, many have graduated and, after receiving Village Capital funding, grown to take on larger investments from well-known social enterprise investors like Calvert Foundation, Investors' Circle, Khosola Ventures, Blue Orchard, Unitas Capital, and others.

Brazil Pilot

In 2011, Village Capital partnered with Brazilian accelerator Artemisia and capital partner Vox Capital to execute a Village Capital cohort in São Paulo, Brazil. Village Capital saw Brazil as a vibrant emerging market with a growing social enterprise sector and abounding opportunities. As a part of the cohort, ten enterprises met four times in three months to work together, challenge each other, and grow their businesses. At the close of the cohort, two businesses emerged: Saútil (see case study 9.2 on Vox Capital) and Quadrado Mágico, a social enterprise that brings affordable, world-class education to low-income Brazilians through online content.

The Challenge

Challenges arose for Village Capital upon the close of the pilot cohort when the organization learned of regulations limiting foreign direct investment in Brazil. Due to Brazilian regulations (specifically resolution 2689), non-Brazilian investors are required to appoint a Brazilian representative, work with an authorized Brazilian financial institution, register with the Brazilian government as a non-Brazilian investor, and be subject to taxes. These additional regulations added greatly to the transaction costs and nearly precluded Village Capital's investment in Brazil.

The Solution/Recommendation

Halloran Philanthropies, a philanthropic actor interested in furthering impact investing in Latin America, stepped in to absorb some of the transaction costs by underwriting the deal with grant funding. Six months after the end of the cohort, Village Capital was finally able to close the deal. Village Capital executive director Ross Baird expressed interest in open-source documents that help investors navigate the complex regulatory environment surrounding impact investing in Latin American countries.

Case Study 9.4   FIS

Background

FIS is an investment fund for the Chilean market that aims to promote investment projects with a social impact (see table 9.4). The private equity fund looks

Table 9.4   The need to bridge the early-stage social enterprise investment gap: Chile

Structure	Limited partnership
Investment Sizes	Equity raised from USD 100,000 to USD 1 million[a]
Industry	Microfinance, education, health, housing, and social and environmental issues
Geographies	Chile

Note: [a]Although Fondo de Inversion investments exceed the level of early-stage impact investment included in this chapter, they are one of the few impact-investing funds in Chile, and their views are very helpful to understanding their own experience as well as the climate for early-stage investing in the country.

to invest in growth-stage social enterprises seeking funding to increase their impact and achieve operational self-sustainability.[24] By investing in sectors such as microfinance, education, health, housing, and social and environmental issues, FIS receives an economic return on its investment while generating a high, quantifiable social impact.

The fund has raised USD 4.5 million since its inception a few years ago. FIS now has two portfolio investments—Promoeduc and Lumni. Promoeduc offers educational resources, counseling services, and educational support, evaluation, and performance management to state-subsidized schools. Lumni seeks to expand access to higher education by investing in human capital. Its aim is to design, structure, and manage investment funds that enable talented low-income young people to access (or continue) higher education studies. Upon receipt of funding, the student agrees to pay a fixed percentage of future gross income for a fixed period.

Challenge

FIS is the first impact-investment firm in Chile. It elected to invest in growth-stage social enterprises because the fund considered early-stage investment a riskier option for establishing credibility as an investor. Like many new and novel impact-investment funds around the world, FIS wants the fund to show positive results and develop a track record that will encourage others to help fund and grow the sector.

After a few years of operations, one of FIS's greatest challenges is developing a strong pipeline of investable opportunities that meet its criteria. Chile has a large early-stage social enterprise–funding gap, and no commercial funds exist to finance the early-stage between start-up (where family and friends provide funding) and FIS's USD 1 million investment level. A few organizations, including NESsT, Accion Joven, and CORFO (the Chilean government), offer grant assistance, but the amounts are either not large enough, or not targeted specifically to social enterprise (in the case of CORFO, though this is changing as described in chap. 7).

Solution/Recommendation

Maria Jose Montero, the fund manager for FIS, is working to convene actors for the early stage in Chile. The support system for early-stage social enterprises would improve greatly with a fund specifically developed to make seed-stage investments and mentor these social enterprises.

CONCLUSIONS AND RECOMMENDATIONS

The experiences of early-stage impact funds demonstrate the importance of encouraging the development and expansion of incubators and accelerators. Investors rely upon Latin American incubators and accelerators like Agora, New Ventures, and Artemisia. Furthermore, there is a symbiotic relationship between incubators/accelerators and investors in Latin America, and in some instances, the lines are becoming increasingly blurry with incubators launching investments funds and investment funds setting up incubators.

Furthermore, transaction costs for impact investors need to be reduced by providing comprehensive legal and investment guides for navigating the investment climate in the many countries that comprise Latin America. This would also increase the profile of Latin America as a desirable investment destination for international impact investors and/or provide support to aspiring indigenous fund managers.

Although there is an increasing interest in Brazil, Colombia, Peru, and Mexico, Latin America is still not as widely considered as other regions. Investors cite a lack of exit opportunities and the lack of a successful track record as contributing to this lower interest. Increasing the profile of the region could come in the form of case studies documenting social enterprise exits and through comprehensive investment guides (as described above). Documenting and sharing examples of creative, entrepreneur-friendly capital investment can accelerate the development of the industry.

Additionally, it is important to promote the emergence of new funds in countries/regions where there are noticeable gaps in the early-stage pipeline for social enterprise investors, specifically in Chile, Colombia, and parts of Central America. Promotion of new funds could be done through financial (e.g., loan guarantees or investment matching) and nonfinancial (e.g., training, resources, etc.) incentives.

As is the case with pioneer philanthropists, early-stage impact investors are also in many ways pioneers. They are working together with pioneer philanthropists and social investors to help create the pipeline of investment-ready social enterprises. Given that international aid continues to leave the region, and that most local philanthropy is still tied to more traditional charitable giving, there is an urgent need to find more entrepreneurial solutions to poverty. Early-stage impact investing, alongside social investing more generally, can certainly address this need.

10

THE ROAD IS WORTH GOING DOWN

Social Enterprise in Emerging Market Countries: No Free Ride puts forth a series of recommendations necessary to build the enabling environment that will allow social enterprises to thrive. The task is complex, with close to 30 recommended opportunities for change at both the supply and demand side of the social enterprise economy (see illustration 1.1). However, there are a number of urgent recommendations that should become the Holy Grail of the sector's development in the next five years if we really are serious about these changes.

Although creating a legal and regulatory framework that would simplify and reduce the confusing and bureaucratic nature of the current system is important, it will take a long time, and putting too much emphasis on this will no doubt lead to frustration and could in many ways backfire and lead to the overregulation of social enterprise. Spending too much time trying to get everyone to agree to a definition of social enterprise could also backfire since it is unlikely that we will ever reach consensus. Instead, for the next five years, greater emphasis should be put on developing procurement and incentive policies that create opportunities to grow social enterprises and their impact. The need to document, learn from, and replicate best practices in this regard is essential.

Strengthening support structures that offer capacity support for social enterprise development is absolutely critical. The economies of scale and efficiencies created by working through intermediaries, leading to mitigation of risks and greater opportunity for systemization of lessons learned, seems to be a no brainer. However, someone needs to pay for this capacity support. Philanthropists have a tremendous opportunity to accelerate the social enterprise pipeline if they are willing to provide philanthropic capital to support the start-up and development of intermediaries. Providing longer-term support with a view to helping these entities become sustainable should be considered.

First-stage scaling is fundamental. It is a critical stage when social enterprises have consolidated, have proof of concept, and are ready to begin the first stage of scaling. However, to do this successfully, they need patient capital and heavy doses of capacity support to move from reaching hundreds to reaching thousands or tens of thousands of beneficiaries. Probably, the most important driver of success is strengthening their middle management teams. Visionary leaders must invest the time and energy needed to create these teams, or bring someone else onboard to do it. Without them, it is unlikely that they will be able to position their social enterprises for real growth.

Pioneer donors need to become the rule rather than the exception. If more philanthropists are willing to enter the earlier stages of social enterprise development to help with first-stage scaling and field building, there will no doubt be a steady flow of high-impact social enterprises. Pioneer donors need to reach out to their peers to convince them to adopt these practices. They also need to support efforts to educate the philanthropic community—particularly the class of new and potential donors in emerging market countries—on the role that they can play in unlocking philanthropic capital in these countries.

Building financial instruments that are appropriate for each stage of social enterprise development is also critical. The use of grants alongside loans is important for underwriting the high social costs of social enterprise. Offering softer and more attractive lending schemes with longer repayment periods or repayment based on performance will go a long way toward helping social enterprises develop. Creating loan funds for higher levels of risk and early-stage funds with longer investing cycles will help generate the needed capital for social enterprises. It is important to keep these instruments simple, making sure to distinguish investment instruments that require a financial return from patient capital that is being underwritten by philanthropy.

As shown in table 10.1, the focus of financing needs to be in the middle of the social enterprise development sector centered on early-stage social and impact investing.

Creating the next generation of social enterprise entrepreneurs and social enterprise sector leaders is critical for the ultimate consolidation of the sector in the emerging market countries. The research conducted for this book demonstrates that much of the thought leadership emanating from the sector is still coming from more developed countries. More academic programs in emerging market countries need to be developed. There is a very concrete opportunity to endow professors and provide scholarships for students who wish to pursue social enterprise as a career. Given the growth of emerging market economies, the time is ripe for this to happen as more young people become interested and are financially able to enter this field.

Underlying these recommendations is the need to build a homegrown social enterprise movement in emerging market countries while leveraging the trends and accomplishments of the global community. The world is too small, resources too scarce, and the potential returns too great not to pursue a local-global strategy. For this, the transfer and adaptation of best practices, investment tools, and expertise will go very far. Working in the local language, within the local context and realities is fundamental. We should ensure that a wide range of local stories and local models are promoted, and that we do not get stuck on the handful of cases that are already proven and that everyone wants to support.

As we move to build the enabling environment for social enterprise, perhaps the best strategy to adopt is to practice what we preach and use the same persistence, the same calculated risks, and the same conviction that social entrepreneurs

Table 10.1 The middle of the social enterprise sector

Field	Philanthropy		Social investing	
Type of donors or investors	Philanthropists	Social investors/venture philanthropists	Early-stage impact investors (fund structures)	Impact investors (fund structures)
Type of financial support	Donation but often with program focus as opposed to social enterprise	Philanthropic capital/patient capital— includes grants, grant loans, soft loans, quasi-equity	Debt and/or equity; usually convertible loans	Debt and/or equity
Levels (USD)	10,000–400,000 usually 1–3 years duration	50,000–300,000	300,000–500,000	500,000+
Capacity support	Often focused on providing training	Often includes ongoing capacity support-building skills, structures, and systems	Includes management assistance	Includes management assistance
Expected returns	Social return	Social return first and more flexible expectation of financial return; doesn't need to happen in case of grants	Social return or financial return first; both are expected	Social return or financial return first; more expectation of financial return
Social enterprise stage	Charities/nonprofits	Nonprofits with earned income activities, early-stage social enterprises, first-stage scaling social enterprises	Investment-ready social enterprises	More mature social enterprises with capacity for exits

use to pursue their goals. Developing the ecosystem for social enterprise promises to be very challenging. However, we are much farther along in this pursuit than we have ever been and what needs to happen is clearer than ever before. Those who have been in this sector for a long time need to build on their knowledge and really push for these changes to happen. They should engage the newcomers and not allow themselves to be discouraged by the naysayers. No one said that this ride would be easy, but the findings presented in *Social Enterprise in Emerging Market Countries: No Free Ride* show that the road does exist and certainly is very much worth going down.

APPENDIX 1: RESEARCH APPROACH AND METHODOLOGY

Social Enterprise in Emerging Market Countries: No Free Ride is the result of extensive research conducted by NESsT in the past five years to inform its own work, as well as the work of the social enterprise sector overall. The research reflects NESsT's belief that for social enterprises to truly thrive and have impact, efforts must focus not only on developing social enterprises, but also on the systemization and dissemination of best practices and the creation of an enabling environment. The book is the final output of a report that was commissioned by the Rockefeller Foundation in 2012 to learn more about the challenges and opportunities for social enterprise development in emerging economies. In 2013, the findings were updated and expanded to develop the final publication.

The book specifically responds to three key sets of questions:

- What are the broader enabling conditions that would support the emergence and long-term sustainability of social enterprises?
- What are the barriers for social enterprises in attracting growth capital? To what extent can technical assistance and tailored financing instruments address these barriers?
- Are there practices that could catalyze the emergence of more social enterprises? What other support mechanisms could increase the number of investment-ready social enterprises?

NESsT approached the research and analysis through a combination of portfolio analysis, desk research, and extensive interviews. It employed qualitative and quantitative analysis to identify, describe, and evaluate the landscape, opportunities, trends, and future path of social enterprise development.

Chapter 2 on the regulatory and policy environment in Latin America entailed in-depth legal research conducted with the input of lawyers in five countries where NESsT operates. Chapter 3 on the European Union (EU) legislation was the result of research and active participation in the policy panels that have been advising the EU on its social enterprise policies. Chapter 4 entailed an assessment of the current support structures in Latin America and more in-depth surveys of certain incubators. Chapter 5 reflects NESsT's own experience of first scaling a cohort of its overall portfolio and the best practices that are needed with this group of enterprises. Chapter 6 entailed an in-depth assessment of NESsT's own donor base of 230 current and prospective Latin American donors in social enterprise over the last ten years. Chapter 7 involved in-depth research and a series of interviews with each of 14 pioneer donors. Chapter 8 is based on two regional studies on social enterprise lending in the last five years and an assessment of investments made with 20 social enterprises. Chapter 9 was a survey of 165 early-stage impact funds and more in-depth study of 19 of them.

The research was intended to survey and capture the experience of a significant sampling of the key stakeholders in the ecosystem including the following:

- *Social entrepreneurs:* Social entrepreneurs address both public and private gaps. On the one hand, they work with people that governments have been unable to reach effectively with basic public goods and services or to overcome challenges that are too risky for them to undertake, and on the other hand, social entrepreneurs address market failures by providing access to private goods and services to locations and communities where business does not operate because the risks are too great and the financial rewards sometimes appear to be too few.

- *Advocates, regulators, and policymakers:* Legislators, policymakers, economic leaders, and social enterprise advocates all play an active role in how the legal and regulatory frameworks for civil society organizations and social enterprises are shaped and established. Empathetic policymakers and an easy to navigate legal system maintain an environment ripe for opportunities and growth. The right policies will make it easier to do business, remove obstacles to external financing, and develop human capital that can be readily harnessed by the entrepreneurial sector.

- *Social enterprise support structures:* Similar to NESsT, incubators and other intermediary organizations work with organizations and entrepreneurs to assess the feasibility of their ideas, providing tailored capacity support and setting the stage for scaling or replication. Intermediaries provide a link between enterprises, their market, and the potential investors who can provide more long-term capital and support. University programs develop the new generation of social entrepreneurs and social investors.

- *Social enterprise donors:* These stakeholders provide seed money and a source of capacity building for small and medium enterprises looking to expand. They include corporate giving programs, foundations, family offices, government programs, individual givers, institutional investors, and multilateral organizations. Their commitment levels vary and their motivations differ. Many are increasingly emphasizing private sector development as the preferred path to growth.

A total of 698 entities were researched, 224 interviews were conducted, and 68 cases are featured in this book (see table A1.1). The research was conducted by NESsT's own team of senior managers with the support of a research and coordination team that was specifically designated for the project.

Table A1.1 Scope of *No Free Ride* Research

	Institutions researched	Interviews	Cases featured
Policymakers and experts	44	14	6
Donors and pioneers	236	15	14
Mixed financial instruments	145	126	20
Social enterprises	36	24	19
Impact investors	158	19	4
Incubators	79	26	7
Total	698	224	68

NOTES

1 THE OPPORTUNITY FOR SOCIAL ENTERPRISE IN EMERGING MARKET COUNTRIES

* Please see glossary of terms for definitions of terms used in this chapter and throughout the book.

1. NESsT focused the research on Latin America and Central Europe, the two regions where it has operated for over 15 years. In particular, the research focuses on Argentina, Brazil, Chile, Ecuador, and Peru, with some cases from other countries in Latin America and Central America, including Colombia Mexico and Nicaragua. For the purpose of illustrating important models and innovative programs and policies, this book also highlights cases and experiences from Central Europe, particularly Croatia, Czech Republic, Hungary, Romania, and Slovakia. There are also cases and policies from the European Union (EU) overall. Both Latin America and Central Europe are at important moments of change and show tremendous opportunity for adopting and adapting new models and practices locally, as well as sharing their experiences with the field on a global scale.

2. NESsT defines impact social enterprises as businesses that solve a critical social problem in a sustainable manner. A consortium of organizations commissioned by the Rockefeller Foundation to research social enterprises across the globe, and which led to the development of this book, used the following definition: A social (impact) enterprise is a financially self-sustaining and scalable, revenue-generating venture that actively manages toward producing net positive changes in well-being for individuals at the base of the pyramid, their communities, and the broader environment. Given the compatibility of the two definitions, for purposes of this book, they are used interchangeably. NESsT invests in those enterprises that move marginalized communities out of poverty and exclusion by providing access to the following: fair employment and sustainable income; quality, affordable, and basic services; improved living conditions; socially and environmentally responsible products and services; and universal rights.

3. CSOs refer to the wide range of not-for-profit, nonstate organizations as well as community-based associations and groups (distinct from both the governmental and business sectors) that advance a collective or public good. These organizations are also referred to as "nonprofit organizations" (NPOs), "nongovernmental organizations" (NGOs), "charities," "voluntary organizations," and so on.

4. "The Social economy in the European Union," CIRIEC, page 48.

5. The United States has a long history of favorable tax laws for individual and corporate donations to eligible NPOs. More recently, Congress created the New Market Tax Credit Program in 2000 to incentivize equity investment in low-income areas. The

program was designed to apply business practices to stimulate investment, and has allocated USD 33 billion in tax credits to Community Development Entities (see the US Treasury Community Development Financial Institutions Fund website, http://cdfifund.gov/). Some states have also passed "B Corporation" legislation and may provide enhanced tax advantages for donations to specific organizations (e.g., see Maryland's Community Tax Credit program at http://www.neighborhoodrevitalization.org/Programs/CITC/CITC.aspx). Although not limited to social enterprises, often federal and state agencies have target percentages of procurement from small, minority-owned, or other categories of businesses.

6. "Ben Thornley: The Facts on U.S. Social Enterprise," *Huffington Post*, http://www.huffingtonpost.com/ben-thornley/social-enterprise_b_2090144.html.
7. See Bridgespan Group, "The MBA Drive for Social Value," April 2009, http://www.bridgespan.org/Publications-and-Tools/Career-Professional-Development/NonprofitCareers/The-MBA-Drive-for-Social-Value.aspx#.UX7UGaJwoyo.
8. All data comes from the World Bank. The Gini index is a measure of inequality that measures the extent to which the distribution of income or consumption expenditure among individuals or households within a country deviates from a perfectly equal distribution.
9. NESsT has created a proven methodology for developing social enterprises that contains three stages: planning, incubation, and first-stage scaling. The process and stages will be discussed in subsequent chapters.

2   THE REGULATORY AND POLICY VACUUM FOR SOCIAL ENTERPRISE IN LATIN AMERICA

* The focus of this chapter is on civil society organization (CSO) social enterprise, as the legal research to date has been conducted mostly with a view to understand this sector.

1. "Poverty, Inequality, and Democracy," A Conference Report of the Network of Democracy Research Institutes (NDRI), Bratislava, Slovakia, April 26–28, 2009.
2. "Latin America: Social Enterprise & Philanthropy," *Financial Times*, December 2, 2011.
3. "Latin America: Social Enterprise & Philanthropy: Fashion for Giving Starts to Catch On," *Financial Times*, December 2, 2011.
4. "Latin America: Social Enterprise & Philanthropy," *Financial Times*.
5. "Latin America: Social Enterprise & Philanthropy: Cultural Legacy Has Created Cautious Attitude to Charity," *Financial Times*, December 2, 2011.
6. "B Corps—Firms with Benefits," http://www.economist.com/node/21542432.
7. Daryl Poon, "The Emergence and Development of Social Enterprise Sectors," University of Pennsylvania, January 1, 2011.
8. "CSO" refers to the wide diversity of not-for-profit, nonstate organizations as well as community-based associations and groups (distinct from both the governmental and business sectors) that advance a collective or public good. These organizations are also referred to as "NPOs," "non-governmental organizations (NGOs)," "charities," "voluntary organizations," and so on.
9. NPOs in the countries researched are for the most part either associations or foundations. Associations represent a union of individuals who decide to set up an entity to address a common cause or interest. Most laws also distinguish between associations whose purpose is to benefit people outside of their interest ("public benefit") and those that are established to aid their own members. Foundations, however, are founded through some of kind of endowment or financial contribution to address a

cause. The laws governing these two types of entities are very similar when it comes to commercial activities, although there are a few exceptions, mostly in the case of Argentina. Also, Argentina adopted many regulations that govern different types of associations, leading to a myriad of organizations that are governed by both the civil code and the particular regulations that apply to them.

10. NESsT based its assessment of the legal and regulatory framework using a typology developed by The International Center for Not-for-Profit Law to classify the use of economic or commercial activities among CSOs.

11. In 2012, Chile passed Law 20.500 whereby the constitution of a foundation or association is no longer based on the approval of the president of the republic, but by a relatively easy procedure that falls under the civil code. The new law also has provisions that recognize the special nature of organizations constituted for the "public interest," to better the rights of citizens, and their educational, health, social, and environmental conditions. This legislation allows these organizations to access funding from a government fund set up to strengthen these organizations.

12. The committee is a NPO formed for a specific and temporary purpose. It is defined in the civil code as an "organization of natural persons or legal entities, or both, dedicated to public fundraising for an altruistic end" (article 111 of the civil code).

13. A CIC is a business with primarily social objectives whose surpluses are principally reinvested for that purpose in the business or in the community, rather than being driven by the need to maximize profit for shareholders and owners. CICs tackle a wide range of social and environmental issues and operate in all parts of the economy. By using business solutions to achieve public good, it is believed that social enterprises have a distinct and valuable role to play in helping create a strong, sustainable, and socially inclusive economy.

    CICs are diverse. They include community enterprises, social firms, mutual organizations such as cooperatives, and large-scale organizations operating locally, regionally, nationally, or internationally.

    There is no single legal model for social enterprise. They include companies limited by guarantee, industrial, and provident societies, and companies limited by shares; some organizations are unincorporated associations and others are registered charities, industrial, and provident societies. (http://en.wikipedia.org/wiki/Community_interest_company.)

14. In 1998, Law 25.063 removed the tax-exempt status from foundations that undertook commercial and/or industrial activities. This situation resulted in many formal complaints from the nonprofit sector to the district attorney and the executive branch, requesting a revision of this law. A reform law was drafted to revoke this ruling: "If the resources obtained are not one hundred percent reinvested in their specific purpose and mission." Unfortunately, this bill, although approved in the House of Representatives, was never passed by the Senate. On July 29, 1999, Law 25.239 was approved and introduced a reform to Law 20.628, by stipulating that this exemption "will not be applicable to foundations and associations or civil entities that are trade associations and carry out commercial and/or industrial activities." A literal interpretation of this regulation, in isolation from other regulations and judicial and administrative jurisprudence, would negatively affect many foundations and associations that operate as trade associations and carry out commercial activities in order to meet their objectives as stipulated in their bylaws.

    Loss of tax-exempt status would also mean loss of exemption from VAT for services rendered, even when these are directly related to the objectives of the organization.

15. For more details, please see the Argentina Legal and Regulatory Framework Guide, NESsT Legal Series, copyright 2009.

16. In Brazil, the constitution grants certain "immunities" that impede the tax authorities from collecting taxes in certain situations. The patrimony, income, and services of nonprofit educational and social service institutions benefit from constitutional tax immunity.

17. Art. 15 da Law n° 9.532, December 10, 1997.

18. Requirements to be met related to good governance and transparency include (a) not paying board of directors in any way for their services; (b) applying resources to the furtherance of its purpose; (c) keeping complete accounting records of receipts and expenses under formal bookkeeping standards, which ensure exactness; (d) maintaining in good order, for five years from the date of inception, documents that show the origin of receipts and amounts spent, as well as records of other acts that change its financial situation; (e) presenting an annual declaration of income following guidelines by the Federal Revenue Department; (f) collecting taxes and social security properly, and comply with the related obligations; and (g) ensuring that its endowment will go to another immune institution or public agency should it incorporate, merge, dissolve, or end its activities (Law n° 9.532/97, Art. 12, § 2).

19. For more details, please see the Brazil Legal and Regulatory Framework Guide, NESsT Legal Series, copyright 2011.

20. For more details, please see the Chile Legal and Regulatory Framework Guide, NESsT Legal Series, copyright 2012.

21. For more details, please see the Ecuador Legal and Regulatory Framework Guide, NESsT Legal Series, copyright 2009.

22. For more details, please see the Peru Legal and Regulatory Framework Guide, NESsT Legal Series, copyright 2007.

23. See also chapter 4 on "The Emergence and Evolution of Social Enterprise Support Structures" for more on this topic.

24. See Ben Thornley, David Wood, Katie Grace, and Sarah Sullivant "Impact Investing: A Framework for Policy Design and Analysis," a collaboration between InSight at Pacific Community Ventures and the Initiative for Responsible Investment at Harvard University and funded by The Rockefeller Foundation, which explores the role of public policy in impact investing. NESsT will be adopting this framework to assess policy that fosters social enterprise development in future research.

25. The assessment mostly focuses on economic or productive activities in the countries, and does not focus on other sectors such as health or education.

26. The "social economy" does not have a universally accepted definition. However, it is generally understood as comprising "third-sector" entities such as foundations, associations, NPOs, cooperatives, and volunteer groups that are neither public nor for-profit private (the first two sectors). These entities emphasize social good above profit, and democratic processes and local control above financial rights and centralized control. NESsT includes for-profit entities as part of the social economy if they are established to solve critical social problems affecting marginalized communities. NESsT also includes government agencies and private for-profit companies that provide financing or technical assistance to the aforementioned organizations as part of the overall social economy. For a more detailed analysis on how the social economy can be viewed, see "Mapping the Social Economy in BC and Alberta: Towards a Strategic Approach," a BALTA working paper by Mike Lewis, BC-Alberta Social Economy Research Alliance, August 2006. Copyright © 2006, Canadian Centre for Community Renewal on behalf of the BC-Alberta Social Economy Research Alliance, http://www.socialeconomy-bcalberta.ca/social-economy/.

27. The full version of this case study is available on the NESsT website. Please see http://
issuu.com/nesster/docs/case_study_38_-_incores_and_actis_a.
28. Income share held by highest 10 percent of the population ranges from a low of
32.3 percent in Argentina to more than 42 percent in both Brazil and Chile. The
percentages in Ecuador and Peru are 39.32 and 36.11, respectively. The percentage
share of income or consumption is the share that accrues to subgroups of population
indicated by deciles or quintiles. The data are from the World Bank, Development
Research Group, and are based on primary household survey data obtained from government statistical agencies and World Bank country departments. For more information and methodology, please see PovcalNet (http://iresearch.worldbank.org
/PovcalNet/index.htm).

3 Trade-offs between Regulation and Fostering of Social Enterprise: The Case of European Union Policies

* This chapter was written by Eva Varga, director of Portfolio Performance for NESsT. Eva
participates on the expert panel on policies promoting social enterprise and appropriate
financing that makes recommendations to the Employment, Social Affairs, and Inclusion
DG of the EU Commission. Many of the policy recommendations made by this panel were
adopted by the commission and are reflected in this chapter.

1. The European Union (EU) officially uses the terms "social entrepreneurship" and
"social enterprise" with a similar definition as that which is being used in this book.
2. Single Market Act, dedicated website, http://ec.europa.eu/internal_market/smact
/index_en.htm; "Twelve Levers to Boost Growth and Strengthen Confidence," April
2011, http://eur-lex.europa.eu/LexUriServ/LexUriServ.do?uri=CELEX:52011DC
0206:EN:NOT.
3. http://eur-lex.europa.eu/Lex-UriServ/LexUriServ.do?uri=COM:2011:0682:FIN:
EN:PDF; SBI website, http://ec.europa.eu/internal_market/social_business/index
_en.htm.
4. http://ec.europa.eu/internal_market/social_business/expertgroup/index_en.htm.
5. http://www.socialfirmsuk.co.uk/about-social-firms/what-social-firm.
6. Social Enterprise UK, http://www.socialenterprise.org.uk/about/about-social-enterprise
/social-enterprise-dictionary#general.
7. "Slovenia's Social Enterprise Act," http://www.euclidnetwork.eu/news-and-events
/sector-news/830-slovenias-social-enterprise-act.html.
8. "What Makes a Social Enterprise?," page 2, Social Enterprise UK, http://www
.socialenterprise.org.uk/uploads/files/2012/04/what_makes_a_social_enterprise
_a_social_enterprise_april_2012.pdf.
9. Lubos Vagac, "Active Labour Market Measures in Slovakia." EU Employment
Observatory, December 2010: 1–15. http://www.eu-employment-observatory.net
/resources/Slovakia-EmploymentServices.Law.pdf.
10. M. A. Peter Meszaros, Background study for the project titled, "Social Economy:
Innovative Model for Economic and Social Development in Slovakia," 3lobit February
2012, http://www.3lobit.sk/.
11. Ibid., referring to Peter Sokol, "The Analysis of the Experience with Introducing of the
Social Economy in Slovakia," *Nová ekonomika*, o.p.s. (obecně prospěšná společnost,
public service company).
12. Act No. 5/2004 Z.z. adopted in April 2008, entered in effect in September 2008.

13. Chapter on Poland by Ewa Les, edited by Jacques DeFourny and Marthe Nyssens, "Social Enterprises in Europe: Recent Trends and Developments," EMES Working paper No. 08/01, page 28.
14. Ibid., page 29.
15. http://ec.europa.eu/internal_market/social_business/index_en.htm.
16. "The Community Interest Company Regulations, 2005 No. 1788," http://www.legislation.gov.uk/uksi/2005/1788/contents/made.
17. http://www.bis.gov.uk/cicregulator/guidance/chapter-6.
18. Ibid.
19. http://www.socialenterprisemark.org.uk/.
20. http://www.socialenterprisemark.org.uk/the-mark/about-us/.
21. Charity Bank Annual Review 2010, published in May 2011.
22. http://www.ceredigioncaresociety.org.uk/index.php/en_US/about-us.html.
23. "The Social Economy in the European Union," CIRIEC, page 48.
24. "Social Enterprise UK: Annual Review 2011," http://www.socialenterprise.org.uk/uploads/files/2012/02/seuk_annual_review_2011.pdf.
25. The estimate is based on positive performance in 2009.
26. Social costs are costs incurred by social enterprises due to their social nature, which are usually not incurred by similar businesses with no social goals. The cost of social workers that assist disabled employees, the cost of creating accessible workplaces for disabled employees, or the cost of environmentally responsible technologies in order to reduce contamination are examples of social costs.
27. http://ec.europa.eu/esf/main.jsp?catId=35&langId=en.
28. Ibid.
29. http://eurlex.europa.eu/LexUriServ/LexUriServ.do?uri=COM:2011:0682:FIN:EN:PDF.
30. This section is not an exhaustive list, but the most important action items are mentioned.
31. Minutes of the June 5, 2012, meeting of the GECES, http://ec.europa.eu/internal_market/social_business/docs/expert-group/050612-minutes-final_en.pdf.
32. On March 12, 2013, the European Parliament voted strongly in favor of the new social investment fund label, thus taking the final legislative step to help the concept move toward implementation. On April 17, 2013, the European Council adopted the regulations. They entered into force 20 days after their publication in the *Official Journal of the European Union*. Text of the regulation as adopted by the European Parliament and the council (April 17, 2013) is available at http://eur-lex.europa.eu/LexUriServ/LexUriServ.do?uri=CELEX:32013R0346:EN:NOT.

4   THE EMERGENCE AND EVOLUTION OF SOCIAL ENTERPRISE SUPPORT STRUCTURES

* This chapter was written by Sebastian Gatica, Adjunct Professor, Business School, and Director, Social Innovation Laboratory, *Pontificia Universidad Católica de Chile*. Special thanks are extended to the Social Innovation Lab team for its contributions to the chapter. The final version was edited by the authors of *Social Enterprise in Emerging Market Countries: No Free Ride*.

1. Henry Etzkowitz and Loet Leydesdorff, "The Dynamics of Innovation: From National Systems and 'Mode 2' to a Triple Helix of University-Industry-Government Relations," *Research Policy* 29, no. 2 (2000): 109–123.

2. Dee Hock, *One from Many: Visa and the Rise of Chaordic Organization*, San Francisco: Berrett-Koehler Publishers, Inc., 2009.
3. Sebastian Gatica, "*Emprendimiento e Innovación Social: construyendo una agenda pública para Chile.*" *Temas de la agenda pública* 6, no. 48 (2011). See also chapter 2.
4. Yves Vaillancourt, "Social Economy in the Co-Construction of Public Policy," *Annals of Public and Cooperative Economics* 80, no. 2 (2009): 275–313.
5. Further information available at http://www.corfo.cl/programas-y-concursos /programas/concurso-innovacion-y-emprendimiento-social.
6. Further information available at http://www.anspe.gov.co/es/programa/innovacion -social.
7. Luisa Fernanda Acevedo, "*Colombia ya tiene su Centro de Innovación Social -CIS-,*" March 2012, Accessed April 19, 2013, http://www.rutanmedellin.org/actualidad /Paginas/centro_de_innovacion_social_cis_colombia_230312.aspx.
8. Heerad Sabeti et al., "The Emerging Fourth Sector," Washington, DC: The Aspen Institute (2010).
9. Further information available at http://www.cicassociation.org.uk/ y en http://www .socialenterprise.org.uk/.
10. Further information available at http://www.euricse.eu/en/journals/impresa-sociale.
11. Further information available at http://www.benefitcorp.net/ and at http://www .bcorporation.net/.
12. Brazil, Decree no. 5, 940, October 25, 2006, Brasilia.
13. Rory P. O'Shea, Thomas J. Allen, and Kenneth Morse, "Creating the Entrepreneurial University: The Case of MIT," presented at Academy of Management Conference, Hawaii, 2005.
14. The first revolution saw the integration of research into what had previously been purely teaching.
15. Henry Etzkowitz, A. Webster, C. Gebhardt, and B. R. C. Terra, "The Future of the University and the University of the Future: Evolution of Ivory Tower to Entrepreneurial Paradigm," *Research Policy* 29, (2000): 313–330. B. R. Clark, *Creating Entrepreneurial Universities*, Oxford, UK: Pergamon, 1998.
16. Further information available at http://www.fundades.org/.
17. Sebastian Gatica et al., *La Innovacion Social en Chile y el Rol del Estado en su desarrollo, Ministerio de Economia*, Santiago: Escuela de Administración de la Pontificia Universidad Católica de Chile, 2012.
18. Further information available at http://www.emes.net.
19. Institute for Social Entrepreneurs, *Evolution of the Social Enterprise Industry: A Chronology of Key Events*, 2008.
20. More information at www.socialenterprise.org.uk/.
21. More information at www.se-alliance.org.
22. More information at http://www.socialinnovationeurope.eu/.
23. More information at http://www.socialinnovationexchange.org/.
24. B Lab 2012 Annual Report, available at www.bcorporation.net.
25. For information on shared value, see "Creating Shared Value" by Michael E. Porter and Mark R. Kramer, *Harvard Business Review*, January 2011.
26. Support Organizations in Latin America: ICESI University, 2010.
27. More information at www.idea.me; www.noblezaobliga.com; www.fondeadora.mx/.
28. Interview of Ricardo Teran, cofounder and managing director of Agora Partnerships, on July 3, 2012.
29. Henry Etzkowitz and Loet Leydesdorff, "The Dynamics of Innovation: From National Systems and 'Mode 2' to a Triple Helix of University–Industry–Government Relations," *Research Policy* 29 (2000): 109–123.

30. Kim Alter, "Social Enterprise Typology," *Virtue Venures LLC* (2004).
31. Julie Battilana, Matthew Lee, John Walker, and Cheryl Dorsey, "In Search of the Hybrid Ideal," *Stanford Social Innovation Review* 10 (2012).
32. Margaret Wheatley and Deborah Frieze, "Using Emergence to Take Social Innovation to Scale," Provo, UT: The Berkana Institute (2006).
33. Mirjam Schöning et al., "The Governance of Social Enterprises Managing Your Organization for Success," Schwab Foundation for Social Entrepreneurship, Geneva, 2012.
34. Marta Curto, *"El Emprendimiento Social: Estructura Organizativa, Retos Y Perspectivas De Futuro."* *Cuadernos de la Cátedra "la Caixa" de Responsabilidad Social de la Empresa y Gobierno Corporativo* no. 14 (2012).
35. Peter Senge, *The Fifth Discipline, The Art and Practice of the Learning Organization*, New York: Currency Doubleday, 1990.
36. More information at http://www.simondecirene.cl/wp-content/uploads/2012/10/2_Manual-para-administrar-Empresas-Sociales.pdf.
37. More information at http://www.artofhosting.org.
38. More information at www.ashoka.org.
39. SESAME, Working in Social Enterprises, Anglia Polytechnic University (2002).

5   First-Stage Scaling: Moving Early-Stage Enterprises to Expansion

1. In some cases, these enterprises will opt to accept a small amount of subsidy for their employees in order to use the income generated by the enterprise for investment and growth purposes.
2. Social drivers are those that focus on achieving social goals and that are tied to the success of the enterprise. For example, the amount of training provided to a marginalized person making them more employable could be considered a social driver.
3. "Argentina—Country Strategy Paper 2007/2013—Mid-Term Review ANNEX," European Union.
4. Desempeño del Mercado Laboral en el Perú, Edwin Poquioma, Asesor de la Secretaría Técnica del Consejo Nacional de Trabajo y Promoción del Empleo, 2007, página 8. (Performance of the Labor Market in Peru, Edwin Poquiom, Advisor to the Technical Secretariat of the National Advisory Group of Work and Promotion of Employment, 2007, page 8.) /http://www.mintra.gob.pe/archivos/file/CNTPE/Desempeno_Mercado_Laboral_en_el_Peru.pdf; Asesor de la Secretaría Técnica del Consejo Nacional de Trabajo y Promoción del Empleo, http://www.mintra.gob.pe/archivos/file/CNTPE/Desempeno_Mercado_Laboral_en_el_Peru.pdf.
5. "Peru: 2011 Findings on the Worst Forms of Child Labor," Bureau of International Labor Affairs, United States Department of Labor, http://www.dol.gov/ilab/programs/ocft/2011TDA/peru.pdf; http://www.dol.gov/ilab/media/reports/iclp/Advancing1/html/peru.htm.
6. "Disability in Latin America & the Caribbean," World Bank Fact Sheet, http://siteresources.worldbank.org/DISABILITY/Resources/Regions/LAC/LACfactsheetEng.pdf.
7. "The Labor Market Situation of Disabled People in European Countries and Implementation of Employment Policies: A Summary of Evidence from Country Reports and Research Studies," report prepared for The Academic Network of European Disability Experts (ANED), 2009.

8. http://www.nesst.org/wp-content/uploads/2012/07/2012-Argentina-Andar-EN
   .pdf; http://www.nesst.org/wp-content/uploads/2012/07/2012-Hungary-Kek-Madar
   -EN.pdf.
9. http://www.conveagro.org.pe/node/8934.
10. http://www.mmediu.ro/vechi/biroul_de_presa/comunicate_de_presa/09
    _Septembrie_2008/02.09.08a.htm.
11. In 2009, Brazil reported an unemployment rate of 17.8 percent among both sexes
    and in the age bracket of 15–24 years. Source: United Nations Statistics Division,
    Millennium Development Goals Database.
12. http://www.anbpr.org.ro/index.php/afiliere/272-baza-de-date-membri.html.
13. http://www.anph.ro/tematica.php?idt.

6   Donor Giving and Social Enterprise in Latin America—a Fragmented Landscape

1. An analysis of NESsT's own database and experience with donors in Latin America is
   relevant to understanding donor support for social enterprise in the region for several
   reasons: (1) since NESsT's core mission is to develop social enterprises, its experience
   with donors directly relates to their support for this strategy and activities related to it;
   (2) NESsT's own work to assist local CSOs and social enterprises to become sustainable has led the organization to conduct numerous studies to better understand the
   challenges to their sustainability and impact in the region; and (3) finally, efforts to
   build an enabling environment for social enterprise in the region have engaged NESsT
   in a constant dialogue with donors regarding this topic and the need for donors to
   further support these efforts. However, the analysis of the NESsT donor database and
   overall experience is a case study to illustrate the funding situation for CSOs in Latin
   America and does not necessarily apply to all organizations and individuals—since
   many operate within specific funding contexts that depend on their mission, country,
   and other factors.
2. Long-term donors, as defined by NESsT, commit to financial contributions for more
   than two years.
3. This small group of pioneer donors will be featured in chapter 7.
4. The European Union (EU) recently announced its bilateral funding withdrawal from
   Colombia by 2014. Development assistance of EUR 40 million will cease to be available to local CSOs. Only bilateral assistance relating to the Colombian conflict will
   remain.
5. "Accelerating Progress towards the Millennium Development Goals through Inclusive
   Business; Delivering Results: Moving towards Scale; Report on an Inclusive Business
   Dialogue," held on September 21, 2010, during the UN Summit on the Millennium
   Development Goals. October 2010.
6. http://www.iadb.org/en/topics/civil-society/call-for-proposals-civil-society-jpo
   /2012-winning-organizations,6433.html.

7   Betting on Higher Social Returns— Pioneer Donors Show the Way

1. Harvey Koh, Ashish Karamchandani, and Robert Katz, "From Blueprint to Scale: The
   Case for Philanthropy in Impact Investing," Executive Summary, Monitor Group,
   April 2012.

2. For more details on engaged philanthropy, see Lee Davis, Nicole Etchart, and Claire Costello, *All in the Same Boat: An Introduction to Engaged Philanthropy*, copyright 2005, San Francisco, CA: NESsT, 2005.
3. The use of the term "social investment" in this chapter and book refers to capital provided by a philanthropist or social investor, who primarily seeks a social return or social impact, and in some cases a modest financial return.
4. As mentioned in chapter 1, early-stage social enterprise development refers to support at start up and incubation and is customarily in the range of USD 50,000–250,000.
5. Of the 14 pioneers, 11 have directly worked in Latin America. CAF Venturesome, KL Felicitas, and RAF are the only organizations without operations in the region. Five are working in Central Europe—Ausherman Family Foundation, Citigroup, KL Felicitas, RAF, and Shell Foundation.
6. SEKN is a collaboration of Latin American business schools and HBS in partnership with the Avina Foundation. It was founded in 2001 to address the need for generating social enterprise intellectual capital in Latin America. See www.sekn.org.
7. See chapter 3 for reference to B Corps.
8. SOCAP is the impact-investing industry global event, which gathers investors, social entrepreneurs, social ventures, government leaders, academics, and other innovators in the sector in order to advance the field.
9. UK Gift Aid increases the value of donations to charities by allowing them to reclaim the basic rate tax on gifts. For donors in higher tax brackets, the donor may claim back the difference between the higher tax rate and the basic rate on the value of the donation. For more information, see http://www.hmrc.gov.uk/individuals/giving/gift-aid.htm.
10. ANDE is a global network of organizations that invest money and expertise to advance entrepreneurship in emerging markets. It is housed within the Aspen Institute and works to dramatically increase the amount and effectiveness of capital and technical/business assistance for entrepreneurs in developing countries. See http://www.aspeninstitute.org/policy-work/aspen-network-development-entrepreneurs.
11. CORFO, www.corfo.cl.
12. http://halloranphilanthropies.org/who_we_are#!mission.
13. John Kohler, Thane Kreiner, and Jessica Sawhney, "Coordinating Impact Capital: A New Approach to Investing in Small and Growing Businesses," Santa Clara University and The Aspen Network of Development Entrepreneurs, July 2011, http://www.scu.edu/socialbenefit/resources/upload/Coordinating-Impact-Capital.pdf.
14. "Our Programmes," Shell Foundation, http://www.shellfoundation.org/pages/corelines_index.php?p=corelines_content.
15. The Momentum Program uses the term "social entrepreneurship" to mean social enterprise as defined in this publication.
16. "Social Venture," BBVA, http://accionistaseinversores.bbva.com/TLBB/micros/informes2011/en/Nonfinancialinformation/SocialVenture.html.
17. http://www.rafonline.org/?lng=&id2=0000.
18. http://www.rafonline.org/?id2=000200000003.
19. Ibid.

8   THE (STAIR)CASE FOR MIXED FINANCIAL INSTRUMENTS

1. Social investment is the provision and use of capital to generate social as well as financial returns. Social investors weigh the social and financial returns they expect from an

investment, and often accept lower financial returns in order to generate greater social impact. Social investment enables social sector organizations to develop activities that generate income used to repay investors. Social sector organizations may generate a surplus through trading activities, contracts for delivering public services, grants and donations, or a combination of some or all of these. See http://www.bigsocietycapital .com/what-social-investment.

2. Like social investing, impact investing consists of investments made into companies, organizations, and funds with the intention to generate measurable social and environmental impact alongside a financial return. Impact investments can be made in both emerging and developed markets, and target a range of returns from below market-to-market rate, depending upon the circumstances. However, impact investing occurs at later stages of business development, the amounts of investment are higher, and also includes "financial first" investments, which is never the case in social investing.

3. Social impact bonds are designed to improve the social outcomes of publicly funded services by making funding conditional on improvements. Investors pay for the project at the start, and then receive a payment based on the results achieved by the project. For more information, see https://www.gov.uk/social-impact-bonds.

4. Investment readiness may be defined as the capacity of a small or medium enterprise, social enterprise, or entrepreneur—who is looking for external finance, in particular equity finance—to understand the specific needs of an investor and to be able to respond to these needs by providing an appropriate structure and relevant information, by being credible and by creating confidence. See http://ec.europa.eu/enter prise/newsroom/cf/_getdocument.cfm?doc_id=1171.

5. NESsT 2008 research of demand for and supply of loans to social enterprises in Central Europe showed that only 25 percent of surveyed social enterprises had used loan finance in the past. At the same time, out of 21 surveyed financial institutions and funds, only 9 had provided loan finance at least once to a nonprofit organization (NPO)/social enterprise. See more detail about the research in the next section.

6. Selling shares may be limited in the case of certain legal forms, for example, the Community Interest Company (CIC) in the United Kingdom. CICs are a type of limited company designed specifically for those wishing to operate for the benefit of the community rather than for the benefit of the owners of the company. For more information, see http://www.bis.gov.uk/cicregulator/about-us.

7. The Social Investment Bank, The Commission on Unclaimed Assess, UK, March 2007, http://socialfinance.ca/knowledge-centre/glossary/term/quasi-equity.

8. This research was conducted in 2008 surveying NESsT's social enterprise portfolio and financial institutions in order to gain insight into the experience with debt financing, the demand for and the supply of loans to social enterprises. The demand side conclusions were based on the results of 56 survey questionnaires filled in by civil society organizations (CSOs), while the supply side analysis included questionnaires and interviews made with 21 banks and specialized loan funds in the region.

9. This includes Czech Republic, Croatia, Hungary, Slovakia, and Romania.

10. The research was conducted in the summer of 2011 in four countries: Chile, Ecuador, Argentina, and Peru. It looked into access to finance for social enterprises on a broader level; not only access to credit, but also all kinds of financial services, including bank accounts, and so on. Conclusions about the demand side were based on findings of 11 in-depth interviews with NESsT portfolio members and 37 organizations were interviewed about the supply side including banks, funds, foundations, venture capital funds, and consultancies.

11. http://www.tise.pl/.

12. http://www.iadb.org/en/about-us/idb-financing/social-entrepreneurship
-program,6064.html.
13. http://www.cepicafe.com.pe/.
14. http://www.asoprof.com/.
15. SITAWI Annual Report 2011, http://sitawi.net/en/wp-content/uploads/2012
/10/20120517-SIT-ANNUAL-REPORT-2011-1.pdf.
16. Muhammad Yunus is a Bangladeshi economist and pioneer of microfinance lending to
the poor. He is the founder of Grameen Bank, which has loaned more than USD 10
billion since the 1970s. Dr. Yunus and Grameen Bank were awarded the Nobel Peace
Prize in 2006.
17. http://www.patriatakarek.hu/patriatakarek/hu/okotakarek/okotakarekoldal.html#az
-okotakarekrol.
18. Social finance is an approach to managing money that delivers social and/or environmental benefits, and in most cases, a financial return. Social finance encourages
positive social or environmental solutions at a scale that neither pure philanthropy nor
traditional investment can reach. http://socialfinance.ca/what-is-social-finance.
19. A "sheltered workshop" refers to a supervised workplace for physically disabled or
mentally handicapped adults.
20. http://www.popular-safi.com/.
21. www.cafonline.org/.
22. http://themidimusiccompany.co.uk/.
23. http://www.kids.org.uk/.
24. Social costs are costs incurred by social enterprises due to their social nature, which
are usually not incurred by other similar business with no social goals. For example,
the cost of social workers that assist disabled employees, the cost of creating accessible
workplaces for disabled employees, or the cost of environmentally responsible technologies in order to reduce contamination.
25. EVPA is a European membership association that works as a network of venture philanthropy organizations. Their objective is to promote the development of social enterprise
and improve the effectiveness and impact of venture philanthropy in Europe. To achieve
their mission, they (1) provide a network where European philanthropists can exchange
ideas about their approach to the social enterprise sector; (2) support members in the
production of workshops and research to foster the sector; and (3) collect data to generate best practices and to improve venture philanthropy and social investment in Europe.
26. "The European Venture Philanthropy Industry 2010/2011," EVPA report, Brussels,
May 2012, page 36.
27. "European Venture Philanthropy and Social Investment 2011/2012," Brussels:
European Venture Philanthropy Association (EVPA), March 2013, page 40.
28. Ibid., page 41.
29. http://www.socialventurefund.com/eng/home/.
30. Investment Example Verba Voice, http://www.socialventurefund.com/eng/social
_entrepreneurship/investment_example_verbavoice/.

9   Early-Stage Impact Investing in Latin America

*This chapter was written by Geoff Schwarten, business manager for NESsT, who is
responsible for overseeing the organization's consulting initiatives around the world. Prior
to joining NESsT, Geoff worked in the private sector leading marketing initiatives for

socially responsible companies like Clif Bar, Better World Books, and many others in a consulting capacity.

1. http://www.thegiin.org/cgi-bin/iowa/resources/spotlight/376.html.
2. http://www.miamiherald.com/2012/04/07/2735585/latin-american-schools-disconnected.html.
3. http://www.miamiherald.com/2012/05/19/2806557/politics-crippling-latin-american.html.
4. http://seaf.com.
5. http://www.runa.org/about-us/.
6. http://www.good.is/post/social-ist-impact-investing-why-ecuador-invested-500–000-in-a-brooklyn-startup/.
7. http://blog.bcorporation.net/2012/01/b-corp-runa-granted-high-profile-investment-representing-new-model-for-developing-nations-to-support-sustainable-business/.
8. Debt is repaid as one lump-sum payment when it reaches maturity. At that point, the investor has the option of asking for repayment of the loan in full, or taking a share in the form of equity in the company. There is always the option of restructuring for a certain period of time.
9. http://www.equitasventures.com/images/EquitasII.pdf.
10. All case studies referenced are found at the end of the chapter.
11. SOCAP, or the Social Capital Markets, is an annual event series that connects global innovators, investors, foundations, institutions, and social entrepreneurs to build the social capital market. http://socialcapitalmarkets.net/. The third Latin America Impact Investment Forum promotes and develops the impact business sector in the region, creating a network among key actors. http://inversiondeimpacto.org/en/forum-2013.html.
12. Fundacion Sistema B has a mission to articulate, enhance, and create new business models that redefine success and solve social and environmental problems for poor and vulnerable populations in Latin America. See http://www.sistemab.org/beta version.

   A "Benefit corporation"—usually referred to as a "B Corp"—creates the legal framework for socially focused enterprises to stay true to their social goals. B Corps make up a specific class of corporation bound by law to create measureable social benefits through its existence and operations, as well as benefits to shareholders. To qualify as a B Corp, a firm must have an explicit social or environmental mission, and a legally binding fiduciary responsibility to take into account the interests of workers, the community, and the environment as well as its shareholders. It must also publish independently verified reports on its social and environmental impact alongside its financial results. For more information, see www.bcorporation.net.
13. http://www.kauffman.org/uploadedfiles/irpr_2012_echecopar.pdf.
14. http://www.creecuador.com.ec.
15. http://blog.bcorporation.net/2012/01/b-corp-runa-granted-high-profile-investment-representing-new-model-for-developing-nations-to-support-sustainable-business/.
16. Vox invests in Minha Casa Minha Vida enterprise, which benefits from government subsidies under the program with the same name. The social enterprise builds and sells houses to low-income families. If the house is under a price cap and the family earns less than a certain amount per month, the government (through its bank Caixa Economica Federal) subsidizes part of the price of the house and finances the rest in up to 35 years (at low interest rates).

17. A SICAV is an open-ended collective investment scheme common in Western Europe, especially Luxembourg, Switzerland, Italy, Spain, Belgium, Malta, France, and Czech Republic. SICAV is an acronym for French *société d'investissement à capital variable*, which can be translated as "investment company with variable capital."

It is similar to an open-ended mutual fund in the United States, while a *sociedad de inversión de capital fijo* or *société d'investissement à capital fixe* (SICAF) is similar to a closed-ended fund. As in the case of other open-end collective investment schemes (such as contractual funds), the investor is in principle entitled at all times to request the redemption of their units and payment of the redemption amount in cash. (http://en.wikipedia.org/wiki/SICAV.)

18. http://www.mim.monitor.com/downloads/Blueprint_To_Scale/From%20Blueprint%20to%20Scale%20-%20Case%20for%20Philanthropy%20in%20Impact%20Investing_Full%20report.pdf.

19. www.investeddevelopment.com.

20. www.frogtek.org.

21. www.tiendatekweb.com.

22. www.voxcapital.com.br.

23. www.vilcap.com.

24. www.fondoinversionsocial.cl.

NESsT Glossary of Terms

Base of the pyramid (BoP): The World Resources Institute defines the base of the economic pyramid (BoP) as those with annual incomes below USD 3,000 in local purchasing power—approximately 4 billion people who live in relative poverty. Their incomes in current US dollars are less than USD 3.35 a day in Brazil, USD 2.11 in China, USD 1.89 in Ghana, and USD 1.56 in India. "The Next 4 Billion: Market Size and Business Strategy at the Base of the Pyramid," Executive Summary, World Resources Institute, http://www.wri .org/publication/content/7790.

Business advisory network (BAN): A group of leaders who provide pro bono advice and assistance to NESsT and the NESsT portfolio of social enterprises.

Business plan: A concrete and comprehensive implementation strategy under-taken by the principal agents of a prospective enterprise to assess the existing market and the enterprise's proposed entrance.

Capacity building or capacity support: The development of an impact/social enterprise's core skills and capabilities—including leadership, management, financing, infrastructure, systems, program implementation, and evaluation—in order to enhance its effectiveness and ability to further its impact.

Civil society organization (CSO): The wide range of not-for-profit, nonstate organizations as well as community-based associations and groups (distinct from both the governmental and business sectors) that advance a collective or pub-lic good. These organizations are also referred to as "nonprofit organizations (NPOs)," "nongovernmental organizations (NGOs)," "charities," "voluntary organizations," and so on.

Corporate social responsibility (CSR): A corporate initiative to assess and take responsibility for the company's effects on the environment and impact on social welfare. The term generally applies to company efforts that go beyond what may be required by regulators or environmental protection groups (http://www .investopedia.com).

Double bottom line: A term referring to businesses that pursue both finan-cial and social goals ("triple bottom line" includes environmental objectives as well).

Early-stage impact enterprise/social enterprise: NESsT defines early-stage enterprises as ones that are one to four years into their development and show potential to be financially self-sustainable and scalable. Some might have started the growth or replication process but are still not ready for a pure market investment and need to rely on patient capital (grants, soft loans, quasi-equity, etc.) and nonfinancial support to get to the next phase of growth.

Equity: Financing in exchange for shares or partial ownership of the impact enterprise/social enterprise. To obtain equity investment, an enterprise must have the appropriate legal form (usually a company). The investor has voting rights and a certain level of control, and may receive dividends if the impact enterprise generates profit. The investor can get the initial investment back if they sell their shares in the company.

Feasibility study: A formal and comprehensive analysis of the viability of a proposed enterprise.

Financial capital: General, multiyear financial support in the form of grants, loans, quasi-equity, or equity from donors and social investors provided to social enterprises to meet business development and operational needs. It is one of three types of capital NESsT and its supporters offer to social enterprises (financial, intellectual, and social). **Financing:** The provision of financial capital for the investment and operational needs of a social enterprise or business.

First-stage scaling: The first true attempt of the social enterprise to evolve its model to grow within their communities and/or replicate from one community to a select number of additional ones. This process leads to significant increases in the level of impact and activities compared to incubation, typically in the order of magnitude of four or five times.

Grants: Monetary aid given from a grantor to a grantee, in many cases a NPO. Grants are usually conditional upon certain qualifications as to the use, maintenance of specified standards, or a proportional contribution by the grantee or other grantor(s).

Guarantees: Promises of payment to support debt-financing applications. The guarantor may guarantee the entire loan request or a portion only. The lender calls upon the guarantee when repayment by the debtor is late or never takes place. Guarantees are used to facilitate loan finance from third-party lenders.

High-net-worth Individuals (HNWI): A person with a high net worth. In the private banking business, these individuals typically are defined as having investable assets in excess of USD 1 million.

Impact enterprise: Businesses designed to solve critical social problems and/or businesses created to further a social purpose in a financially sustainable way—another term for social enterprise.

Impact investment: Impact investing consists of investments made into companies, organizations, and funds with the intention to generate measurable social and environmental impact alongside a financial return. Impact investments can be made in both emerging and developed markets, and target a range of returns from below market-to-market rate, depending upon the circumstances. Impact investing occurs at later stages of business development, the amounts of investment are higher and can include "financial first" investments, where the financial return supersedes the social return.

Inclusive business: A business initiative that reduces poverty through the inclusion of low-income communities in its value chain.

Incubation stage: Stage following business planning of the NESsT portfolio approach, providing tailor-made capacity-building support, mentoring, and financing to launch and consolidate the impact enterprise/social enterprise.

Intellectual capital: Pro bono advice provided to social enterprises and their support structures by donors and social investors that includes assessing business plans, providing coaching or mentoring, and assisting with investment decisions. It is one of three types of capital NESsT and its supporters offer to social enterprises (financial, intellectual, and social).

Intermediaries: Organizations whose purpose is to provide or channel financial and capacity support to social enterprises and/or to provide information and vehicles for others to provide this support. Intermediaries include incubators and accelerators, loan funds, and venture philanthropy funds among others.

Investment readiness: "Investment-ready" means that the social enterprise has the financial performance, leadership, and systems in place to receive commercial loans or equity investments based on investor expectations of market returns.

Loans: Repayable forms of finance with varying structures, depending on the purpose (investment vs. working capital) and the provider(s) of the loan finance. Loans carry interest, which has to be paid to the lender on a regular basis, often along with regular installments of the principal (initially borrowed amount).

Microenterprise: A microenterprise is usually defined according to its level of investment, sales, or employment, but definitions vary widely from developed to developing countries. For the World Bank, microenterprises have fewer than 10 employees and less than USD 100,000 in assets or sales. For the European Union (EU), the employment criterion is the same, but sales can reach up to about USD 2.5 million annually.

NESsT portfolio: NESsT's own portfolio of impact/social enterprises that receive mixed financial and tailored capacity-building support at planning, incubation, and scaling stages.

Organizational readiness: An analysis of readiness of an organization or entrepreneur to develop, lead, and manage a social enterprise upon entering the NESsT portfolio. This entails a due diligence process that assesses leadership and management capacities and ability to undergo rigorous and objective business planning. Methodology is applicable to all NESsT target groups.

Patient capital: Capital investment designed to finance higher-risk enterprises for a longer term so that an enterprise can achieve sustained growth, making it more desirable for loan finance and commercial finance.

Pipeline development: Activities taken by investors and incubators/accelerators to develop a stream of investment-ready and/or scalable enterprises.

Planning stage: First stage of the portfolio approach, which includes a series of training workshops and one-on-one support to provide teams with the tools needed to assess and develop a social enterprise idea, assess the feasibility of the market, and create a business plan.

Prefeasibility study: An initial investigation of the viability of an enterprise idea to determine if additional time, effort, and research are worth pursuing.

Private equity shares: A NESsT program that invites private equity professional and firms to provide their intellectual, social, and financial capital to help develop and grow social enterprises. The program is designed to make philanthropic giving easy and effective for the private equity industry and to promote excellence in philanthropy within the private equity industry and beyond.

Quasi-equity: A special form of financing for impact/social enterprises that fills the gap that exists between grants/loans and equity. It has equity-like qualities without conferring ownership rights to the investor. Forms of quasi-equity include use of underwriting, royalty share finance, and repayable grants. It should be noted that some current definitions of quasi-equity also embrace the use of subordinated, unsecured debt.

Scaling stage: Third stage of the portfolio approach aimed at significantly growing and/or replicating a consolidated impact/social enterprise to achieve greater social impact.

Self-financing: Refers to a variety of types of entrepreneurial activities, including both mission-related and non-mission-related activities aimed at generating revenues (membership dues, fees for service, use of "soft" assets, use of "hard" assets, ancillary business enterprises, investment dividends, etc.). Unlike social enterprise, self-financing does not have to have significant mission impact.

Social capital: Social capital leverages the networks and contacts of donors and investors to cannel financial and in-kind resources to social enterprises. It is one of three types of capital NESsT and its supporters offer to social entrepreneurs (financial, intellectual, and social).

Social change organization: An organization that addresses systemic-level political, social, and/or economic problems through innovative strategies designed to address the root causes of these problems.

Social costs: Costs incurred by social enterprises due to their social nature, which are usually not incurred by other similar business with no social goals. For example, the cost of social workers that assist disabled employees, the cost of creating accessible workplaces for disabled employees, or the cost of environmentally responsible technologies in order to reduce contamination.

Social enterprise: Defined by NESsT as a business that solves a critical social problem in a sustainable manner. NESsT expects social enterprises to be well planned and have significant impact. A social enterprise is also referred to as an "impact enterprise," "nonprofit enterprise," "social-purpose business," or "revenue-generating venture" that operates with a "double bottom line" of generating financial return while simultaneously advancing a social mission.

Social entrepreneur: Visionary or leader who addresses a critical social problem entrepreneurially. The social entrepreneur does not always use social enterprise or business to do this.

Social investment: Social investment is the provision and use of capital to generate social as well as financial returns. Social investors weigh the social and financial returns they expect from an investment, and often accept lower financial returns in order to generate greater social impact. Social investment enables social sector organizations to develop activities that generate income used to repay investors. Social sector organizations may generate a surplus through trading (commercial) activities, contracts for delivering public services, grants, and donations, or a combination of some or all of these (http://www.bigsocietycapital.com/what-social-investment).

Social finance: An approach to managing money that delivers social and/or environmental benefits, and in most cases, a financial return. Social finance encourages positive social or environmental solutions at a scale that neither purely philanthropic supports nor traditional investment can reach.

Strategic partner: A key ally capable of providing targeted and timely support to a social enterprise or to any of the types of structures that develop and support social enterprises.

Strategic plan: An outline of future goals, methods, and actions designed to guide an organization in pursuing its mission.

Traditional philanthropy: Traditional grant making in which donor organizations (i.e., private foundations, trusts, etc.) contribute a fixed sum of money over a defined period of time to support CSOs; often consists of a onetime grant with the expectation that an alternative source, such as the government, will provide matching or continued funding.

Venture grants: Grants provided by NESsT to assist with the launch, incubation, and scaling of a social enterprise. These grants are often used to pay for social costs associated with the enterprise (see definition of social costs).

Venture philanthropy: Sometimes called "engaged philanthropy," an emerging field of philanthropic investment that combines the policies and practices of long-term, engaged investment and venture capital models of the for-profit sector with the principles and public-benefit missions of the nonprofit sector. Venture philanthropy strategies combine financial capital "investments" with some form of additional capacity building or technical assistance to the NPOs they support.

Bibliography

Print References

Alter, Kim. "Social Enterprise Typology." *Virtue Venures LLC* (2004).

Battilana, Julie, Matthew Lee, John Walker, and Cheryl Dorsey. "In Search of the Hybrid Ideal." *Stanford Social Innovation Review* 10 (2012).

Bello, Juan Luis Dammert. *Actividades de autofinanciamiento de las organizaciones de la sociedad civil en Perú: NESsT Country Assessment*. NESsT Learning Series. Lima: NESsT, 2007.

Brazil. Decree no. 5,940. Brasilia: October 25, 2006.

Budani, Agustina, Maximiliano Luft, and Carmen López. *Main Philanthropy Trends in Latin America*. Avina Foundation and the Inter-American Development Bank, August 2010.

"Catalyzing and Scaling Impact Enterprises to Benefit Poor and Vulnerable Communities: Impact Enterprise Working Definition and Summary of Research" (internal document). William Davidson Institute, University of Michigan, April 4, 2012.

Charity Bank Annual Review 2010. Kent, UK: The Charity Bank Limited, May 2011.

Clark, B. R. *Creating Entrepreneurial Universities: Organizational Pathways to Transformation*. Oxford, UK; New York; Tokyo: IAU Press and Pergamon, 1998.

Comolli, Loïc, Eva Varga, and Peter Varga. *Hit the Ground Running: Getting a Head Start with Local Lessons for Sustainable Social Enterprise*. NESsT Practitioner Series. Santiago: NESsT, 2011.

Davis, Lee. *End of the Rainbow: Increasing the Sustainability of LGBT Organizations through Social Enterprise*. NESsT Practitioner Series. San Francisco, CA: NESsT, 2008.

Davis, Lee, Nicole Etchart, and Claire Costello. *All in the Same Boat: An Introduction to Engaged Philanthropy*. NESsT Practitioner Series. San Francisco, CA: NESsT, 2005.

Davis, Lee, Nicole Etchart, María Cecelia Jara, and Brian Milder. *Risky Business: The Impacts of Merging Mission and Market*. NESsT Learning Series. Santiago: NESsT, 2003.

Davis, Lee, Nicole Etchart, María Cecelia Jara, and Joanna Messing. *Get Ready Get Set: Starting Down the Road to Self-Financing*. NESsT Practitioner Series. Santiago: NESsT, 2004.

DeFournay, Jacques, and Marthe Nyssens, eds. "Social Enterprises in Europe: Recent Trends and Developments," EMES Working Paper No. 08/01 (transversal paper). Liege (Sart-Tilman), Belgium, 2008.

Edwards, J. *Hybrid Organizations: Social Enterprise and Social Entrepreneurship*. Lulu. com. 2008, 71.

Etzkowitz, H., A.Webster, C. Gebhardt, and B. R. C. Terra. "The Future of the University and the University of the Future: Evolution of Ivory Tower to Entrepreneurial Paradigm." *Research Policy* 29 (2000): 313–330.

Etzkowitz, H., and L. Leydesdorff. "The Dynamics of Innovation: From National Systems and 'Mode 2' to a Triple Helix of University-Industry-Government Relations." *Research Policy* 29, no. 2 (2000): 109–123.

"The European Venture Philanthropy Industry 2010/2011." Brussels: European Venture Philanthropy Association (EVPA), May 2012, 36.

"European Venture Philanthropy and Social Investment 2011/2012." Brussels: European Venture Philanthropy Association (EVPA), March 2013, 40–41.

"Evolution of the Social Enterprise Industry: A Chronology of Key Events." Institute for Social Entrepreneurs, 2008.

Freeman, Chris. "The National System of Innovation: A Historical Perspective." *Cambridge Journal of Economics* 19 (1995): 5–24.

Gatica, S. "Emprendimiento e Innovación Social: construyendo una agenda pública para Chile." *Temas de la agenda pública* 6, no. 48 (2011): 1–15.

Gatica S. et al. *La Innovacion Social en Chile y el Rol del Estado en su desarrollo, Ministerio de Economia.* Santiago: Escuela de Administración de la Pontificia Universidad Católica de Chile, 2012.

Grau, Curto. *"El Emprendimiento Social: Estructura Organizativa, Retos Y Perspectivas De Futuro." Cuadernos de la Cátedra "la Caixa" de Responsabilidad Social de la Empresa y Gobierno Corporativo,* no. 14 (2012).

Hock, D. *One from Many: Visa and the Rise of Chaordic Organization.* San Francisco: Berrett-Koehler Publishers, Inc., 2009.

Hwang, V., and G. Horowitt. *The Rainforest: The Secret to Building the Next Silicon Valley.* Los Altos Hills, CA: Regenwald, 2012.

"The Impact Investor: People & Practices Delivering Exceptional Financial & Social Returns." Pacific Community Ventures, Inc., ImpactAssets, and CASE Center for the Advancement of Social Entrepreneurship, San Francisco, CA, March 2012.

Koh, Harvey, Ashish Karamchandani, and Robert Katz. "From Blueprint to Scale: The Case for Philanthropy in Impact Investing." Monitor Institute and Acumen Fund, San Francisco, CA, April 2012.

Lalkaka, Rustam. "Technology Business Incubators to Help Build an Innovation-Based Economy." *Journal of Change Management* 3, no. 2 (2002): 167–176.

"Latin America: Social Enterprise & Philanthropy." *Financial Times*, December 2, 2011.

"Latin America: Social Enterprise & Philanthropy: Cultural Legacy Has Created Cautious Attitude to Charity." *Financial Times*, December 2, 2011.

"Latin America: Social Enterprise & Philanthropy: Fashion for Giving Starts to Catch On." *Financial Times*, December 2, 2011.

Leadbeater, C. "Social Enterprises and Social Innovation: Strategies for the Next Ten Years." A social enterprise think piece for the cabinet office of the third sector, London, 2007."

Les, Ewa. "Poland." In "Social Enterprises in Europe: Recent Trends and Developments," edited by Jacques DeFourny and Marthe Nyssens, EMES Working paper No. 08/01, 28.

"Making the Grade: 2010–2011." NESsT report to supporters of the Private Equity Shares Campaign for Central and Eastern Europe, 2012.

Messing, Joanna, and Nicole Etchart. *Real Sustainability for Virtual Projects: A Guide to Self-Financing for Non-profit Websites.* NESsT Practitioner Series. Riga: Centre for Public Policy PROVIDUS, 2003.

Messing, Joanna, Nicole Etchart, and Lee Davis. *Enterprising Mentality: A Social Enterprise Guide for Mental Health and Intellectual Disabilities Organizations.* NESsT Practitioner Series. Santiago: NESsT, 2005.

La Morada: The Challenges of Adopting an Entrepreneurial Culture in a Social Change Organization. NESsT Case Study Series No. 17, 2007.

NESsT Case Study Series No. 1–35. Santiago: NESsT, 2000–2011.

NESsT, Global Proceedings, Social Enterprise World Forum, Rio de Janeiro, 2012.

NESsT Legal Series. (currently available for Argentina, Brazil, Chile, Colombia, Croatia, Czech Republic, Hungary, Ecuador, Peru, Romania). Santiago: NESsT, 2007–2011.

Nicholls, Alex. "The Landscape of Social Investment: A Holistic Topology of Opportunities and Challenges." Skoll Centre for Social Entrepreneurship, SAID business school, Oxford University, 2008.

———. "The Legitimacy of Social Entrepreneurship: Reflexive Isomorphism in a Pre-Paradigmatic Field." *Entrepreneurship Theory and Practice* 34, no. 4 (2010): 611–633.

Nordskog, Julie. *Donors to Latin American and the Caribbean Civil Society.* Fundación AVINA, 2010.

Novogratz, Jacqueline. "Meeting Urgent Needs with Patient Capital." *Innovations* 2, no. 1–2 (Winter/Spring 2007): 19–30.

Noya, A., ed. *Local Economic and Employment Development (LEED). The Changing Boundaries of Social Enterprises.* Boston, MA: OECD Publishing, 2009.

Nyssens, M. *Social Enterprise: At the Crossroads of Market, Public Policies and Civil Society.* London; New York: Routledge, 2006.

O'Shea, R., Allen, T. and Morse, K. "Creating the Entrepreneurial University: The Case of MIT." Presented at Academy of Management Conference, Hawaii, 2005.

Poon, Daryl. "The Emergence and Development of Social Enterprise Sectors." University of Pennsylvania, January 1, 2011.

Porter, Michael E., and Mark R. Kramer. "The Big Idea: Creating Shared Value. How to Reinvent Capitalism—and Unleash a Wave of Innovation and Growth." *Harvard Business Review* 89, no. 1–2 (2011).

"Poverty, Inequality, and Democracy." A Conference Report of the Network of Democracy Research Institutes (NDRI), Bratislava, Slovakia, April 26–28, 2009.

Prahalad, C. K. *The Fortune at the Bottom of the Pyramid.* Upper Saddle River, NJ: Pearson Prentice Hall, 2006.

"Programa para el escalamiento de Innovaciones rurales—Anexo2: Buenas prácticas para el escalamiento de innovaciones de base tecnológica en América Latina." NESsT report supported by the IDRC and the International Fund for Agricultural Development, 2011.

"Quasi-Equity: Case Study in Using Revenue Participation Agreements." Venturesome (an initiative of the Charities Aid Foundation), London, March 2008.

Sabeti, H. et al. "The Emerging Fourth Sector." Washington, DC: The Aspen Institute, 2010.

Schöning, Mirjam, Abigail Noble, Andreas Heinecke, Ann-Kristin Achleitner, and Judith Mayer. "The Governance of Social Enterprises: Managing Your Organization for Success." Schwab Foundation for Social Entrepreneurship, Geneva, 2012.

Senge, P. *The Fifth Discipline: The Art and Practice of the Learning Organization.* New York: Currency Doubleday, 1990.

Smallbone, D. "The Distinctiveness of Entrepreneurship in Transition Economies." *Small Business Economics* 16, no. 4 (2001): 249–262.

Smilor, R. W., D. V. Gibson, and G. B. Dietrich. "University Spin-Out Companies: Technology Start-Ups from UT Austin." *Journal of Business Venturing* 5 (1990): 63–76.

"The Social Economy in the European Union." International Centre of Research and Information on the Public, Social and Cooperative Economy (CIRIEC), CIRIEC-España and University of Valencia, 2007.

"The Social Investment Bank: Its Organisation and Role in Driving Development of the Third Sector." The Commission on Unclaimed Assets, London, March 2007.

Vaillancourt, Yves. "Social Economy in the Co-Construction of Public Policy." *Annals of Public and Cooperative Economics* 80, no. 2 (2009): 275–313.

Wengner, Etienne C., and William M Snyder. "Communities of Practice: The organizational Frontier." *Harvard Business Review* (2000): 139–145.

Wheatley, M., and D. Frieze. *Using Emergence to Take Social Innovation to Scale.* Provo, UT: The Berkana Institute, 2006.

"Working in Social Enteprises," Anglia Polytechnic University, SESAME, 2002.

Zurbano, M., G. Henry, and Ail Urszela. "El Cuarto Sector en Euskadi." Zamudio: Innobasque, 2012.

Web References

The website information contained in this book was gathered from March 2012 through April 2013. For purposes of the bibliography, all website information has been cited as of July 2012, unless otherwise noted.

"Accelerating Progress towards the Millennium Development Goals through Inclusive Business; Delivering Results: Moving towards Scale; Report on an Inclusive Business Dialogue." During the UN Summit on the Millennium Development Goals, held on September 21, 2010. The United Nations Development Program. October 2010. http://api.ning.com/files/f5EkJDqrBb9jySj-LXOrgBH1WbrsCdtSZRwGZghOE5qQ9rWyr BZuTIe4Vop-jfrL7RcCkfnGLGVGZ8YDxye-qRcI5*fZ9gLH/DeliveringResults _MovingTowardsScaleFINALHR.pdf.

Acevedo, L. F., "Colombia ya tiene su Centro de Innovación Social -CIS-." March 2012. Accessed April 19, 2013. http://www.rutanmedellin.org/actualidad/Paginas/centro _de_innovacion_social_cis_colombia_230312.aspx.

Actis. Accessed July 31, 2012. http://www.act.is/.

Agora Partnerships. Accessed July 31, 2012, and March 1, 2013. http://www.agorapartner ships.org/.

"Annual Review 2011." Social Enterprise UK. February 2012. Accessed July 31, 2012. http://www.socialenterprise.org.uk/uploads/files/2012/02/seuk_annual_review _2011.pdf.

"Approach." Omidyar Network. Accessed July 31, 2012. http://www.omidyar.com /approach.

"Annex: Mid-Term Review and National Indicative Programme, 2011–2013, Argentina." European Union. Accessed July 31, 2012. http://eeas.europa.eu/argentina/csp/11 _13_mtr_en.pdf.

Artemisia. Accessed July 31, 2012. http://www.artemisia.org.br/pdf/siteenglish.pdf.

ASOPROF. Accessed July 31, 2012. http://www.asoprof.com.

Ausherman Family Foundation. Accessed July 31, 2012. http://www.aushermanfamily foundation.org/.

AVINA Foundation. Accessed July 31, 2012. http://www.avina.net/esp/.

"B Corp Runa Granted High Profile Investment, Representing New Model for Developing Nations to Support Sustainable Business." B Corporation. January 11, 2012. Accessed July 31, 2012. http://blog.bcorporation.net/2012/01/b-corp-runa-granted-high -profile-investment-representing-new-model-for-developing-nations-to-support-sustainable -business/.

Bannick, Matt, and Paula Goldman. "Priming the Pump: The Case for a Sector Based Approach to Impact Investing." Omidyar Network. September 2012. Accessed March 1, 2013.

http://www.omidyar.com/sites/default/files/Priming%20the%20Pump_Omidyar%20Network_Sept_2012.pdf.

Bridgespan Group. "The MBA Drive for Social Value." April 2009. Accessed July 31, 2012. http://www.bridgespan.org/Publications-and-Tools/Career-Professional-Develop ment/NonprofitCareers/The-MBA-Drive-for-Social-Value.aspx#.UX7UGaJwoyo.

CEPICAFE. Accessed July 31, 2012. http://www.cepicafe.com.pe/.

"Chapter Six: The Asset Lock." Department for Business Innovation and Skills. Accessed July 31, 2012. http://www.bis.gov.uk/cicregulator/guidance/chapter-6.

"Child Labor in Peru." United States Department of Labor, Bureau of International Labor Affairs. http://www.dol.gov/ilab/media/reports/iclp/Advancing1/html/peru.htm.

"Communication from the Commission to the European Parliament, the Council, the Economic and Social Committee and the Committee of the Regions—Single Market Act." European Commission. April 13, 2011. Accessed July 31, 2012. http://eur-lex .europa.eu/LexUriServ/LexUriServ.do?uri=COM:2011:0206:FIN:EN:PDF.

"Communication from the Commission to the European Parliament, the Council, the Economic and Social Committee and the Committee of the Regions—Social Business Initiative." European Commission. October 25, 2011. Accessed July 31, 2012. http:// eur-lex.europa.eu/LexUriServ/LexUriServ.do?uri=COM:2011:0682:FIN:EN:PDF.

"The Community Interest Company Regulations 2005." United Kingdom legislation. Accessed July 31, 2012. http://www.legislation.gov.uk/uksi/2005/1788/contents /made.

CORFO. Accessed July 31, 2012. http://www.corfo.cl/.

CreEcuador. Accessed July 31, 2012. http://www.creecuador.com.ec.

"The eBay Way." Bloomberg Businessweek, November 28, 2004. Accessed July 31, 2012. http://www.businessweek.com/stories/2004-11-28/the-ebay-way.

"Disability in Latin American & the Caribbean." Fact Sheet, The World Bank. Accessed July 31, 2012. http://siteresources.worldbank.org/DISABILITY/Resources/Regions /LAC/LACfactsheetEng.pdf.

Echecopar, German, Sharon Matusik, Carla Bustamante, and Santiago Mingo. "Public Policy for Entrepreneurial Finance: A Comparative Assessment of the U.S. and Chile's Risk Capital Industries." The Kauffman Foundation. Accessed July 31, 2012. http:// www.kauffman.org/uploadedfiles/irpr_2012_echecopar.pdf.

"Equitas II—Impact Investment Fund." Equitas. Accessed July 31, 2012. http://www .equitasventures.com/images/EquitasII.pdf.

"The EU Single Market—Expert Group (Social Business)." Accessed July 31, 2012. http://ec.europa.eu/internal_market/social_business/expert-group/index_en.htm.

"The EU Single Market—The Single Market Act." European Commission. Accessed July 31, 2012. http://ec.europa.eu/internal_market/smact/index_en.htm.

"The EU Single Market—Social Business." European Commission. November 7, 2011. Accessed July 31, 2012. http://ec.europa.eu/internal_market/social_business/index _en.htm.

"Firms with Benefits." The Economist, January 7, 2012. Accessed July 31, 2012. http:// www.economist.com/node/21542432.

"Fondo Inversión Social." Claro y Asociados. Accessed July 31, 2012. http://www.claroya sociados.cl/?page_id=501.

Fondo Inversion Social. Accessed July 31, 2012. http://www.fondoinversionsocial.cl/.

Frogtek. Accessed July 31, 2012. http://www.frogtek.org/.

Fundes. Accessed July 31, 2012. http://www.fundes.org/.

Goldmark, Alex. "Social(ist) Impact Investing: Why Ecuador Invested $500,000 in a Brooklyn Startup," Good, January 3, 2012. Accessed July 31, 2012. http://www.good

.is/post/social-ist-impact-investing-why-ecuador-invested-500–000-in-a-brooklyn
-startup/.

"Impact." Multilateral Investment Fund. Accessed July 31, 2012. http://www5.iadb
.org/mif/HOME/Impact/tabid/398/language/en-US/Default.aspx.

"Impact Investment: What Investees Think." Keystone Performance Surveys, Keystone
Accountability. March 2013. Accessed March 1, 2013. http://www.keystoneaccount
ability.org/sites/default/files/What%20Investees%20Think.pdf.

International Development Research Centre. Accessed July 31, 2012. http://www
.idrc.ca/.

Invested Development. Accessed July 31, 2012. www.investeddevelopment.com.

Investment Ready Program. Accessed July 31, 2012. www.investment-ready.org.

"Investment Ready Program: Because Impact Matters." Investment Ready Program.
Accessed July 31, 2012. http://www.investment-ready.org/docs/Delivery_Partner.pdf.

"Investor Spotlight: Inter-American Development Bank Group." GIIN, February 28,
2012. Accessed July 31, 2012. http://www.thegiin.org/cgi-bin/iowa/resources
/spotlight/376.html.

Jaquier, Julia Balandina. "Avoiding Traps in Impact Investing: Lessons Learned." Credit
Suisse. January 2012, pp. 37–41. Accessed July 31, 2012. http://infocus.creditsuisse.
com/data/_product_documents/_shop/336096/investing_for_impact.pdf.

Kohler, John, Thane Kreiner, and Jessica Sawhney. "Coordinating Impact Capital: A New
Approach to Investing in Small and Growing Businesses." Santa Clara University and
The Aspen Network of Development Entrepreneurs. July 2011. Accessed July 31, 2012.
http://www.scu.edu/socialbenefit/resources/upload/Coordinating-Impact-Capital
.pdf.

Korodi, Attila. Romanian Minister of Environment and Sustainable Development Ministry
of Environment. Comments at event on biodegradable bags. September 9, 2008.
Accessed July 31, 2012. http://www.mmediu.ro/vechi/biroul_de_presa/comunicate
_de_presa/09_Septembrie_2008/02.09.08a.htm.

"The Labor Market Situation of Disabled People in European Countries and Implementation
of Employment Policies: A Summary of Evidence from Country Reports and Research
Studies." Report prepared for The Academic Network of European Disability Experts
(ANED), 2009. Accessed July 31, 2012. http://www.disability-europe.net/.

Lewis, Mike. "Mapping the Social Economy in BC and Alberta: Towards a Strategic
Approach" (working paper). Copyright © 2006, Canadian Centre for Community
Renewal on behalf of the B.C.-Alberta Social/Economy Research Alliance. Accessed
July 31, 2012. http://www.socialeconomy-bcalberta.ca/social-economy/.

"Minutes of the 5 June, 2012 Meeting of the *Groupe d'experts de la Commission sur
l'entrepreneuriat social* (GECES)." European Commission. Accessed July 31, 2012.
http://ec.europa.eu/internal_market/social_business/docs/expert-group/050612
-minutes-final_en.pdf.

Monitor Inclusive Markets. Monitor Group. Accessed July 31, 2012. http://www.mim
.monitor.com/.

"About NBIA." NBIA. Accessed July 31, 2012. http://www.nbia.org/about_nbia/.

Njambre. Accessed July 31, 2012. http://www.njambre.org.

Oppenheimer, Andres. "Latin American Schools: Disconnected." *The Miami Herald*,
April 7, 2012. Accessed July 31, 2012. http://www.miamiherald.com/2012/04/07
/2735585/latin-american-schools-disconnected.html.

———. "Politics Crippling Latin American Universities." *The Miami Herald*, May 19,
2012. Accessed July 31, 2012. http://www.miamiherald.com/2012/05/19/2806557
/politics-crippling-latin-american.html.

"Our Programmes," Shell Foundation. Accessed July 31, 2012. http://www.shellfoundation.org/pages/corelines_index.php?p=corelines_content.

"Our Projects." Multilateral Investment Fund. Accessed July 31, 2012. http://www5.iadb.org/FOMIN/Projects/tabid/400/language/en-US/Default.aspx.

"Perú: Perfil de la pobreza por departamentos, 2004–2008." El Instituto Nacional de Estadística e Informática (INEI), Lima, Peru. 2009. Accessed July 31, 2012. http://www.inei.gob.pe/biblioineipub/bancopub/Est/Lib0878/index.htm.

Popular SAFI. Accessed July 31, 2012. http://www.popular-safi.com/.

"Productores, Gremios y Cocineros Demandan Politicas de Promocion de Granos Andinos." La Convención Nacional del Agro Peruano (CONVEAGRO). Accessed July 31, 2012. http://www.conveagro.org.pe/node/8934.

"Quasi-Equity." SocialFinance.ca. Accessed July 31, 2012. http://socialfinance.ca/knowledge-centre/glossary/term/quasi-equity.

Ramp Perú. Accessed July 31, 2012. http://ramp-peru.org.pe/portal/.

Romanian Ministry of Labor, Family, and Social Protection. National Authority for People with Disabilities. Accessed July 31, 2012. http://www.anph.ro/tematica.php?idt.

Runa. Accessed July 31, 2012. http://www.runa.org/about-us/.

Ruttman, Robert. "Unlocking Capital to Drive Social Impact." Credit Suisse. January 2012. Accessed July 31, 2012. http://infocus.creditsuisse.com/data/_product_documents/_shop/336096/investing_for_impact.pdf.

SEBRAE. Accessed July 31, 2012, and March 1, 2013. http://www.sebrae.com.br/.

Sitawi. Accessed July 31, 2012. http://www.sitawi.net/.

"Social Enterprise Dictionary." Social Enterprise UK. Accessed July 31, 2012. http://www.socialenterprise.org.uk/about/about-social-enterprise/social-enterprise-dictionary#general.

Social Enterprise Mark. Accessed July 31, 2012. http://www.socialenterprisemark.org.uk.

"Social Entrepreneurship—Investment Example Verbavoice." Social Venture Fund. Accessed July 31, 2012. http://www.socialventurefund.com/eng/social_entrepreneurship/investment_example_verbavoice/.

"Social Entrepreneurship Program." IDB. Accessed July 31, 2012. http://www.iadb.org/en/about-us/idb-financing/social-entrepreneurship-program,6064.html.

"Social Entrepreneurship Program." Multilateral Investment Fund. Accessed July 31, 2012. http://www5.iadb.org/FOMIN/Projects/Financing/SocialEntrepreneurshipProgram/tabid/424/language/en-US/Default.aspx.

"Social Investment Manual: An Introduction for Social Entrepreneurs." Schwab Foundation for Social Entrepreneurship. September 2011. Accessed July 31, 2012. http://www.schwabfound.org/pdf/schwabfound/SocialInvestmentManual.pdf.

"Social Venture." BBVA. Accessed July 31, 2012. http://accionistaseinversores.bbva.com/TLBB/micros/informes2011/en/Nonfinancialinformation/SocialVenture.html.

Social Venture Fund. Accessed July 31, 2012. http://www.socialventurefund.com/eng/home/.

Thornley, Ben. "The Facts on U.S. Social Enterprise." *Huffington Post*, November 8, 2012. Accessed March 1, 2013. http://www.huffingtonpost.com/ben-thornley/social-enterprise_b_2090144.html.

Thornley, Ben, David Wood, Katie Grace, and Sarah Sullivant. "Impact Investing: A Framework for Policy Design and Analysis." Insight at Pacific Community Ventures and the Initiative for Responsible Investment at Harvard University. January 2011. Accessed July 31, 2012. http://www.rockefellerfoundation.org/uploads/files/88fdd93f-b778-461e-828c-5c526ffed184-impact.pdf.

Tiendatek en la web. Accessed July 31, 2012. http://www.tiendatekweb.com/.

Tinker Foundation. Accessed July 31, 2012. http://www.tinker.org/.

United Nations Statistics Division, Millennium Development Goals Database. 2009 Brazil unemployment rate among both sexes and in the age bracket of 15–24 years. Accessed July 1, 2012. http://www.anbpr.org.ro/index.php/afiliere/272-baza-de-date-membri .html.

TISE. Grupa Credit Cooperatif. Accessed July 31, 2012. http://www.tise.pl/.

Uradni list, Republike Slovenije. Accessed July 31, 2012. http://www.uradni-list.si /_pdf/2011/Ur/u2011020.pdf.

Vagac, Lubos. "Active Labour Market measures in Slovakia." EU Employment Observatory, December 2010: 1–15. http://www.eu-employment-observatory.net/resources /Slovakia-EmploymentServices.Law.pdf.

Village Capital. Accessed July 31, 2012. http://www.vilcap.com/.

Vox Capital. Accessed July 31, 2012, and March 1, 2013. www.voxcapital.com.br.

"What Is a Social Firm?" Social Firms UK. Accessed July 31, 2012. http://www.social firmsuk.co.uk/about-social-firms/what-social-firm.

"What Makes a Social Enterprise a Social Enterprise?" Social Enterprise UK. Accessed July 31, 2012. http://www.socialenterprise.org.uk/uploads/files/2012/04/what _makes_a_social_enterprise_a_social_enterprise_april_2012.pdf.

"Who We Are." Halloran Philanthropies. Accessed July 31, 2012. http://halloranphilan thropies.org/who_we_are#!mission.

The World Bank, Development Research Group, using PovcalNet (data on levels of poverty and income). Accessed March 1, 2013. http://iresearch.worldbank.org/PovcalNet /index.htm.

INDEX

Printed in the United States of America